# IN THE DAYS OF RAIN

# IN THE DAYS OF RAIN

REBECCA STOTT

4th ESTATE • *London*

4th Estate
An imprint of HarperCollins*Publishers*
1 London Bridge Street
London SE1 9GF

www.4thestate.co.uk

First published in Great Britain in 2017 by 4th Estate

Copyright © Rebecca Stott 2017

1

Rebecca Stott asserts the moral right to be identified
as the author of this work in accordance with the
Copyright, Design and Patents Act 1988

A catalogue record for this book is
available from the British Library

Hardback ISBN 978-0-00-820916-2
Trade paperback ISBN 978-0-00-820917-9

Printed and bound in Great Britain by
Clays Ltd, St Ives plc

# CONTENTS

# RECKONING

# I

My father did the six weeks of his dying – raging, reciting poetry, and finally pacified by morphine – in a remote eighteenth-century windmill on the East Anglian fens. It had been built to provide wind power to help drain the land, but by the time my father and stepmother bought it, the sails and cogwheels were long gone. A previous owner had stripped out the rusting machinery, added a low nave with extra rooms and painted it a dusky pink. From a distance and with the paint flaking off, it looked like a church washed up on the banks of a river. When the local farmer covered the black fields in every direction with plastic sheeting that miraged into floodwater in certain lights, the building always looked to me like a boat, or an ark, untethered from its moorings.

It was so far from civilisation that it did not figure on GPS systems: the undertakers took four hours to reach us.

Since they'd moved into it six years earlier, my father had turned the Mill into a pagan shrine, pasting its round, six-foot-thick walls with passages from Eliot's *Four Quartets* and from Yeats's last poems, owl feathers and Celtic symbols. He glued the lines of poetry onto the plaster, and when the damp made the paper curl off he'd hammer in huge nails that made the plaster crack.

They'd bought the house on a whim a year after their wedding. They both wanted to live on flat land, he said. They both liked big skies.

'It's on the banks of a fen river,' he said, when he phoned to say they'd found the perfect house. 'The Romans used it to ship building materials across the fens. During the war a farmer ploughed up a hoard of Roman silver plates covered in tritons and sea gods just a couple of fields away, and the local Baptists used to do their baptisms here. There's a mooring platform, so we can buy a *boat*.'

*But you've got no money*, I muttered to myself. *How exactly are you going to buy a boat?*

They drove me up to see it. We climbed through nettles and peered in through cobwebbed windows. It was beautiful, but it was also eerie and unsettling. All that sky. All that black soil. American bombers crossed the land on their flightpath from the Mildenhall airbase. Falcons hung low over the riverbank or scrutinised the fields from their posts on electricity cables.

Four months later my stepmother had turned the small circle of long-neglected riverside land into the beginnings of a garden. My father beat down the nettles with sticks. He borrowed a plough from a neighbouring farmer and broke it within a few hours. The farmer patched up the worst parts of the road. My father planted beech hedges and supervised local lads in the laying out of a lawn. He ordered and planted a grove of white birches at the far end of the garden as a birthday present for my stepmother. Their white trunks were magnificent, luminous against the black soil of the fen fields, especially at dusk.

'He's always had a thing for silver birches,' she told me. 'I prefer willows.'

My father was built on a different scale to the rest of us. In 2007, the year of his dying, he was sixty-eight, six foot four, and twenty stone. His long snow-white hair and beard would have made him look like an Old Testament prophet if it wasn't for the combat jacket he'd taken to wearing. He'd bought it from the Army and Navy Stores to audition for the part of Mark Antony in a production of Shakespeare's *Antony and Cleopatra*, and now wore it all the time. He thought of himself as an ageing Antony, but to me he was Sir Andrew Aguecheek, sometimes a Falstaff, occasionally a Lear. We called him Roger in our teens, and later Rodge or Dodge or The Big Man, never Dad. He wasn't a dad, at least not in the way that most people meant it. I'd usually just refer to him as 'my father' – Roger seemed an absurd name for a man built on his scale.

His head was twice the size of mine. When he'd had money he'd bought his clothes from an outsize shop called High and Mighty, but now that he was poor, most of his clothes – and my stepmother's – came from charity shops. When he split the seams of his trousers he'd staple them back together again. It was far quicker and more efficient than sewing, he insisted when I asked what he was doing with the stapler in one hand and the washing basket in the other. My stepmother flashed me a look that meant hold your tongue. When he broke his glasses, he taped the arms back on. She flashed me a look about that too.

He had a set of dentures that had replaced some of his back teeth, and sometimes he'd take them out when he was speaking fast or reciting poetry. He'd place them on the table between us. Sometimes he'd do this in restaurants or pubs. He'd belch, too – at home and in public. His belches were loud, elongated, and reverberated like a long rumble of thunder. He belched, I think, as an act of defiance against all forms of gentility and because it made us laugh. My brothers – and then my son – competed to imitate those sounds. It became a tribal thing.

Through that final winter, increasingly lame, bilious and irascible, his pancreas riddled with the still-undetected cancer, my father – the great limping bulk of him – walked the bank of the River Lark for hours every day, following the line of the river across the fens listening to Joyce's *Ulysses* on his head-phones for the seventh time. He and my stepmother had planted hundreds of bulbs – fritillaries and parrot tulips – on the path up to the Mill door and in rows on the riverbank. By February they were pushing up shoots.

On Valentine's Day in a hospital in Bury St Edmunds, doctors had finally used the word 'cancer' at the end of several weeks of euphemisms that had begun with 'inflammation' and then progressed to 'blockage', then 'lump', and then finally 'tumour'.

'Seems they manage bad news by drip-feeding it here,' my father said. 'It's exactly three centimetres by six centimetres,' he added, indulging his obsession for numbers, tracing the edges of the shadow on the ultrasound scan printout. 'They don't know how long I have. But they've given me a counsellor. That's not good, is it?'

He'd have to finish his memoir now, he said, when he'd been allowed to go home and when he'd stopped swearing, raving, and thumping walls and tables with his fist. He'd begun to think about what it might mean to put his affairs in order. When he told me he was going to need my help to finish that book of his, my heart sank.

He'd started writing it eight years earlier, shortly before meeting my stepmother. He'd called it 'The Iron Room', after the corrugated-iron Meeting Room where he and his parents and siblings had worshipped five or six times a week when he was growing up. For the first three years he'd talked about his memoir all the time. Every spare hour he took away from his paid work as a freelance copyeditor he'd be at it: ten steps back into rewriting; one step forward into new writing. He'd sent me scores of drafts, each only slightly different from the last. I came to dread the sight of his emails in my inbox.

'I can't see the wood for the trees any more,' I pleaded. 'Let me read it when it's finished. Then I'd be a fresh pair of eyes.'

I was relieved when the emails stopped coming, when he'd been distracted by the Mill, the garden, the broken plough, and the question of where to put the silver birches.

It was when he hit the 1960s, he said, that he'd run into trouble. He hadn't been able to get any further. I did the calculations. That was a shortfall of forty-nine years. How long would that take him – or me – to write?

'The *Nazi* decade,' he added, as if it were an explanation, and I nodded, telling myself the morphine was addling his head. Everything *after* 1960 had turned into a *thicket*, he whispered, through tears and expletives, whilst uncorking what was probably the third bottle of wine that afternoon. But he was going to finish it, he said. He *had* to. He wasn't going to let Death win that sodding chess game. He thumped his huge fist down on the arm of his chair again. *Not any time soon.*

He gestured at the television, a forty-two-inch flatscreen, the only piece of equipment in the cool damp interior of the curved Mill walls, on which he'd paused a scene from Ingmar Bergman's *The Seventh Seal*. Within the black-and-white frame two men dressed in medieval clothes sat playing chess against a wild sea.

'So long as the knight keeps playing the game of chess,' my father said, 'Death can't take him.'

He was damn well going to watch all fifty-eight of Bergman's films again now, he declared.

Of all the things I might have guessed my father might have wanted to do with his remaining days, watching Ingmar Bergman films wasn't one of them. I could only remember seven films that Bergman had directed. My father had made me watch them when I was sixteen, on afternoons when he persuaded me to skip school during my O-Levels: *Wild Strawberries*, *Autumn Sonata*, *Cries and Whispers*, *The Seventh Seal*, *Winter Light*, *The Silence* and *Through a Glass Darkly*. He'd buy red wine, huge loaves of still-warm bread and slabs of ham, and open a jar of his favourite wholegrain English mustard. We'd watch those films in his dusty, post-divorce flat, sitting on the floor amid piles of unpaid bills and documents and scatterings of poems. I'd go back to school – or to my mother's house – slightly drunk, my head spinning.

I started a list on the day he showed me Death playing chess on the TV screen. *Ingmar Bergman: 58*, I wrote at the top of the page in my notebook, thinking I'd order them online. I'd forgotten that my father had more than forty of them in a cupboard in the Mill, that he'd been collecting them since he'd stolen into the back row of a cinema to see *Wild Strawberries* at the age of eighteen.

Fifty-eight. How many films could you watch in a day?

My younger brother, travelling across New Zealand on sabbatical from work, flew home and moved into the Mill. I stayed as often as I could, driving up from Cambridge every other day, leaving notes for my ex-husband and babysitters, managing a job and publishers from a phone and an internet connection that rarely worked. My sister flew over from France. My two other brothers came as often as their jobs and young families allowed them. The five of us gathered around, steeled ourselves. My stepmother ordered in food and more cases of wine and turned the thermostat dial to Constant.

In the crypt light of the Mill tower, through late February and March, we watched Bergman films together, interspersed with long hours of cricket – the World Cup had just started. We played Mozart, drank wine, cooked, and ate together at a table that seated fifteen, only a few feet from my father's reclining chair, which was now permanently horizontal. It snowed. My son and I drove across fen dirt tracks in the dark to fetch foil boxes of Gressingham duck prepared for my father by the cooks at the White Pheasant pub at Fordham, but though he wanted to eat he had no appetite. He worked away at his memoir for several hours a day for the first week, propped up on pillows, but then, once the Macmillan nurse had increased his daily doses of morphine, he was too tired to write.

Then there was the day he told me, tears in his eyes, that he didn't think he could finish his memoir after all. He'd gone back into the thicket, but he couldn't face it: *the muddle, the cruelty, the madness of it all.* And even if he *could* describe those years, he whispered, as if someone might be listening in, he'd never be able to close the great gap in time, get from 1960 to now, to *this.*

'Shandy's dilemma,' I said, and he smiled darkly. For decades he'd been persuading me to read his favourite books. Many had become my household gods now too. A webwork of in-jokes and literary references had grown up between us. We'd both read Lawrence Sterne's mad fictional eighteenth-century memoir *The Life and Opinions of Tristram Shandy, Gentleman.* But now that he had only weeks to live, the similarities between *Tristram Shandy* and my father's own unfinished fictional memoir struck me as both tragic and ridiculous.

Poor Tristram finds he's written several hundred pages before he's even been born. Convinced that the oddities of his personality were caused by the fact that his father was interrupted while having sex with his mother on the night of his conception by his mother asking if he had forgotten to wind the clock, Tristram then has to explain about the clock, and to do that he has to explain about Uncle Toby, his father's brother … and while he is trying to explain all of this, and as the pages are mounting up, there's a knock at the door and Death is there on the threshold – cloak, scythe and all. Tristram leaps from the window and gallops to Dover to take a boat to Calais. Death takes up pursuit.

I took the bus from my house into town to buy a portable tape recorder.

'If I ask you questions,' I said to him as he disappeared into another cricket match, 'it might be easier. You wouldn't get so tired. Then I could transcribe it later. We could do short bursts, when you felt like it.'

I had bought a black tape recorder. Out in the Mill dust coated everything in hours, and I had to keep wiping the machine down. The dust bothered me. I'd never noticed it before. Dust and, even in March, fruit flies. The house was full of them. My father had started to keep a tally of the number he'd find in his wine glass. The fruit fly count joined all the other reckonings in his notebooks: daily calorie counts, his gambling winnings and losings, the daily diabetes count, the cricket scores. My stepmother just put an old beermat over her glass. She didn't much like wine.

But although the tape recorder had been easy enough to choose in the department store that day, I hadn't anticipated that the tapes would stupefy me. How many did I need? They came in packs of four or eight or twelve. Each of them could hold eight hours of recording. How long did he have? How far would he get? I stood in front of the display case in the shop for twenty minutes trying to do multiplication sums in my head. I picked up three packets of twelve: thirty-six tapes. That was 288 hours; 17,280 minutes.

I now have two tapes in my study drawer, next to the old tape recorder. One is full, the other only partly full. I gave the unused ones away. My father got from 1960 to 1966, two years after my birth. He ran out of time. Like Tristram Shandy, like the knight in *The Seventh Seal*, he didn't get to finish his story once Death had got into the house.

What he had to tell me was far worse than I could have imagined. No wonder he'd got stuck.

When we began, I pictured my father and me in that thicket together, with scythes, torches and protective clothing, and then, triumphant, finally scaling the castle walls. We'd do whatever was needed – cut through the thorns, slay the dragon, rescue the princess – *together*. But we didn't make it.

Day by day he grew quieter. His reclining chair remained in its horizontal position and his morphine-induced sleeps lasted longer. I slipped the tape recorder and the pack of tapes into the back of the cupboard where he kept his dusty film collection and his store of Spanish reds.

In the fourth week of his six weeks of dying, my father, laid out at the centre of the Mill tower, opened his eyes and summoned my brother and me, his executors. He had already given me instructions about what to do about his memorial stone, the funeral, and his extensive debts. He was struggling hard to surface from his drug-inspired dreams, to keep his eyes open, to sit up. We moved in closer.

'This is very important,' he stressed, raising an arm from the bed and jabbing his finger into the air with all the strength he had, his white beard and hair wild, his jaundice-yellowed eyes bloodshot.

'You can't leave any of those bastards alone with me when I'm asleep. You understand? You know what they're like. They'll take advantage. They're like vultures.'

He knew all too well from his fifteen years as a ministering brother in the Exclusive Brethren that the distant family members who were now visiting every day as the end grew nearer would want to pray over him, help him find his way back to the Lord. He was having none of that.

Dutifully, we warned the cousins who came carrying Bibles and hymnbooks. How do you tell a Christian not to pray?

What else were they supposed to do? Leave the dying man to the tortures of hellfire?

We asked them to respect his wishes. They were offended and baffled. They'd driven a long way. Many had got lost when their GPS systems had begun to tell them to turn around and make for the nearest road. They drank tea and examined the strange pagan grotto of the Mill and its many false idols. I watched a distant cousin run her eyes down the lines from *Four Quartets* my father had pasted above the door, her brow furrowed.

He was right to warn us to be vigilant. Despite our requests, there were two or three times when we dropped our guard. On one occasion we saw the lips of one of the visiting cousins, a kind elderly woman, pressed up against my father's ear, while he lay commanding the room even in sleep, laid out like a fallen tree or an oversized, dusty and yellowing tomb effigy. She was whispering to him.

'Excuse me,' my brother said, glancing anxiously at me, embarrassed. 'Please don't do that.'

The promise we'd made had probably already been broken.

We never left him alone with visitors again. His eyes flickered open once to tell me as I leant across him that I was *so beautiful*. He woke another time to implore me to keep the scale of his gambling debts secret from my stepmother. On the night before the equinox I left the house for the first time in weeks. I'd been invited to interview for a job I'd applied for months before at the University of East Anglia. The nurse had taken me aside.

'I'm sure he'd want you to go,' she said. 'He'd want you to have a good shot at it.'

From a building on the Norfolk campus, surrounded by lush green hummocks overrun with rabbits, I rang my brother every two hours. I stood in the empty toilet trying to apply make-up to my swollen face minutes before the interview, talking to my father in the mirror.

'You've never been arrogant enough,' I heard him say to me as he'd so often done. 'Be arrogant. Nail it.'

When I got back late that night, my brother told me my father was still alive, although the nurse had said he probably wouldn't last to the morning. I volunteered to take the night watch. No one argued; they were all exhausted. My father's breaths rattled, paused, rattled, gasped, and began again.

'Get him to *let go*,' my brother whispered, after my step-mother had left the room. 'He'll listen to you.' He helped me drag the sofa across the room so that I could sleep next to my father's reclining chair, and then my brother was gone, the lights in the house out.

The wind rattled the windows. It was snowing again. I steadied my breathing in the darkness to match my father's breaths; I held my breath when his stopped. I told him about the interview. I told him I'd been arrogant, that I'd done a good job. Then I told him he could let go. Immediately I wished I hadn't said it.

My mobile rang. It was an old friend who I'd not heard from in years. He was walking home from a pub through the snow along a riverbank in the southern fens, he told me. He'd called to find out if I was all right. Startled by the sound of my sobs and my father's laboured breathing, he stayed on the phone, talking softly about anything that came into his head until the first birds began to sing, when I finally fell asleep.

When the vice-chancellor rang early the next morning to offer me the job, I asked if I could have a few days to get back to him. My father was about to die, I said. *About to die* struck me as an odd phrase. I wanted to tell him how strange it was to watch death fighting to take possession of a body, of how my father's body and the blackening ridges of his fingernails made me think of the colour and texture of a felled oak I'd once seen out on the fens, but instead I said *thank you*. I told him that I was, of course, *delighted*. I would get back to him. I just needed to attend to this particular day. Take your time, he said. Take as much time as you need.

My brother and I played Chopin in the late afternoon. At around five, the light began to fade. My stepmother and sister-in-law set out to drive the six miles across the fens to buy milk. The phone rang. I walked from my father's chair through the nave of the Mill to the sitting room at the far end of the building to take the call. It was an old friend of my father's asking how he was.

Across the fields in the half-light I could just make out something moving in the distance, a flash of white against the darkening trees. It was a barn owl, flying low through the dusk, following the path of the river, heading straight for the Mill, heading straight for us. I walked back down the long corridor to where my father lay breathing in rasps, my brother reading the newspaper beside him.

'It's coming,' I said.

I have no idea what I thought the 'It' was. My brother put his newspaper down, I opened the window and we each picked up one of my father's great gnarled hands, just as the owl passed by the front door, just as my father took his last breath, just as my stepmother opened the door with the milk, just as a great congregation of crows, lapwings and blackbirds took up their positions in rows along the electricity cables and pylons. The owl circled the house for twenty minutes and then disappeared.

Twilight on the equinox, with an owl, by a river. It was just as my father would have conjured it.

# 2

No one would have guessed that I'd been raised in a Christian fundamentalist cult, or that my father and grandfather were ministering brothers in one of the most reclusive and savage Protestant sects in British history. So it would always be my fault if the subject came up. It might be because I'd dropped my guard, got bored, or told a story from my childhood. Of course, once it did come up, it would always be difficult to make it go away again. People were interested; they asked questions. I'd never learned how to steer around the subject.

You can't tell just bits of it, I'd remind myself. Once you get started the whole thing starts unravelling, like a stitch in a scarf, or a story that has no beginning, middle or end. Best not to start at all. Best to keep quiet.

No matter how many times I'd try to tell it, in pieces or at length, I'd always end up baffled, feeling as though there was a part I'd left out or forgotten, a lost moral or a punchline.

'I was raised in a cult,' I'd say, and then I'd recoil, embarrassed by the melodrama of the words I'd used. Were the Brethren a cult? I didn't know. What was the difference between a sect and a cult? Was there a point on a spectrum where a sect became a cult?

'We wore headscarves,' I'd say. 'We weren't allowed to cut our hair. We weren't allowed television, newspapers, radios, cinemas, holidays, pets, wristwatches.'

The list of prohibitions always seemed endless. I'd watch people's eyes open wider. They'd look at me askance, then compete to ask questions, and I'd think, *Oh no, not this again.*

'We weren't allowed to talk to the other children at school,' I'd say. 'They told us that everyone outside the Brethren was part of Satan's army and they were all out to get us. They called them "worldly", or "worldlies". If you didn't do exactly what they said, they'd expel you. Then your family wouldn't be allowed to speak to you ever again. People committed suicide. People went mad. Yes, this was Brighton. Yes, this was Brighton in the sixties. Yes, during flower power. In the suburbs. During the sexual revolution. Yes. It's hard to explain.'

'You were raised *Plymouth Brethren*?' people would say. They would have heard about the Plymouth Brethren. Some might even have read *Father and Son*, Edmund Gosse's beautiful memoir about growing up in a nineteenth-century Plymouth Brethren assembly. And I'd hear myself reply with a hint of superiority, 'We weren't *Plymouth* Brethren. We were *Exclusive* Brethren.'

'My people were the hardliners,' I'd say. 'Gosse was in the *Open* Brethren. That was nothing. They were virtually *Baptist*. They had pulpits and priests and adult baptisms. They were allowed to talk to worldly people, even eat with them.'

*My people? Had I really just said 'my people'?*

But even if the subject didn't come up, my Brethren childhood would rear up like Banquo's ghost at the dinner table, refusing to be buried. At university, when I made new friends and confidantes, I couldn't explain how I'd become a teenage mother, or shoplifted books for years, or why I was reckless, impatient, afraid of the dark, and had a compulsion to rescue people, without explaining the Brethren, the God they made for us, and the Rapture they told us was coming.

But then, I couldn't really talk about the Brethren without explaining about my father, how he'd been a ministering brother and then become addicted to roulette when he left the sect and stopped believing in God. I'd have to explain how he'd gone to prison for embezzlement and fraud and then ended up making films for the BBC, and that on his deathbed he'd talked about a 'Nazi decade' and made us promise not to let anyone pray over his sleeping body.

And I could never really tell my father's story without telling my grandfather's – how the Scottish ships' chandler had migrated south to supply food to the hotels of Brighton and had ended up one of the ruling members of the Brethren and running the publishing house that printed Brethren ministries.

And to explain Brethren women, I'd have to tell the story of how my great-grandmother had been sent to an asylum in Australia for forty years by her Brethren husband not just because she had epilepsy, but because she was considered too *wilful*. Wilfulness isn't allowed in Brethren women, I'd say, and then I'd realise that I didn't really know what kind of wilful she'd been.

My family, I'd tell them, have been caught up in the Brethren for a hundred years. And then I'd notice I'd just used that funny old-fashioned phrase my mother always used: *caught up in*.

'But back then, of course,' she'd say when she was remembering something about rationing or the air raids, 'we were caught up in the Brethren.'

My family hadn't *belonged to* the Brethren, we'd been *caught up in* them. Caught up like a coat catching on thorns. Caught up in a scandal. Caught up in the arms of the Lord. Whichever way you phrased it, it meant you didn't get to choose, and that there was no getting away.

And then I'd be five years old again, sitting in Meeting, listening to my grandfather preaching about the Rapture. The Lord Jesus was going to take us with him up into the air in the middle of the night, he'd say. We'd be *caught up in* his arms. My grandfather's usually harsh Scottish preaching voice would go soft when he talked about the Rapture. And I'd be sitting there swinging my legs on the chair in the Meeting Room, wondering how the Lord Jesus was going to lift all of us up at the same time – there were some large and sweaty people in our fellowship. The Lord Jesus would have to be a giant to be strong enough to lift my father off the ground. I'd never seen anyone do that.

After we left the cult my father sometimes tried to explain about the Brethren to people who'd never heard of them. Though he was a man who'd seize any opportunity to hold the floor, his eyes always seemed to glaze over when anyone asked him about it, as if he was bored or reading from a script. He complained that when he tried to write an Exclusive-Brethren-in-a-nutshell section in his memoir it just came out as a lump of gawky exposition. My mother refused to talk about it at all. Best to draw a line under all of that, she'd say. No use going back in there. It won't do any good.

# 3

After the funeral and the wake and the speeches and the fire we burned his chair in, my brother and I ventured into my father's study, stacked high with papers. It all had to be cleared out, my stepmother said, if the Mill was to be sold. We rescued anything that looked important from piles of unpaid bills, receipts, photographs, and instructions for long-dead appliances.

If I was going to finish his book, I told my brother, I was going to need everything that looked as if it had anything to do with the Brethren. So we shoved stacks of letters and diaries and yellowed documents into boxes without sorting through them. My brother and my son helped me carry the six boxes up three flights of stairs in my Cambridge house and slip them into the dark and dusty space under my Victorian iron bed. I'd deal with them later, I told myself. When I was ready, when I had time.

A month after my father's funeral, my stepmother rang to say that she'd been to see the doctors about her stomach cramps. After a series of tests they had diagnosed her with bowel cancer. She'd be fine, she said. She had her cousins nearby. There'd be a course of chemo. Her cousins would drive her back and forth from the Mill to the chemo sessions. Friends would come in to help with the garden. She didn't need me to come out there. She didn't need anything from any of us for now. She'd let us know if she did.

How could two newlyweds, living out an Indian summer, planting a garden on the banks of a river, *both* have been incubating cancerous growths, his pancreatic, hers bowel? Did his cancer explain the biliousness of his behaviour, his rants and storms, the way he'd started to talk to her in those last years, his complaints about how she refused to sit and watch Shakespeare with him?

'Perhaps she just doesn't like Shakespeare,' I'd said to him. 'It's not a crime.'

'*Midsomer Murders,*' he said. '*Midsomer* bloody *Murders.* That's the level of philistinism we are talking about here.'

'I'd watch *Midsomer Murders*,' I thought to myself, 'if the alternative was listening to you lecture me about Wilson Knight and the late plays of Shakespeare for the fourteenth time.'

I wanted to help my stepmother. We all did. But though I drove up every few weeks, I now dreaded the sight of the Mill. *Puddleglum*, the little second-hand cabin boat my father and I had bought together, moored on the river under the willow tree, was now covered in mildew and leaves. The lawn grass was running to seed, the birch trees wilting in the sun. The pyre where we'd burned my father's chair had left a scorch mark and stumps of charcoaled wood on the grass. Someone needed to rake it all in and put some grass seed down.

My stepmother was struggling not just with the chemo but also with the bank. My father had left her almost penniless. I printed out the bank statement from my father's computer a week after the funeral. He'd placed scores of online bets in those final days, most made in the middle of the night when we'd all been asleep. Just one big win, he would have been telling himself. Just one big win so that he could leave my stepmother some money with which to pay off the debts.

I reckoned up the bets. He'd spent thousands of pounds in those last weeks by moving money from one credit card to another. It wasn't even his money; it was the last of my stepmother's small inheritance.

I volunteered to spend an afternoon at the Mill when my stepmother was in the hospital and her cousins were away for their summer holidays. I'd mow the lawn and water the birches, I told her. It was the least I could do.

I drove slowly up the long lane that gave way to the dirt track that followed the course of the river, coal-black fen fields in one direction and rising corn in the other. I parked the car and let myself in using the key she kept under a rock near the back door. I found the mower in the shed, the blades encrusted with dried grass.

When the mower started up, the sound seemed a rude imposition on the birdsong and silence, but the smell and the stripes of mowed grass made me feel I was pushing the encroaching wilderness back a little, that I could make all of this tidy again, at least for now.

Somewhere in the heat of the day, amid the smell of cut grass and the roar of the machine, I strayed into a corner of a flower-bed. On the edge of my vision a black cloud rose up and hummed low and close, smoke-dark against the white of the birch trunks. The first sharp sting of venom broke my concentration. The second made me release the handle of the mower. It wasn't until I'd run screaming through the empty garden, casting off my clothes, and taken refuge in the sitting room, shaking, hurt and enraged, that I examined my skin in the mirror. I counted twenty-one stings, raised, hot mounds on my arms, neck, hands. I'd run over a wasps' nest in the dark fen soil of that garden, in the twilight of its grieving afternoon.

Can a dead man conjure wasps? Can an owl flying at dusk take a dying man's soul? Out there in that pagan fen landscape that disgorged Roman silver plates on the ploughshare, anything seemed possible. Like the house in Alan Garner's *The Owl*

*Service*, there were unaccountable scratchings in the eaves of the Mill now, presences everywhere.

'Leave me alone,' I said to the empty air. 'Leave me a-*lone*. I'll finish your book when I'm ready. You can't *make* me.'

The contents of those six boxes under the bed made me think of chaos, the spillage of my father's body after his death, the gritty cremation ashes we'd scattered on the river by the Mill, the mess of his life, the impossibility of telling the Brethren story, and my own grief. They stayed down there – under the bed, gaffer-taped up.

There was so much else to do. A new job and a commute, teenagers to cook for, homework to supervise, deadlines to meet, students to teach, lectures to write and a mortgage to pay. It was two years before the letters from debt collectors and credit card companies and court summonses stopped coming, and before I stopped posting out the photocopies of my father's death certificate with the covering letter that explained that he'd died *without assets*, that his debts and bills could not be paid. By then the Mill had been sold and my stepmother had gone to Australia to live near her family.

What had I actually promised him, I began to wonder. If I was going to finish his book, I'd have to describe what happened in the sixties, in that decade he couldn't bear to look at. No one could understand the recklessness of his behaviour without understanding that. But I didn't want to revisit that decade any more than he had. No one in the family wanted to go back there. Sometimes my father's cousins would refer to the years we were 'caught up in the Brethren', or 'living in the Jims', or 'living under The System'. Most of them seemed ashamed that they hadn't seen through it at the time; some clearly felt angry and duped. Most wanted to tell me that they should have got out earlier. But no one knew, they'd say. No one knew how bad it was going to get. Then they'd change the subject. Best not to dwell on the past. Better to focus on the future.

Even if I did get a book written, the Brethren were rich and powerful. They attacked people who criticised them. They employed legal teams. When I'd once written about growing up in the Brethren for a Sunday magazine, a Brethren ministering brother had sent me a letter to say they were praying for me; that meant they knew where I lived. I'd moved house since then, but I knew they could track me down if they wanted to, wherever I was. What would my family have to say if I started asking questions about that history now? And I'd have to find a way of not writing about my mother, of steering around her, because she wouldn't want me to make her remember any of that.

If I was going to finish my father's story, I'd have to write about the girl I'd been in the Brethren too, because we'd both lived in that thicket, and we'd both got caught up in its cruel aftermath. I'd have to think about the days I spent listening out for the sound of Satan's hooves on the paving stones of Brighton, for instance, or making deals with the Lord, or hoarding tins of corned beef and condensed milk in prepara-tion for the Tribulation. I didn't want to think about that Brethren girl in her red cardigan with brass buttons, wearing her headscarf and clutching her Bible. I'd drawn a line between me and her. My mother was right. Perhaps it was all best left well alone.

# 4

Four years after my father died I won a place at a month-long silent writers' retreat in a fifteenth-century castle just south of Edinburgh. I was supposed to be writing a novel set in nineteenth-century London, but after a week sitting at a desk staring down over the castle grounds I was deleting everything I wrote, and that wasn't much. Every paragraph felt hollowed out; every sentence threw me off.

When I walked the castle grounds at dusk, down through the bracken and the fallen and rotting trees to the peat-red river, up to the edge of the mown lawns and the flowerbeds and back round again, I heard my father reciting parts of *Revelation* or *Ezekiel*, or Yeats's 'The Wild Swans at Coole', or talking about that thicket of his. His voice echoed through the east and west wings of the castle, through the woods, in the wind. These were just aural grief hallucinations, I told myself, just flickers in my neural pathways. They were nothing out of the ordinary, nothing to worry about.

In the final week of the retreat I joined the other four writers at dusk to swim in the river that curled wide and red-brown over rocks and pebbles through the castle woods. After we'd climbed from the freezing water and pulled our towels and robes around us, we followed the path up the steep riverbank into the darkening wood. I fixed my eyes on the poet's feet ahead of me, now level with my head, as they pressed into the leaves and bracken. When his foot slipped and he stumbled slightly, I saw, or thought I saw, a plume of smoke rising slowly from a hole in the ground that he'd disturbed.

I felt the scratchings and rustlings in my hair. The first stings began. The poet behind me, dressed in a red robe, had also been engulfed. We ran through the wood back to the castle, tripping over undergrowth in the darkness, shaking our hair and pulling off our clothes, until we were sure we'd outrun them.

We'd had a lucky escape, we told ourselves over dinner. Was it, someone asked, lemon juice or ice you were supposed to put on wasp stings? Someone passed me a tumbler of whisky. I took myself to bed early. The whisky must have addled my head, I thought, because I seemed to be hearing voices that weren't there.

At three in the morning I woke, my pulse drumming wildly in my ears, fireworks exploding behind my eyelids. When I stumbled to a mirror to prise open a single eye, my face and neck were so swollen, taut and shiny that I stumbled backwards in shock. I was struggling to breathe.

Two days later it was all over: the early-morning drive through the dark to the emergency surgery in the director's car, the steroids, the dosage of antihistamines large enough to floor an elephant, the semi-coma I slipped into for twenty-four hours. The doctor had counted up the hard lumps on my scalp and neck. Twenty-five stings. Enough to kill someone with an allergy, almost enough to kill someone who'd been stung before in an empty garden when a smoky swarm had risen like a ghost from a hole in the ground.

Not enough to kill, I thought, but enough to make a point.

A few years earlier, I'd discovered that the man dressed in a turquoise and pink Hawaiian shirt sitting opposite me at a Cambridge dinner party was a world expert on shamanism. I'd plagued him with questions, and if I'd failed to observe the to-and-fro turn-taking of dinner-party etiquette, I was not the only one. None of us wanted to talk about anything else.

For fifteen summers he'd lived with a shamanic tribe on the Russian steppes, he told us. He'd studied shamans as they talked their dead down.

'Talking down,' I said. 'What does that mean?' Death for me had been all about going *up there*, the transcendent sucking *up* into the air, into the arms of Jesus. I thought again of the impossibility of that body-weight of my father's going *up there*, going up *anywhere*. Even in the blood-red plastic cremation jar his ashes had been a ton weight.

The shaman expert told us that the bereaved Sora used the shaman as an intermediary to persuade the dead person to go down into the next world.

'Like laying a ghost?' I asked.

'Something like that,' he said. 'Though it works both ways for them. The dead and the living both have to convince the other to let them go. It takes a long time.'

Until the relatives had talked down the dead person, he told us, their spirit would be hanging around the village doing bad things, provoking, making people sick, causing the crops to fail. They had to be talked down and into the ground.

In that moment I saw my huge father up on a cliff ledge somewhere, slightly drunk, swaying close to the edge, holding forth, and my siblings and me talking him down. Or trying to. Hadn't we done that? I asked myself. Isn't that what we'd done out there at the Mill with the Bergman and the cricket?

But I hadn't even started. My father was still roaming. Still talking. There were swarms of wasps, acts of provocation. It would get worse. *Someone* was going to have to talk him down.

# 5

Six years after my father died, my daughter Kezia, nineteen and home from university for the summer, went looking for an electric fan that I told her had been dismantled and would be in a cupboard somewhere. It was impossible to think, she'd complained the day before, up in my study with the summer sun beating at the closed shutters.

She texted me at the desk where I was working a mile away in the cool of the British Library.

'I found Grandpa's boxes,' she wrote. 'Can I open them?'

It took me a while to reply.

'It's a mess in there,' I texted back. 'But maybe you could sort the papers into some kind of order, if you've got time.'

When I came back to the house several hours later Kez was sitting in the top-floor study, shutters closed, among neat piles of papers. Knife-thin shafts of light, pouring in through the gaps in the shutters, lit up the dust. Orlando, my elderly marmalade-striped cat, tiptoed over and between the piles of papers, trying to get himself into the path of her intense attention. The fan parts lay discarded, unassembled, on the floor.

She'd gone to the pound shop round the corner and bought Post-it notes and plastic filing sleeves and filing boxes.

'I started in 1953,' she said, flushed. 'There's letters from South Africa and Grandpa's prison diary in that file. There's this letter he wrote to Granny when he tells her he wants a divorce and he says he wants to discuss which of you stays with her and which one goes with him. There's all these lists of Brethren rules and pamphlets. Mad stuff. Weird. I didn't know half of this. You've never told me.'

'You can't just tell it in bits,' I said, though I knew I could have tried. Why hadn't I told my children about the Brethren? Because I didn't know how to begin to answer the questions I knew they'd ask, questions that I'd avoided for years. How do cults work? How had our family got caught up in such an extreme Protestant sect in the first place? Why would anyone have wanted to join the Brethren? How did the men get such power over the women? Why didn't anyone rebel?

And then the girl in the red cardigan and headscarf is in the room with me again. The girl I'd once been. She's furious. She's sitting in Meeting listening to the men preach, and she's trying to figure out what 'heavenly citizenship' is, or what it means for a house to be 'hallowed', or whether the Holy Spirit is male or female and how transparent it is. And she wants to know why the women aren't allowed to speak. But she knows she can't ask questions about that because she's a girl and she's not allowed to speak either. And she's wondering why none of the women are standing up and shouting and stamping their feet like she wants to do, telling the men to stop talking all that nonsense.

My father might have died before he'd been able to face his questions, but I still had time. This was going to be *my* story as well as his. I might be afraid of those bullying men and their lawyers, but I'd face them down. *Let* them come and find me.

Kez agreed to be my research assistant for a few weeks that summer. She'd make an archive in a series of box files, label everything. While I began to piece a history together, Kez found a website.

'They've renamed themselves the Plymouth Brethren Christian Church,' she said, passing me her laptop.

'You must have found the wrong Brethren,' I told her. 'Exclusive Brethren never go anywhere near the internet. Mobile phones and computers are all banned. Bruce Hales

– that's their current leader – once described the internet as "pipelines of filth". They'd *never* have their own website.'

But Kez was right. This *was* the same Exclusive Brethren that three generations of my family and I had all been born into: same leaders, same values, same rules. There were, according to Wikipedia, 46,000 of them, living in fellowship across nineteen different countries, 16,000 in the UK. The leader, Bruce Hales, was the nephew of the man who'd been in charge when I was growing up. They'd turned it into a family dynasty and rebranded – expensively. They must have renamed themselves to throw off the bad publicity they'd been attracting for decades, I told Kez. But why would they have spent that much money? They'd never cared about public opinion before.

The website had photographs and videos of Brethren Rapid Response Teams – young people dressed in high-visibility jackets – setting up travelling kitchens to feed people who'd lost their homes in bushfires in Australia or in flooding in the UK, handing out brownies to baffled fire crews or bottles of water to commuters at King's Cross station during a heatwave. There were photographs of choirs of Brethren girls in long skirts and headscarves singing hymns to old people in care homes. It made the hairs on the back of my neck stand up.

*Family is at the heart of everything we believe and everything we do*, one caption read, printed over a close-up photograph of a small girl running her hand through ears of corn. I felt a sudden flare of fury. How dare they? I thought of the suicides; the thousands of families that the Brethren had tortured and broken up over the decades; the scores of ex-Brethren I knew who would never see their parents or their siblings again. Did the members of the PR company have any idea about the group they'd agreed to promote?

But when Kez and I looked at news archives, we found that the Brethren were still getting bad press. In 2009 an Australian investigative journalist had published a best-selling book about Brethren tax-avoidance schemes. He'd exposed their aggressive political lobbying in Australia; he'd interviewed hundreds of ex-Brethren about suicides, excommunications, severed families, and post-traumatic stress.[1] The then Australian prime minister Kevin Rudd had described them as 'an extremist cult that breaks up families and is bad for Australia'.[2]

British investigative journalists had been on their backs too. Newspaper articles about Brethren faith schools and tax-avoidance schemes had dented their reputation. In 2012 Britain's charity watchdog had denied charitable status to the Brethren for one of their trusts in Devon. They risked losing millions of pounds in tax breaks as a result. So they'd appealed against the decision, and started up that PR and lobbying campaign to get their charitable status reinstated. But, British journalists wrote, these were no little guys being picked on by the Charity Commission. These people preached hate.

'We have to get a hatred, an utter hatred of the world,' Hales had told a large Brethren audience in 2006. 'Unless you've come to a hatred of the world you're likely to be sucked in by it, and seduced by it.'[3]

British Brethren lobbyists had been more than usually aggressive in their campaign to get their charitable status reinstated. Two *Times* journalists had got hold of minutes from a meeting in which Hales had urged Brethren lobbyists to apply 'extreme pressure' to William Shawcross, the head of the Charity Commission; 'Go for the jugular,' he told them, 'go for the underbelly.' It made me shiver.

'That's in hand,' one lobbyist had replied.[4]

For Hales and his followers, Shawcross was a non-Brethren 'worldy', an agent of Satan's system and thus fair game.

When I read that the Charity Commission *had* renewed the Brethren's charitable status in 2014 I began to wonder what they'd done to Shawcross's jugular. Then I began to wonder what they might do to mine. I could see Kez was thinking the same thing.

'Shit,' she said. 'This is scary.'


Over the next few weeks Kez labelled the box files 'Before', 'During' and 'After'.

'You can change it later,' she said. 'It's just a way of dividing up the time for now.'

I nodded. The girl in the red cardigan was in the room again.

'You might prefer "Aftermath",' Kez said, 'rather than "After". It gives more of a sense of consequence … You know – that what happens to you and your father after is a result of the screws gradually tightening in the "Before" and "During" parts.'

'Of course,' I said. I was remembering the feel of the headscarf knot pressing at the back of my neck and the weight of my uncut hair hanging down my back in braided ropes. 'Yes. That's good.'

I made a note to watch *Wild Strawberries* with Kez. She's never seen any Bergman.

A month after we started, I dreamt Kez and I were lowering ourselves down into a dark network of caves on a long rope. She was ahead of me. She had the torch. She made me think of those old stories where an innocent girl has to slay a dragon to break a curse.

Her young handwriting layered over my father's when she put his letters in order. 'This one's interesting,' she'd write on a label on the plastic sleeve. 'He was preaching out in the black townships during apartheid.' On the letter that my father had written to my mother about divorce, Kez wrote: 'This one might be hard to read.'

'Break bread?' Kez says. 'What's that?' She's secular. I've raised her that way.

'Transubstantiation,' I tell her. 'Jesus died on the cross and left instructions that people were to remember his death, his *sacrifice*, by eating bread and drinking wine. The bread was supposed to be his body and the wine his blood. We called it breaking bread.'

'I'll look it up,' she said.

I'm already back there, kneading the tiny piece of warm bread in my fingers in the early hours of the morning. It's winter. It's the first Meeting of the day and it's still dark outside. I'm in my headscarf and my Best Dress and I'm holding my Bible in one hand and my doll in the other.

'We called it breaking bread,' I'd told Kez. Who, I wondered, was this *we* I kept slipping back into?

# BEFORE

# I

I was born fourth-generation Brethren. Hanging up there on all the branches of the family tree are generations of Brethren on both my mother's and father's sides, and before that several generations of French Huguenots, Calvinist émigrés who fled waves of Catholic persecution. If you've been born into a group like the Brethren, and everyone you know – parents, friends, work colleagues, siblings, grandparents, great-grandparents, cousins – is living by Brethren rules, you assume it's completely normal. It's the people *outside* your assembly who seem strange.

That long Brethren inheritance was a badge of honour in our household. It was held in place by the stories we were told and the objects and keepsakes in our home. An enormous oil paint-ing of my eminent great-great-grandfather, Grandpa Mallalieu, my grandmother's grandfather, hung over the fireplace in our sitting room. It would have reminded the Brethren guests who came for tea between Meetings of our distinguished bloodline. Arthur Lee Mallalieu had 'taken the ministry' across Australia, set up tent meetings and tin tabernacles and helped to establish the first Brethren assemblies in Adelaide, Canberra, Melbourne and Sydney. When my mother toasted crumpets on the fire for us on cold winter days I'd look up and he'd be looking straight back down at me.

It was not an especially stern portrait. Grandpa Mallalieu was tall and handsome. In the painting he seemed to have just looked up from reading his Bible; his head rested thoughtfully on his hand. But you could never escape Grandpa Mallalieu's eyes. Growing up I tried standing in every corner of our sitting room to find a spot where I might avoid them. There wasn't one.

There was always someone watching: God from above and Grandpa Mallalieu from the sitting-room wall.

'Grandpa Mallalieu'

The portrait had been painted over another painting, my mother said, but she could not remember what it was. As a small child I imagined there was a ship under Grandpa Mallalieu, battling high waves, riding the wind.

In the kitchen my mother had hung a large framed print of Vermeer's *The Milkmaid*. She loved the cobalt blue of the young woman's apron, she said. It was her favourite colour.

The milkmaid stood at a window, pouring milk at a table piled high with freshly baked bread. She didn't watch me like Grandpa Mallalieu did. Her eyes were down; she was rapt in her own daydreams, just as my mother often was. I watched the milkmaid from the kitchen table when my father was giving thanks before dinner, when my siblings and I were supposed to be praying with our eyes closed. Her milk poured from the mouth of her jug into that terracotta bowl below, *without end*. With her head covered like that and her table full of freshly made bread, I always assumed she was a Brethren sister, just like my mother and aunts, busy preparing the bread for the Lord's Day Meeting. While the men were discussing ministries or disciplinary decisions in the adjoining room as they did in our house, she was snatching a private moment, secret and off in her dreams.

But there was a wooden box in the lower right corner of the picture that filled me with dread. Recently I read that it was probably a seventeenth-century foot warmer, but back then I imagined it was a trap or an instrument of torture. It meant that this dreaming, fleshy, cobalt-blue-wrapped girl was going to get caught.

* * *

Brethren were proud of their roots. My father would defend the radical puritanism of the very first Brethren, sometimes passionately, long after he'd left the Brethren and given up his belief in God.

'It started out right-minded,' he'd say. 'But it went wrong. They weren't intending to start their own Church. They were just good men walking in the Lord together, trying to find a way of living according to Paul's gospel.'

If I had any chance of understanding what my father had called the Nazi decade and its aftermath – the turbulence we lived through as a family in the 1960s, seventies and eighties, the separations, the suicides, the scandal, the schisms, the gambling, my father's addictions, embezzlement and prison sentence – I was going to have to understand how the Brethren crossed the line from being right-minded, as my father had put it, to being wrong-minded. I needed to find out how they turned into a cult.

The handful of Brethren history books I consulted all confirmed my father's story. In the late 1820s a few young men, repelled by the corruption, decadence and in-fighting they saw in the Anglican and Catholic Churches, had come together to break bread in sitting rooms and hired halls in Dublin. Certain that the world was fast approaching its end, they decided to return to the principles of the early Christian Church as laid out by Paul's gospel – adapted, as they thought fit, for nineteenth-century believers:

No priests.

No ritual.

No intermediaries.

No incense.

No hierarchy.

No sacred ground.

No altars or pulpits.

They were not a denomination, they insisted. They were simply following The Spirit, and preparing for the End Times.

A charismatic ex-barrister and ex-curate, John Nelson Darby, had eventually taken a lead. None of them would be saved, he told his followers, unless they separated completely from the rest of the world. They had to prepare a clean house for the Lord's coming.

When I was growing up there were framed photographs of Darby on the walls of most Brethren sitting rooms. Two elderly Brethren sisters called the Miss Ellimans used to give us sweets on the Lord's Day from a drawer under a glass-fronted cabinet in which they kept their framed photograph of Darby. Though Brethren talked about him as a kind of saint, he always looked to me, as he glowered out from behind the glass door of the cabinet, like the kind of man who'd shout at you if he opened his mouth.

Darby is famous for having 'invented' the idea of the Rapture. He'd had a vision, he told his followers, that there would be *two* Second Comings, not just one. First, Christ would arrive and take the Brethren off the planet, in a sudden, secret exodus to heaven. It was all there in the scriptures; hadn't

John Nelson Darby

the Apostle Paul told the Thessalonians that the Lord's people would be 'caught up' into the air? As soon as the Rapture had taken place, all the people left behind, the worldly people, would suffer the Great Tribulation. The Bible didn't specify what this was exactly, but we all understood there'd be terrible storms, earthquakes, plagues and famines.[1]

Christ would return a second time, Darby wrote, for the Judgement Day reckonings. There would be people saved at that point, but they'd be in the second ranking. The most privileged of the residents of heaven would be the Rapture people, the ones who'd gone in the first exodus: the elite, the first-class travellers, the emigrants.

That was *us*, my people, the Brethren.

They told us children that all we had to do was take the Lord Jesus into our hearts and 'withdraw from iniquity' to be certain of a place in the much-longed-for upward rush of the Rapture. But despite my most strenuous efforts, I never managed to withdraw from iniquity for very long – and that meant, of course, that I knew I'd be left behind.

The Brethren visitors who came to our house for tea between Meetings were from all over the world. Once people like Grandpa Mallalieu had started the missionary work back in the nineteenth century, Brethrenism had gone everywhere. By 1845 there were 1,200 Brethren breaking bread together in a hall in Plymouth. By the end of the nineteenth century there were assemblies right across Europe, in Australia, New Zealand, America, Jamaica and Canada, Brethren breaking bread in tents, or assembling in corrugated-iron churches built from kits, in fields and jungles and in the outback.

There were quarrels and schisms right from the start. When Darby returned from preaching in Europe in 1845 and found that the Brethren at Plymouth had reintroduced priests, he first denounced them, and then withdrew from them. This was the first withdrawal of many. The religious-tract war that followed, with Darby accusing his adversaries' leader, Benjamin Newton, of being 'a blind instrument of Satan', led to new rifts. When the Brethren of the Bethesda assembly in Bristol broke bread with some of Newton's followers, Darby withdrew from all of them. He wrote to all the rest of the Brethren assemblies around the world, telling them that 'to receive anyone from Bethesda is opening the door now to the infection of the abominable evil from which at so much painful cost we have been delivered'.[2]

*Abominable evil. Infection.* That was the way they talked. When we left the Brethren I was surprised to discover the rest of the world didn't talk like we did. Darby's way of seeing the world was absolute. He was certain he was right. Evil was real, he told his followers. It was everywhere.

The Brethren tract wars attracted newspaper attention from the start. In 1869 James Grant, editor of the *Morning Advertiser*, described Brethren as living in 'a state of constant antagonism' with each other and with the world. He reported the violent behaviour he'd seen at Brethren conferences; but it was, he wrote, 'the effect of Darbyism on family life' that was 'perhaps its most awful feature'.[3] He reported numerous cases of families broken up by Brethren rules.

Brethrenism has always devastated families. It's a measure of the Brethren's faith, they say, that they are prepared to put the Lord before 'natural ties'. When they say 'natural ties' they mean family bonds, those complex threads of affection and loyalty that weave between siblings and parents and children. Those threads are good, they believe, but not if they lead to Brethren rules being broken. That's when you have to take a knife to them.

My father always had a bit of a thing for Darby's black-and-white, brooking-no-compromise asceticism. I was impressed by it too in my teens; it reminds me of the excitement I felt when I later read Ralph Waldo Emerson or Henry David Thoreau on civil disobedience. There was something brave and bold, I thought, about these people refusing to kowtow to the Church authorities, rejecting the incense, the idolatry, the angels-on-a-pinhead High Church nonsense of it all. They'd gone their own way; they'd done their own thing. I liked that.

But the trouble is that if you persuade people that this world is a mere waiting room for the next, they'll come to despise it; if you teach people to believe that Satan is using all of the people outside your Meeting Room to try to stop you from going up in the Rapture, they'll come to think that all those people are tricksters and devils, or infected with evil; and if the promised Rapture doesn't come, pretty soon they'll become paranoid, impatient and obsessive, and they'll be looking for ways to separate *harder*.

# 2

I found the Dublin auction house – one of the places where those first Brethren had met together in the 1830s – on Google Street View. It had become a shop. I scrolled in close, but couldn't get past the door. I would have liked to have gone inside to find the room where the Brethren brothers and sisters had laid out a circle of chairs around a table, shaken out a white cloth, and placed a freshly baked loaf and a cup of wine in the centre, *just as we had done*. Afterwards, I knew, they'd have stepped out into the noisy street, clutching their Bibles, feeling purged and clean, steeling themselves against Satan's world out there, the dirt and the devil of it, just as we had done.

My father grew up a hundred or so years later amongst Brethren who broke bread in the Iron Room in Kenilworth, a corrugated-iron shed assembled on wasteland down by the river, one of many Brethren tin tabernacles across the world, either purpose-built or requisitioned from other dissenting groups who'd traded up or shut down. At the centre of all that corrugated iron there was always a table with a white cloth, a freshly baked loaf and a collection box, inside a circle of chairs.

The Iron Room had once stood at the end of a terrace of Victorian houses called The Close, but it was demolished in 1982. When I went to Kenilworth to try to find it, the man who worked the adjoining allotment full of sweet peas and cabbages told me he kept pulling up sections of corrugated iron from his soil, even the occasional window frame. It had mystified him. He had no idea that he had the remains of a church underneath his dahlias. A local historian found a photograph for me.

The corrugated iron of Brethren Meeting Rooms testified to the sect's indifference to the world and its materialism. Their God didn't need fan vaulting or gold leaf. He came because of *them*. Nor did they need to consider longevity when they built these rooms – they didn't think about rust, mould, leaks, heating, or frozen pipes – because they were certain the Rapture was only weeks or months away. Eventually, of course, the pipes froze, the windows leaked, the iron rusted, paint flaked, mould spread; journalists came and angled their long-distance lenses to peer in through those high windows. To keep them out, the

'The Iron Room' in Kenilworth before it was demolished as part
of a drive to amalgamate small Brethren assemblies in the 1960s

Brethren frosted their glass, fitted curtain rails inside and rail-
ings and razor wire outside.[4]

Satan is abroad, Darby had told Brethren. Satan is stalking
the streets of Dublin, Paris, London, New York. He's got into
the churches, he's in the pubs, the law courts, the pulpits, the
theatres. 'Satan is the god of this world,' he wrote, 'the prince
of the power of the air, and the manager of this stupendous
system.' And Brethren, he preached, had to separate themselves
completely from all this. They had to disconnect from 'business, politics, education, governments, science, inventions,
railroads, telegraphs, social arrangements, charitable institu-
tions, reforms, religion'.[5] Telegraphs, invented in the 1830s,
were a particular obsession for Darby, certain proof that Satan
had got hold of the air.

There were so many things to separate from. Even the air. It all required so much vigilance.

Splitting, withdrawing – sometimes Brethren called it 'circumcision' – became the Brethren way. They did it dramatically, defiantly, over and over again. It happened all the time in our Meeting when I was growing up. There were always people my grandparents would be tutting about or praying over, sometimes people I knew, or people in other Meetings I'd heard about. If my grandparents were praying for someone it usually meant they were in big trouble. It almost always meant they'd be withdrawn from, and then we wouldn't see them again.

After Darby and his followers split from the large Brethren assemblies in Plymouth and Bristol in 1848, people began to call them the Darbyite Brethren, the Exclusive, or the Close, or Closed, Brethren.

When I think of the word 'close', I hear *Keep close, Come close, Be close, We're close*. There's a hushed, whispered sanctuary to it, something intimate, protective and secretive, warm, perhaps with a hint of stale air. When I think of the word 'closed', I hear doors banging, gates slamming, drawbridges shuddering into place, keys turning. *Closed room. Closed shop.* Closed is not the same as private or keep out. It means *We were open once but now we're closed. We might once have let you in but now we won't.*

The Exclusive Brethren went from close to closed. They went from drawing close to shutting out. In or around 1848 this strict, close community began to *shun*.

I'm stepping gingerly here, because I hear Brethren women – cousins, aunts, ancestors – gathering in the wings. They have something to say. They're whispering that Darby was right; they're telling me why my educated, sceptical, secular way of seeing things is so impoverished. They want to tell me that God loves me, that he wants to make everything right in the world, that he suffers with us, with me, that he died for my sins. They remind me that everything and everybody in this world, including me, is riddled with sin, and only Jesus can redeem us from that. They tell me to look at the pornography, the internet, the self-harm, the levels of depression and the empty churches. These are all signs of Satan's dominion, sure signs of his evil working in the world.

These women have my big bones and wild hair; they are serene, gracious, dignified. My grandmother is in the room. I can hear the swish of her silk skirts, can smell her lily-of-the-valley talcum powder, I can hear her talking about the Lord Jesus as I stand on a chair at her kitchen sink blowing bubbles through my tiny fingers. They'd tell a different story if I let them. But I have to tell my father's story. And mine.

# 3

The Rapture was coming. It might come next week or next year, but it was always coming. I was sure I wouldn't be the only one left behind when it came. I was pretty certain that my brothers and most of the Brethren children in our assembly wouldn't make it either.

Once all those thousands of Brethren grown-ups around the world had disappeared up into the clouds with their Bibles, I knew my brothers and I would have to get through the Tribulation as best we could. The trouble was that not only the not-good-enough Brethren, but all those dangerous worldly people outside the Brethren would be left behind too. We'd have to find a way of hiding from them and getting to high ground so we wouldn't drown when the tidal waves came. I thought about that almost every day.

I knew my brothers wouldn't be much good in an emergency. I'd have to take charge when the time came, find a place for us to hide. I'd gone to look at the coal bunker in our house, but decided against it. It was too dark and dirty. There were spiders. It would flood too when the tidal waves came. The garage at my grandparents' house was a much better proposition. It was higher up. There'd be less chance of flooding. My grandmother kept stacks of crates of strawberry pop in little glass bottles there; there were candles and boxes of jam tarts from the family business. I knew where she kept the key. We'd be fine there for a few weeks, I thought, if we were careful not to be seen going in.

Because I knew I'd be left behind, I spent much of my childhood preparing for the Tribulation. My dreams were full of floods and lightning and earthquakes. Most of the games I played had boats in them. They were thrilling.

When I was growing up in the 1960s, my father and grandfather ran a Brethren wholesale grocery called Stott and Sons from a cavernous and labyrinthine old warehouse in Shirley Street in Hove. If my father had sole charge of me and my brothers, he would sometimes leave us to play unsupervised in the darkened storerooms while he did something 'important' in the office next door. We were not to tell our mother.

Though the Stott and Sons warehouse drivers who came and went would protest about our safety, we'd scramble up the cliffs made by stacks of rice and flour sacks, slip over the top and down into the inner chambers we found or made there. We'd squeeze down rockfaces made by piled-high boxes of tinned asparagus or tomatoes, and hoist ourselves up on the chain winches that ran through the trapdoors in the wooden ceiling to the upper rooms where the boxes of sweets and crisps were kept. We'd hide under crates in dusty back rooms we'd found up tiny staircases that seemed to appear from nowhere. There were no eyes on us in the warehouse.

Before we went to school, my brothers and I had no children's stories or fairy tales or cartoons to shape our play. They were banned. Instead we made up games based on mixed-up Bible stories from the Old and New Testaments. We transformed the darkened rice mountains and valleys and walls of boxes of the warehouse into the landscapes of the Holy Land. We'd march round the walls of Jericho, wade across the Jordan, rescue Jonah from the whale and then raise Lazarus so he could fight alongside David as he took on Goliath.

While my brothers were fencing with swords they'd made from sticks of wood I'd be scrambling up those rice-sack mountains, scraping my knees raw on the rough hessian, fleeing lashing rain and rising floodwater. I'd make arks out of any inner chamber I found, pulling old sacks across the top to keep out the relentless rain and lightning. As the smells of muscovado sugar or paprika or brown rice rose up around me, I'd be pressed into the ark's hold, feeling the swell of the waves or easing a white dove through an imaginary porthole. Or I'd be Jonah inside the belly of the whale, listening out for the sound of gulls through the whale's flanks, sounds that would tell me we were near land.

That ark was mine. I unfurled the sails. I stood at the helm on the deck. I got to decide which way we sailed.

Sometimes beautiful and incomprehensible lines from the Bible drifted into my daydreams or play: 'Hast thou entered into the storehouses of the snow,' the Lord had asked Job as he and Satan took turns to torment him, 'and hast thou seen the treasuries of the hail? … By what way is the light parted, [and] the east wind scattered upon the earth?' Or I'd repeat my favourite sentence from the Bible, four words that come after verse after verse of flooding, wind and rain, destruction and desolation:

'And-God-re-mem-bered-No-ah.'

During those long hours spent listening to Biblical exegesis in Meeting, I could take myself to the imaginary salty, spice-scented hold of my boat or into the whale's belly as if they were parallel worlds. I can still smell the inside of that ark nearly fifty years later, the feel of the hessian sacks against my knees.

It came as no surprise to me then to discover that those Brethren ancestors of mine were fishing folk, that they'd lived on the edge of the sea and the land since 1800. Boats and fish were in my bloodline, too, not just in my Tribulation-survival dreams.

I was the fourth generation of the Brethren Stotts. Unlike the rest of us who had been born into the Brethren, my great-grandfather, David Fairbairn Stott, a Scottish sailmaker, had chosen to join. He was the first. He'd made a choice that would shape the lives of all his children, grandchildren and great-grandchildren, because, due to the severity of Brethren rules, if you were born into the cult you'd have to be steely-willed to be able – or allowed – to leave it.

Could that austere Protestantism linger as a kind of tribal consciousness, I'd begun to wonder – like my boat imaginings – long after I'd left the Brethren? If I avoided friends who'd said something that had offended me, if I neglected to return their emails, was that a Brethren thing, or just a human thing?

I found David Fairbairn Stott on the 1890 census return, where he was listed as an apprentice sailmaker in Eyemouth, a fishing village on the coast fifty miles south-east of Edinburgh, located at the point just north of the border between England and Scotland where the River Eye joins the sea – hence the Eye and the Mouth.

As far as I could trace from the records, in the nineteenth century these Eyemouth Stotts had either fished or made barrels or sails. When they were not following the herring, they scanned the sea and sky for signs of changes in the weather; they tapped barometers, they mended nets; they baited lines, hauled barrels, and dragged nets.

For weeks I sat behind a pile of books at a desk in the British Library – sailmaking manuals, books about witchcraft and smuggling and Scottish dissenting groups – reading about the Lowland clearances and how sails were made and how the herring were gutted and preserved in barrels of salt. When I looked at my hands scribbling notes, I thought about the women I was descended from who'd gutted fish for ten hours a day in the fish yard, their hands cut and bleeding from their sharp knives. They must have been in pain every minute of the day from plunging those raw hands in and out of the salt.

Why would someone – anyone – from an already hard life like this have *wanted* to join the Brethren? The nineteenth-century Eyemouth I was reading about didn't seem to be a particularly religious place. It was a frontier town, a hard-drinking, law-defying town. There were Primitive Methodists here in the 1830s; Baptists and Presbyterians too. But most of the fishermen and fisherwomen in Eyemouth were in constant battle with the Kirk – the Church of Scotland – because it collected large tithes or taxes from their profits. The minister patrolled the harbour when the boats came in to make sure no one tried to cheat him of his dues.

Eyemouth people seemed to be more superstitious than devout. The local history books include lists of things that sailors avoided before the boats sailed. Women were bad luck. So were pigs, hares, white cats, and apples. It was unlucky to give away salt. It was unlucky to give your mother change from your pocket. If a sailor said the wrong thing, an unlucky thing, he had to touch cold iron.

The devil could snatch you. The sea could swallow you. In Eyemouth, staying alive seemed to be a matter of luck, and making sure you didn't test it.

# 4

It's easy to be romantic about lives lived out on the edge of the sea. The history books told me something darker. In the seventeenth century, several Eyemouth residents, almost all of them women, were tortured, tried, condemned and burned as witches, or torn limb from limb because someone had testified to seeing them consorting with the devil.[6] Local ministers ran the witch-hunts, it seemed, not just to drive out the devil, but also to sustain their own power, just as Brethren leaders would do with their own witch-hunts and expulsions generations later.

These were closed communities; people covered for each other. In the seventeenth century, villagers smuggled contraband lace or brandy and hid it in passageways dug through the rock, or stowed it inside hidden chambers they'd made in their chimneys or under floorboards. They'd be hanged if they were caught. The town had its own Masonic lodge, established in the mid-eighteenth century; its members included both smugglers and excisemen, all committed, just as the Closed Brethren were later, not just to religious worship but to sustaining close, secret and lucrative business networks.

But the nineteenth-century documents told me nothing about my family's religious affiliations. The census officers who'd visited the Eyemouth fishermen and women had asked them about parents, children, birthplace, birth date, even about blindness or madness, but they hadn't asked about God. So though I found David Fairbairn Stott on the census returns, I was still no wiser about what he thought about the Tribulation or the Rapture, or where he went on Sunday mornings, or whether he called Sunday Sunday or the Lord's Day.

I would have to drive north, I realised, to find out what took David Fairbairn Stott across the threshold of a Brethren Meeting Room for the first time. The books and historical records weren't going to tell me.

I'd found his grandmother listed as the widowed innkeeper of the Whale on Eyemouth harbourfront, a ten-bedroomed inn with a bar. How – and why – had the grandson of an innkeeper in a rough town like Eyemouth become a leading member of the Brethren? I'd found scores of Brethren Meeting Rooms further north along the coast, but none in Eyemouth. Perhaps if I went to the town it would give me something to go on.

I followed the road east to Eyemouth from Edinburgh through the border towns and villages where I'd found Stotts in the library records: Haddington, East Linton, Dunbar, Dunglass, Cockburnspath and Coldingham. The road wound through high moorland and wooded dells, past the high walls and gatehouses of great estates, down to sandy coves and inlets where fishing villages huddled against the sides of black cliffs studded with nesting seabirds, and back up again to high moor and big sky. The sea came in and out of view as I drove, the low sun gilding mudflats, white sand dunes or black rocks down below.

On the outskirts of Eyemouth the road passed through grey pebbledash suburbs and caravan parks. Along the harbour road the fishing sheds and warehouses gave way to a row of old pubs and inns facing the sea. Among them was the Whale, its windows and doors boarded up, one of three semi-derelict public houses still standing on the harbourfront.

I parked the car, and stepped out into a cold sea wind laced with the harbour smells of engine oil, petrol and fish from the fish yards. I walked around the perimeter of the inn, looking for gaps in the boarding, wading through the rubbish piled up around its walls, under the gaze of a group of fishermen smoking outside the adjacent pub. How had a forty-year-old widow, my ancestor, raised five children, managed the drunken sailors and the brawls and run a ten-bedroom inn here singlehandedly?

I ordered a glass of beer from the landlord in the pub next door. Inside, half a dozen local fishermen and construction workers sat hunched over crosswords or watched football on a television screen. The Whale had been closed for twenty years or more, the landlord told me. A developer from Hull owned the building now. It was a listed building, he said, protected by law, so the owner was probably waiting for it to become derelict enough for the council to allow him to knock it down. Then he'd build something that would make him some *real* money. He laughed.

When I asked for the name of this Hull developer, four or five men lifted their heads from their newspapers and looked in my direction. Was I a journalist, the landlord asked, looking away. I had planned to tell him how Margaret Stott, my great-great-grandmother, had run the Whale in the 1850s, but now I thought better of it. I was just doing some family-history research, I said, and changed the subject.

Eyemouth would have been packed with people at the height of the herring season, I reminded myself as I took pictures of the now almost empty harbour outside; there would have been carts coming and going, clusters of young women working against the clock to gut the fish and get them barrelled up and onto the backs of the waiting carts. During the 1850s, David Fairbairn's future father, the teenaged Robert Stott, an apprentice barrelmaker, would have presided over those herring packing girls, the ones with the cut and salted hands.

It was difficult to imagine this sleepy town as a once dangerous and violent place, the site of political protests and demonstrations. In the 1850s and sixties, after years of struggle, the Eyemouth fishermen and fisherwomen had finally refused to pay the tithe the Kirk demanded from them. Robert Stott, the apprentice cooper, and his fishing cousins had marched with the two thousand protesters along this harbourfront behind an enormous green banner embroidered with the words 'Pay No Tithe'. Robert would have been just fifteen when the local men stoned the police who came to arrest the charismatic leader of the protest, William 'The Kingfisher' Stearnes.

At the age of nineteen, when the police standoffs, protests and demonstrations were still playing out in Eyemouth, Robert had been courting one of the girls of the gutting yards, Lizzie Fairbairn, the eldest daughter of one of the largest fishing families in town. She was eighteen, and seven months pregnant, when they married. Her own mother was also pregnant with her twelfth child, so, with no room left at home, Lizzie moved into the Whale with her husband's mother and his three siblings. She gave birth to Agnes there in 1862, behind one of those boarded-up windows I stood beneath. I could see her now, walking out from the inn with her baby strapped to her back, swaddled against the wind, her much younger siblings running from all directions to cluster around her skirts.

I reached for the phone to call my father and tell him about Agnes and David, before I remembered: I couldn't call my father any more. He was dead. I couldn't tell him about the Whale Inn or his great-grandfather's run-ins with the Kirk, or how – when I'd seen that old inn all boarded up like that – I'd wanted to find a way to buy it and rescue it from the Hull developer, get the windows mended and the roof fixed. I couldn't tell him that for a moment I'd thought I'd seen Lizzie as if she were still alive, striding along the harbour wall.

My father had always been very proud of this Scottish ship-chandler inheritance of ours. When he and I had bought the little cabin boat together, and moored it on the river a few yards from the Mill door, he'd driven me across the fens to the ships' chandlers in Ely. We needed stocking up, he told my stepmother. He was in one of his extreme spending moods; she and I both knew there was no reasoning with him when he was like that. I followed him through the narrow aisles of the Ely ship chandlers as he selected objects that interested him, regard-less of price or usefulness: a stove, a ladder, spare buoys, a captain's hat, an extra-large waterproof coat.

'Stott and Sons,' he said when the shop owner took his credit card. 'Scottish ships' chandlers,' he added, as if he expected the shopkeeper to doff his cap or give him a discount. I winced, but the shopkeeper was charmed. They had already begun to exchange stories.

What would my father have thought of this messy and scattered older family history I'd now found in Eyemouth? What would he have made of the riots and his intemperate great-grandfather Robert? Would he have seen himself in Robert's reflection, as I was beginning to do?

At twenty-one years old, Robert, most likely in trouble with the police for his part in the anti-Kirk protests and stonings, or in debt to the local moneylender, decided it was time to leave town. According to the census returns he moved Lizzie and baby Agnes into one of the upper floors of a tenement in Edinburgh, where he'd taken a job as a cooper in a large brewery. By the time Lizzie was twenty-nine she was managing six children under the age of eight, carrying water and small infants up and down the steep stairs of the tenement and sharing an outside toilet with several neighbouring families.

After nine years in Edinburgh, Robert moved his family three hundred miles south to Grimsby, one of the biggest new dockyards in the world. The Stotts moved into one of the hundreds of small terraces newly built to house the 2,000 workers needed by the dockyards. Lizzie gave birth to two more boys here, Robert and David Fairbairn Stott. Then in January 1876, at the age of thirty-four, she died in the Grimsby terrace while giving birth to her ninth child. The baby did not survive.

For a year, Agnes, now thirteen, and her sisters, eleven-year-old Margaret and nine-year-old Isabella, must have cleaned and fed and cared for their younger brothers and sisters in that overcrowded terrace in Grimsby, doing laundry, keeping house, making ends meet as best they could while their father made barrels down in the dockyard. Their grandmother Margaret died that summer back in Eyemouth. Unmarried Aunt Isabella had taken over the management of the Whale from her mother, but running the inn on her own, she would not have been in a position to take in any of her older brother's city-born children.

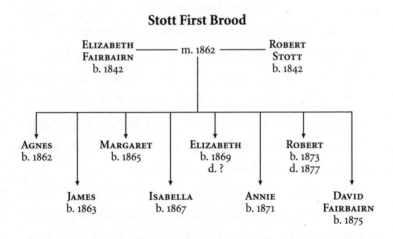

**Stott First Brood**

ELIZABETH FAIRBAIRN b. 1842 ———— m. 1862 ———— ROBERT STOTT b. 1842

AGNES b. 1862

JAMES b. 1863

MARGARET b. 1865

ISABELLA b. 1867

ELIZABETH b. 1869 d. ?

ANNIE b. 1871

ROBERT b. 1873 d. 1877

DAVID FAIRBAIRN b. 1875

Back in the Grimsby terrace, baby Robert died that winter, only three years old. Eight-year-old Elizabeth slips off the records around this time, probably a victim of one of the epidemics that swept the town. Remarkably, David Fairbairn

Stott, the youngest, survived. Having buried two of their siblings that winter, and their mother only a year before that, Agnes and her sisters must have been tending their baby brother with special care. What would they have made of the heavily pregnant stepmother their father brought home to live with them, another Elizabeth, a twenty-nine-year-old Lincolnshire woman who'd been working as a scullery maid since she was fourteen? Her first baby, born in December 1877 and christened Mary, did not survive the winter.

Now Aunt Isabella sent for her brother's four oldest children – Agnes, James, Margaret and Isabella. The next census, taken in April 1881, looks better for all of them. Margaret and Isabella are listed as living at the Whale Inn, working as domestic servants. James, the eldest boy, had joined an Eyemouth fishing crew. Agnes, eighteen, had married a sailmaker called John Wilson, and had a baby son. The couple were living in their own house down near Eyemouth marketplace. Annie and David Fairbairn, the two youngest surviving members of the first brood of Stotts, had stayed on down in Grimsby with their father and stepmother and two new siblings. They were both attending school.

Might those older Stott children, I wondered, have finally found refuge after all those years of poverty, migration and loss? But I'd forgotten about the storm.

When the hurricane, one of the most violent in British history, hit the east coast six months later, Agnes, nineteen and pregnant with her second child, would have been among the crowd of Eyemouth women standing on the harbour wall

Eyemouth harbour. The Whale Inn can be seen between
the boat and the car

outside the Whale as the fleet of battered fishing boats tried to
make it back into the harbour through the towering waves.
One hundred and twenty-nine brothers, uncles, cousins, sons
and fathers were killed in a few hours that afternoon in 1881,
thrown from boats, drowned, or smashed against the rocks or
the harbour wall. Among them were Agnes's three young Stott
cousins and three of her Fairbairn uncles. For weeks afterwards
the bodies of those Eyemouth men washed up in coves and on
beaches, limbs missing, faces unrecognisable.

I do the maths. That's ten, perhaps eleven, family members
Agnes had lost: mother Lizzie, grandmother Margaret, baby
brother Robert, sister Eliza, baby half-sister Mary, three Stott
cousins, three Fairbairn uncles. And she was still only
nineteen.

# 5

A gnes must have considered herself lucky to have married a sailmaker and not a sailor, lucky that her sisters hadn't married sailors, that they'd been spared the fate of the eighty-two widows of Eyemouth. According to the records I'd found in the Eyemouth fishing museum, many of those women were, like Agnes, pregnant when they buried their husbands. They named their newborn babies after their dead fathers. Now I understood why Robert had named his new daughter, born two years after the disaster, Adelina Purves Spouse Stott. It had always struck me as such an odd name. James Purves and Thomas Spouse had been Robert's childhood friends, and they'd died in the storm. Adelina Purves Spouse Stott was Robert's twelfth child.

Few Eyemouth families escaped the long aftermath of the storm. With the fishing fleet largely destroyed, John Wilson's sailmaking business, like all the businesses in the town, was soon on a knife edge. Within four years he'd been listed in the Glasgow *Herald* as a 'Scotch Bankrupt'.[7] He was one of many from the town. If they'd built a new harbour instead of having to fight the Kirk all those years, historians say, those fishermen would probably still be alive. They'd only gone out in that storm because they had to, because they had children to feed and the Kirk tithe to pay.

John and Agnes moved forty miles east along the coast to start up a new sailmaking business in Port Seton, a small fishing village outside Edinburgh. Since its new harbour had opened in 1880, thirty-five boats had been registered there. The population had tripled in twenty years. It was an industrious town, the history books claim, and, compared to Eyemouth, a Godfearing town. New churches were going up everywhere.

But things just kept getting worse for Agnes and John. They and their two small children had only been in Port Seton for four years when news came from Agnes's younger sister Annie down in Grimsby that their father had died, at only forty-six years old. Robert Stott died, his son David always told people, *a drinker's death*. Five months later, his widow Elizabeth died in childbirth, leaving seven orphaned children in the Grimsby terrace.

### Stott Second Brood

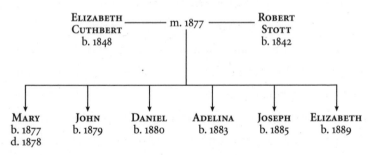

| ELIZABETH CUTHBERT b. 1848 | m. 1877 | ROBERT STOTT b. 1842 |
|---|---|---|

| MARY b. 1877 d. 1878 | JOHN b. 1879 | DANIEL b. 1880 | ADELINA b. 1883 | JOSEPH b. 1885 | ELIZABETH b. 1889 |

Within weeks all seven had been taken in – adopted by their older brothers or sisters, or put to work. Agnes took her fourteen-year-old brother David and her four-year-old half-brother Joseph to live with her in Port Seton. Her husband would take David on as apprentice in the Wilson sail sheds.

Could any of these Stott children read? If the older ones had been taught their letters it would have been at one of the many Grimsby Sunday schools, like the one the Primitive Methodists had opened in 1867, just a few streets away from the Stott house. The younger children were luckier. Annie and David had just enough time between their mother's death in 1876 and their father and stepmother's death in 1889 to attend the new public-funded school. They had learned to read, write, and do sums.

I was the oldest girl in a family of five children, with an absent father and a hardworking, sleep-deprived mother. I knew that Agnes and her young sisters would have been carrying those babies around in Grimsby, mashing up food, wiping noses, cleaning up cuts, singing songs, telling stories, just as I did. I helped my mother feed my adored twin brother and sister, born when I was nearly six, and I read to them and listened to them read when they were old enough.

But there were older Brethren 'sisters' who helped my mother – shadowy, kind women who baked and stitched, who took us out for picnics or to the beach. My mother had electricity, a washing machine, a sewing machine and a food mixer; she had powdered mashed-potato mix, tins of Spam and sliced pineapples in her kitchen cupboards, and her own car parked outside. She taught me to read long before I went to school. I'd like to think that at least some of those Grimsby Stott children had books stowed under their pillows as I did.

But though they'd suffered through those early years, Agnes and David must have considered themselves on safe and solid ground in their new house in bustling Port Seton, with its brand-new harbour and all those boats out there bringing in trade to the Wilson sailmaking sheds.

# 6

The disorder of Agnes and David's early life in Grimsby was due in part to the alcoholism of their father and the worn-down compliance of their mother and stepmother. But now that I'd been to the Eyemouth fishing museum and read the local history books, I was beginning to see a bigger picture. The chaos and bereavement the Stotts had lived through was also caused, at least to some extent, by the Lowland Clearances that propelled so many Scots from their farms into a migrant life in search of work or towards one of the emigration ships sailing to New Zealand, Canada or America. The destiny of the Stotts, like millions of their fellow Scots, had been determined by violent historical forces.

From the mid-eighteenth century, as part of what historians call the Clearances, the owners of large Scottish estates began to clear the 'peasants' off the land and put sheep in their place, to maximise profits. In the Lowlands, near the Borders where my family lived, small tenant or landowning farmers were forced off their farms not by violent eviction, as happened in the later Highland Clearances, but by *stealth*. Landowners

hiked rents, and eventually farms and businesses went bankrupt. Tens of thousands of Lowland cottars moved to newly-
built villages or to cities in search of work or to the coast to fish,
and thousands emigrated.[8]

The Stotts had once been tenant farmers too. I'd found
Robert's grandfather, James Stott, listed as a tenant cattle-farmer
living in Gairmuir near Lauder in the Borders in the 1790s,
thirty-five miles inland from Eyemouth. He'd been declared
bankrupt in 1799, five years after the Earl of Lauderdale's agents
had decided to hike the rents. Like thousands of other bankrupt
labourers and tenants, James gave up his farm and went to the
city to look for work. He set up as a butcher in Edinburgh,
while his three sons later left for Eyemouth to look for work as
fishermen or drovers. The family had stayed put until the storm
of 1881 forced them to migrate again.

I stood on the edge of the remote drovers' road etched into
the hills in the rough high moor at Gairmuir, watching it
undulate through the heather and gorse and disappear into the
mist. This was the road my drover ancestors walked alongside
their cattle to the Edinburgh cattle market. They'd called it the
Thieves' Road, a farmer told me. Robbers attacked the drovers
at night when they returned from the city carrying the money
they'd made at market.

The rain began, lashing diagonally in great lines, bringing
the night down with it. Up on the hill a mile away, lights
glowed in the windows of a remote farmhouse. You'd be glad to
see the light from your home, I thought, if you were a young
drover out here alone in the rain with the dark closing in on

you. You'd be glad to get inside and bolt the door against the robbers and the night.

Of course the displaced labourers and tenant farmers weren't just looking for security when they joined the Presbyterians, the Baptists, the Free Church, or the Open or Closed Brethren in their thousands in the religious revivals of the 1880s. Joining a non-conformist Church must also have been a way of rebelling, of *closing their doors* on all outside authority, refusing to rent a seat in a pew or to pay tithes to a corrupt Church or to kowtow to a landowner who had cleared them off their land.[9] What looked like an act of extreme religious dissent was also a political one.

By the time Agnes and John Wilson arrived in Port Seton in 1885, five years after the new harbour had been built there, and at a time when migrants from all over Scotland were flocking to the town, there were hymns being sung out of *six* buildings on Sunday mornings, including *two* Brethren Meeting Rooms, a Methodist Hall and a Mission Hall. Around the corner local builders were digging the foundations for what is listed as a Fishermen's Bethel, a chapel for sailors.

Brethren were kin; they were in fellowship together. They shut out the rest of the world, but they looked after each other. Brethren married other Brethren and had large numbers of children. They worked hard. They prospered. They kept themselves apart. After the chaos Agnes and David had lived through, they must have been looking not just for stability and faith, but also for a door to close defiantly against the turmoil. Of all the religious groups in Port Seton they might have joined, the Closed Brethren offered them the greatest degree of separation from the world.

# 7

'Were your folk Red-Tilers or Blue-Tilers?' the Port Seton fishmonger asked me when I asked for directions to the Brethren Meeting Room. He'd looked up from the parcel of crab he was wrapping for me and raised an eyebrow. 'Brethren Meeting Rooms are ten-a-penny round here. Red-Tilers don't talk to Blue-Tilers. No one knows what that's all about. Queer folk.'

He pointed in one direction to a building with a red-tiled roof, and in the other to one with a blue-tiled roof. Despite all the detective work I'd done, I had no idea which one my family had belonged to. Where had Agnes and David Fairbairn Stott broken bread?

It proved easier to figure out than I had feared. The noticeboard outside the red-tiled Meeting Room did not welcome visitors, so I knew it belonged to the Closed Brethren. The blue-tiled Meeting Room did welcome visitors, so it must belong to the Plymouth – or Open – Brethren. My folk, then, had been Red-Tilers.

It must have been difficult to live in Port Seton in the 1880s, I thought, without attending one of these churches and chapels. Agnes and her husband were probably breaking bread with the Red-Tilers before her two orphaned brothers stepped off the boat. The Port Seton Brethren had most likely helped John set up his new sailmaking business. Even if they hadn't helped out financially, they would have told the family that if they were prepared to give up their will to the Lord, they'd find a better life to come once he had taken them skyward in the Rapture. Agnes would see her mother and grandmother in heaven, and all those siblings and cousins she'd lost.

If Agnes had taken David and four-year-old Joseph along to the red-tiled Meeting Room, the boys would have been treated kindly, helped along, listened to, given a seat in the centre circle. Eventually they'd be asked to break bread, and then to preach. It would have given them a strong sense of belonging, safety and purpose, a conviction that they were the chosen ones and that the Rapture was coming soon.

From the census returns of 1901 I could see that David Fairbairn Stott had married Lizzie Durham, the eldest daughter of a prosperous fishing family. They'd been Brethren too. The census officers recorded that David was running both his own sailmaking shed on the harbourfront and a shop that sold shipping tackle. He'd become well-to-do. When he bought the first car in Port Seton, cousins had told me, Lizzie wouldn't get into it in front of the house. She was afraid the neighbours would think she was putting on airs, so her husband and children had to pick her up at the edge of the village. It was the Protestant way. Work hard, save money, do well, but don't flaunt your wealth.

Though David now had security, prosperity, community, wife and family, he still had to watch his back. He knew the Brethren assembly might withdraw from him at any moment if he didn't comply with the rules. Brethren used the verb 'to withdraw' to mean 'to separate from someone unclean', but really withdrawal meant expulsion. If you were withdrawn from you couldn't break bread, you were out of fellowship, you'd lose everyone you trusted, everyone you knew, immediately and for always, and you'd be forced to live among the unclean people, Satan's footsoldiers. Sometimes a single individual might be withdrawn from; sometimes whole assemblies.

So, in 1905, when Lizzie and David Stott and the other Port Seton Red-Tilers heard about an acrimonious Brethren rift in a small Northumberland market town called Alnwick, just seventy miles south, they'd have talked and prayed about little else. They'd seen it happen before; they knew that rifts like these could get out of hand and spread, engulfing neighbouring assemblies. It never ended well.

The trouble in the Alnwick assembly had, according to Brethren pamphlets I'd found, been caused, as usual, by disagreements about degrees of separation. One group of Brethren believed they should be out in the world saving souls; the other insisted that they withdraw from iniquity and prepare for the Rapture. Thomas Pringle, one of the older ministering brothers, locked the nineteen dissenters out of Green Batt Hall, their Meeting Room, and issued a letter excommunicating them.

The distressed 'outs' followed Brethren rules and wrote to the neighbouring Brethren in the tiny village of Glanton, eight miles away, asking for guidance about what to do. The Glantons, also following Brethren rules, urged them to seek reconciliation, but would not break bread with them.

Three years passed. Thomas Pringle refused to retract his excommunication. Most of the remaining Brethren in Alnwick left to join the defectors. Soon Pringle was breaking bread with only one or two other Brethren in Green Batt Hall, but he was still certain he was right.

Although David and Lizzie Stott and the other Port Seton Red-Tilers were sympathetic to the Alnwick 'outs', and frustrated by the way Pringle was behaving, Brethren rules stipulated that they were not to get involved. If they did, they might find themselves withdrawn from too.

In 1908 Brethren leaders in London took Alnwick off the list of approved assemblies. With so few Brethren left breaking bread together there, it was no longer viable. The Brethren in Glanton decided they could now break bread with the Alnwick 'outs'. It proved to be a disastrous decision. Other Brethren in neighbouring assemblies declared that the Glantons had broken Brethren rules; they were now unclean too.

Once Brethren assemblies across the north of England and southern Scotland had started taking sides, the trouble spread south. A Brethren woman who belonged to an Edinburgh assembly that had taken a fierce anti-Glanton stand visited Stoke Newington in north London. The Stoke Newington Brethren appealed to Brethren leaders in the nearby Park Street, Islington, assembly. Was it safe to break bread with her? If they did, would they be excommunicated?

The London Brethren patriarchs consulted, prayed and debated. Thomas Pringle, they finally ruled, had been right to pull up the drawbridge on the Alnwick defectors; the 'outs' had been dangerously 'intercommunional'. The Glantons, in supporting the Alnwick defectors, had broken Brethren rules too.

The London Brethren excommunicated not just the entire Glanton assembly but also all the Brethren up and down the country who'd supported them, including, of course, the Red-Tilers in Port Seton – among them Lizzie and David and their little growing family.

In this new large-scale rift, the Glanton sympathisers in Port Seton, held on to the red-tiled Meeting Room. The smaller number of hardliners, now calling themselves the London Brethren, took over the former Fishermen's Bethel on South Doors, a six-minute walk to the west. From satellite view on Google Maps it seems that this building had a *grey-tiled* roof. So there were now three Brethren Meeting Rooms in Port Seton, with blue-, red- and grey-tiled roofs.

All this excommunication was not just chillingly familiar to me – I'd watched the ministering brothers in our assembly suddenly turn on and expel once-respectable members of our fellowship – it was beginning to look like some kind of collective psychosis.[10] The fact that there were three Brethren Meeting Rooms in this tiny fishing village was not just absurd, it was shameful.

The crab parcel in my rucksack had leaked in my bag. It had seeped through the pages of my copy of Murakami's *The*

*Wind-Up Bird Chronicle* and stained them brown. It felt appropriate. The intense and small-minded sectarianism of these people turned my stomach like the crab-juice stains on the pages of my book.

The Glanton rift must have affected the whole village in those years before the Great War. There would have been trouble amongst the newly divided fishing crews, daily tensions in the Stott store on the harbourfront, and tight lips on Main Street on the Lord's Day as three Brethren groups made their separate ways to the Plymouth, Glanton and London Brethren Meeting Rooms: red, blue, and now grey. Didn't these people have enough on their plates just surviving the winters and feeding their children without having to engage in religious feuds as well?

### David Fairbairn Stott's Family

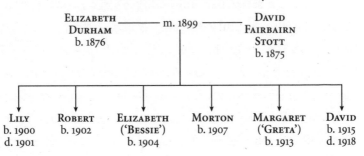

| ELIZABETH DURHAM b. 1876 | — m. 1899 — | DAVID FAIRBAIRN STOTT b. 1875 |

| LILY b. 1900 d. 1901 | ROBERT b. 1902 | ELIZABETH ('BESSIE') b. 1904 | MORTON b. 1907 | MARGARET ('GRETA') b. 1913 | DAVID b. 1915 d. 1918 |

My family, Lizzie and David and their children, my cousins tell me, were 'in the Glantons' for only four years. David and Lizzie Stott, increasingly uncomfortable with the intercommunional ways of the Glanton Brethren, rejoined the hardliners over in South Doors. My great-aunt Greta, their fourth surviving child, born in 1913, would tell people proudly that she was the only one of the family who'd *never* been 'in Glanton Brethren'. By this she meant that she'd never breathed the 'liberal' Glanton air; she'd been born after the family returned to the hardline Brethren. She was pure Brethren, pure *Exclusive* Brethren. During the later years of extreme separation that pure blood would matter.[11]

# 8

The Great War broke out in 1914, but as an older man David Fairbairn Stott wasn't called up until 1916. Following the Biblical injunction 'Thou Shalt Not Kill', he refused to fight, and was one of hundreds of Plymouth and Closed Brethren sent south to Wormwood Scrubs prison in London to await military tribunal. He served out his sentence of hard labour in Dartmoor prison along with other religious and political conscientious objectors.

The coincidence was striking. Sixty-three years later my own father would be sent to Wormwood Scrubs too – sentenced not for conscientious objection, but for embezzling money to feed his roulette habit. I was sixteen when my father went to 'the Scrubs', as it was known. My grandfather Robert had been fourteen when his father was sent there. He'd been forced to leave school to take care of the shop because his mother had three-year-old Greta and one-year-old David to mind. Our household had suffered too. While I was studying for my A-Levels my mother had bailiffs and debt collectors calling at our door.

My father did not like his father, Robert, but in his dying days he talked about him tenderly. He empathised with him. 'It must have been hard being the son of a conscientious objector in a fishing village like Port Seton,' he said, looking at the photographs I'd found of his father as a young man wearing a suit, his hair slicked back with oil, trying to look older than his years. 'Before the war he'd written poetry and hymns. He was learning fine lettering so he could paint signs for local shops, but when the war came he had to stop all that and mind the shop. Customers gave him a hard time; many of the villagers boycotted the shop. He was only fourteen. My Auntie Bessie used to say that sometimes he'd lose his temper and hurl tins like missiles across the shop.'

My father smiled.

Like father like son, I thought.

'Things got worse,' my father said, trying to sit up so he could rummage through the shoebox of photographs. 'While my grandfather was in prison, my father's younger brother Morton – he was only ten then – contracted a bacterial infection in his leg; the doctors rushed him to the hospital in Edinburgh. My grandmother had to travel back and forth to visit him every day with baby David in his pram. The doctors had to cut out a chunk of Morton's leg to drain the poison. They said he wouldn't recover. When they sent him home they expected him to die.'

There was a little white coffin in this story, I remembered. A little white coffin and a Brethren procession. I'd heard my father tell this story before. But now that he was dying, I knew this would be the last time I'd hear him tell it.

'The prison warden allowed my grandfather to go home,' he continued, lost in a photograph of Lizzie pushing the pram along the seafront at Port Seton during the war, 'so that he could see his son one last time. But by the time he'd got all the way from Dartmoor to Scotland – and it must have taken days in wartime – baby David had died instead.'

'Meningitis,' I say, remembering, thinking about how poor Lizzie must have had to break the news to her husband.

'The Brethren,' my father went on, 'carried the little white coffin along the coast to the graveyard in the next village. Then David had to go all the way back to Dartmoor, leaving Lizzie to teach Morton to walk again.'

I'm thinking about Robert trapped behind that shop counter, an open target for the taunts of local lads. Did those boys say the words that all the village must have been thinking – that David's death and Morton's leg had been a punishment for his father's cowardice? That it served those nose-in-the-air Stotts right? Robert must have hurled a fair few more tins then, perhaps even cursed his father. But there would have been older Brethren men looking out for him, I remind myself, and the Brethren sisters would have been helping Lizzie. That's what

Brethren did. At least the Stotts knew they weren't on their own.

The social stigma would have lasted for a long time after the war ended. Conscientious objectors describe being ostracised for decades: people wouldn't shake your hand; with a prison record you couldn't get a job; if you ran a business people wouldn't buy from you.

The Stotts decided to move the family business south. It wasn't just the shame of David's having been a conscientious objector that was making life difficult in Port Seton, my father said. The great herring gold-rush was over, the stocks depleted by overfishing. Neighbours were shutting up shop, selling their boats where they could find people to buy them, moving away. Lizzie's youngest brother had decided to emigrate to Australia. One of her cousins had moved to Hastings on the south coast of England.

'My father knew he and his siblings would never find Brethren to marry in Port Seton,' my father said. 'There were just not enough young Brethren left. If they wanted families they'd *have* to go south. My father had been taking the train down to London several times a year for the big London Brethren Meetings. He'd even starting seeing a Brethren girl in London, but he'd kept that secret from his parents. He got his sisters to cover for him.'

I found a photograph of the family taken a year or two before they left Port Seton to go south. They'd dressed up, I guess, for the picture, gone out into the garden behind the shop to get the best of the light. They look nervous and awkward, unsure where to put their hands. Except for my grandfather. He's standing behind his father, looking straight at the camera. He's carefully dressed and groomed, sure of himself. He looks like a man who wants to impress. He looks like a man who might have a secret romance.

In 1927 the Stotts moved to Brighton, a seaside town a hundred times bigger and worldlier than Port Seton. Lizzie had cousins thirty miles along the coast in Hastings, but a Brighton Brethren builder had offered the two Stott brothers work on a building site and found them somewhere to live. I imagine the

The Stotts photographed in 1925. From left: Lizzie, Morton, Greta, Bessie, Robert, and David Fairbairn Stott

four young Stotts walking amongst day trippers, both fascinated and shocked by street gang fights, piers, parks and a royal
palace. Their Scottish accents would have singled them out
amongst Brighton Brethren as well as in local shops. They'd
have caused a stir in the Brighton Meeting Room.

While Robert and Morton worked on the building site,
Greta and Bessie went to Pitman's College to study secretarial
skills and accountancy. After a year, Hastings Brethren helped
David to buy a wholesale chemist's business in the town. The
family moved into a flat above the shop and joined the Hastings
Brethren assembly. The two Stott brothers, by now in their
twenties, would have been looking about for potential Brethren
wives. Brethren fathers would have been sizing them up too.

In 1930 a well-known Australian ministering brother called
Hugh Wasson arrived in Hastings with his two pretty daughters, Kathleen and Betty. He'd grown up in a big family in
Northern Ireland before emigrating to Australia, and he'd
promised his daughters a grand tour of Great Britain and
Ireland. Robert and Morton offered to accompany the Wassons
when they visited the Highlands. Two years later Kathleen
sailed halfway round the world again, from Adelaide to Tilbury
Docks, to marry Robert. Betty followed two years after that, to
marry Morton.

My father's memoir had begun here, with my grandmother's
sea voyage. Kathleen Wasson, exotic, elegantly but demurely
dressed, the daughter of an eminent and established Australian
Brethren brother, the granddaughter of a Brethren missionary,
had sailed across the world to marry my Scottish grandfather.

# 9

He had painted signs and sold rope, sailcloth and groceries in Port Seton, worked on building sites in Brighton; now Brighton Brethren helped my grandfather secure a job as a travelling salesman for Dubarry, the perfumers. He was going up in the world. During the week he drove hundreds of miles in his company car to peddle fancy perfumes and soaps with French names that promised Compelling Loveliness, Soft White Hands, or a Matte, Velvety Complexion. On the weekends and in the evenings he preached.

Three years later, when he took a sales job at Roger et Gallet, the French soapmakers, he virtually tripled his salary. He and Kathleen bought a detached house in Kenilworth in the Midlands, right in the midpoint of the country, far from the sea, at the centre of Robert's new sales territory. They painted a nursery for their baby, David, employed a nursery-maid, and parked the shiny family Austin outside. Robert stacked the perfume, talc and soap samples in all the spare cupboards and in the attic. Three times a week, sometimes more, they put on their best clothes and hats and pushed the pram the short distance to worship with the Kenilworth assembly in the Iron Room down on the allotment land by the brook.

Brethren were expected to live in detached houses as near to the local Meeting Room as possible, because detached houses minimised contact with worldly people, and proximity kept the local fellowship *close* and in sight. Robert Stott was now the head of his detached household, a respected ministering brother of the Iron Room and at the centre of a commercial sales network that stretched north beyond the border between England and Scotland.

My father was born in June 1938. Although my grandparents gave their other two children Biblical names, they must have named my father Roger after the fancy French perfume company that paid my grandfather's wages. There's no other explanation for this worldly name. Was it a curse or a blessing? Did it set him at odds from the start? Did that account for him being the rule-breaking, hedonistic cuckoo in the nest, the aesthete born amongst puritans? Was it an ill omen, or the best kind of one?

# 10

My Australian grandmother Kathleen had intonations in her voice that were different from everyone else I'd heard. Her father was Northern Irish. Her mother's father, the man in the portrait on our sitting-room wall, the man we called Grandpa Mallalieu, had been born in Leeds, and in the 1880s had emigrated to Australia, where he'd established all those Brethren tent assemblies. People sometimes stop me and ask where I'm from: South Africa? they say, Australia? My voice has my grandmother's mongrel tones too.

She'd show me on the atlas where she'd been born and all the places where she'd lived. She talked to me about the Lord Jesus and about her mother, who'd been taken away to an asylum. She'd lift me onto a chair so I could blow bubbles between my fingers at the kitchen sink. She taught me how to cut crosses into the base of Brussels sprouts. She showed me how to use her hostess trolley, the one she used for entertaining Brethren guests and Brethren visitors from overseas. Her house was always full of guests. She was, other Brethren women told me, an especially spiritual woman.

When she was eighty-eight years old she sent me the transcript of an interview she'd just given to the local oral history group. Now that she was very old, she told me when I visited, her memory was doing strange things. When she sat in her room at the back of my aunts' house looking out over the garden, watching the birds fly between the feeders, she'd suddenly find that she was looking out over the grounds of one of the houses she'd lived in as a child in Melbourne or Adelaide. Or she'd wake up staring at the patterned wallpaper of her bedroom in the Adelaide house. When she closed her eyes she saw giant redwoods, she told me. She could smell eucalyptus.

My grandmother had told the interviewer that when her mother had been sent almost a hundred miles away from their home in Melbourne to a mental asylum at Ballarat in 1914, she and her sister, then nine and six years old, were sent to live with Aunt Marguerite, their mother's sister, who ran a school in a tiny timber-mill town called Beech Forest on Cape Otway, two hundred miles south, in a redwood forest right at the tip of one of the southernmost peninsulas in Australia.

I liked the sound of Aunt Marguerite. She'd lost a leg in her childhood – no one knew how – but, my grandmother said, that had never stopped her from doing anything. The two Mallalieu sisters, Ada-Louise and Marguerite, had been raised among the Box Hill Brethren in a suburb of Melbourne. Marguerite had studied hard, become a school teacher and then in her early twenties married a young labourer who wasn't in the Brethren, and who already had a prison record. She had her first and only child, a daughter, a year later, and when her husband disappeared she'd taken a job in a school as far from her father's preaching territory as she could. She never remarried.

Brethren relatives called Aunt Marguerite 'the man hater', but she seemed like a pirate adventurer to me. I imagined her striding out to school in that remote town along the railway sidings between the tall trees, her wooden leg hidden under her long skirts, her daughter running beside her. The school had fourteen pupils; most of them travelled long distances from outlying farms every day on horseback through the forest to reach it.

My grandmother told the interviewer about the bullock wagon that came to meet her and her sister Betty at the station, and the journey along what she called 'corduroyed roads' – muddy tracks with wooden slats laid across them – through giant redwoods and past waterfalls.

Kathleen and Betty spent the summers with their young cousin wandering the forests between the scattered farms on horseback: 'There were big bushfires sometimes,' she told the interviewer. 'At night we saw showers of sparks where branches suddenly broke off in the fires on the hills.'

My grandmother might have remembered those bushfires when, decades later, she and her husband and sons crouched under the kitchen table during the air raids on nearby Coventry, their eyes fixed on the explosions in the sky beyond the window. Robert, her husband, was at home in Kenilworth throughout the Second World War, working as a firewatcher, too old to be drafted into the army or to register as a conscientious objector. When the planes came, she told my father, Robert read from the Psalms by the light of his torch under the kitchen table.

My father made up a prayer for his memoir to illustrate the kind of Brethren prayer his father gave under that kitchen table where the family took shelter during the bombing raids. 'Our God and Father we cry to Thee,' he wrote, 'we cry to Thee that Thy protecting hand may be over us in this house tonight. We pray that Thou wilt use this fear and our sense of danger to make us more dependent on Thee. Help us to realise Thy power as well as Thy love and mercy. We think of all the saints who love Thee and we ask Thee to have them especially in Thy care. And that men and women who do not know Thee may repent and turn to Thee in their hour of need.'

My father must have learned to speak – or mimic – this language long before he could read. He would have heard so much of it, just as I had. All the Brethren men made the same strange sing-song noises when they preached, pausing for long periods of time, tuning in so that the Lord could guide the direction they were taking, then starting up the zig-zag cadences again. Ministry was impromptu. That was the Brethren way, though some of the longer addresses must have been pre-scripted. In the circles of seats, Brethren brothers and sisters said amen or made assenting noises that sounded like half-awake hums, or quiet moans, or almost a kind of singing. You were supposed to make those sounds, my father said, once you were 'in the Spirit'.

When I read the prayer my father put in his memoir, it's my father's voice I hear, with that strange tremor that would appear occasionally when something in the scriptures moved him and he seemed about to cry.

# II

The Brethren childhood that my father described in his memoir was very similar to my own, but much less circumscribed. Brethren rules were strict in the forties, but nothing compared to the prohibitions introduced in the sixties, when I was born.

What had it been like to grow up as a boy in the Brethren? I'd always felt so cross as a small Brethren girl – not a sulky, smouldering kind of cross, but a fire-out-of-control-sweeping-across-landscapes kind of cross. But I did not dare show it. I was supposed to like being subject. My grandmother did. She'd lower her head when my grandfather was having one of his rages, as if submitting to her bullying husband was a way of serving the Lord Jesus. Sometimes I'd have to bite my lip so I wouldn't howl with rage when I watched her. It was so unfair. Why did women have to do exactly as the men said? Just because Paul had said so? Who was Paul, that he could say such things and have everyone follow his instructions blindly like that? Even thinking those thoughts was a terrible sin, my grandmother would have told me. It was against scripture.

But what if I'd been a Brethren boy? My father would have grown up knowing he'd be head of his household one day, head of the family business, even an important ministering brother if he was good enough at talking about the scriptures. He could preach in Meeting. He could shout in his house. I didn't much like any of the Brethren boys I knew. They called me 'just a girl', and I grew up knowing that I'd be 'just a girl' until I became 'just a woman'. Would I have liked the Brethren boy my father had been? I don't think so. He'd have probably called me 'just a girl' too.

'If we were at home for the Lord's Day,' my father wrote, 'we set out on foot for the eleven o'clock Meeting at The Iron Room. We were expected to walk quietly and sensibly: my brother and I usually walked ahead and my father and mother followed, pushing my baby sister in the pram. Each of us

carried a hymnbook and a Bible. This was part of our testimony
– *amongst whom ye shine as lights in the world.*

'But there weren't many people about to shine on,' my father
complained. 'There'd have been Baptist and Methodist services
in Kenilworth at the same time and there was certainly a Holy
Communion at St John's Church in the other direction but,' he
wrote, 'we only ever saw Mr and Mrs Bert Clayton and Mr and
Mrs Foster, the two Brethren couples who also lived in Waverley
Road. They were either ahead or behind walking on the other
side of the road. We never walked with them. I have no idea
why. Mr Foster had a long neck and a very prominent Adam's
apple. He was tall and thin and he walked quickly in a kind of
stalking manner. His much shorter wife struggled to keep up
with him. My father called them "the long and the short of it".'

In the forties and fifties all the Brethren sisters wore hats. In
the scriptures, the Apostle Paul had stipulated that women's
heads should be covered when they were 'in the temple', my
father explained, but that men were to have their heads uncovered. For a group of post-war fundamentalists living in the
British suburbs two thousand years later, this injunction of
Paul's proved difficult to follow. One of the early Brethren leaders had made a rule that if men were supposed to have their
heads *uncovered* in the temple, they should have their heads
*covered* on their way *to* it. So the brothers wore hats to the
Meeting, and hung them on the rows of hooks at the back of
the Iron Room.

When my father was a child, the lack of symmetry in this
hat rule had vexed him. He'd asked my grandfather why the

sisters weren't carrying their hats to the Meeting and putting them on when they went in. His grandfather laughed, but didn't answer the question. My father wasn't sure he knew the answer. He'd begun to wonder if there were other things his father did not know.

'The Morning Meeting in The Iron Room,' my father remembered, 'lasted for just over an hour. Brethren boys had to make sure that all the sisters had any cushions they wanted before the Meeting started, and a hassock, or footstool. Hassocks were piled at the back of the Room, fat and thick and stuffed with some kind of coarse material, some patterned, some plain. All the sisters had to have one to put their feet on. The chairs were arranged in a circle around a table covered in a white cloth. On the table there was a goblet, a loaf of freshly baked bread in a basket, and a collection box.'

First, a brother 'gave out the notices'. These included the times of the following week's Meetings, who was giving the address in the Iron Room that night, and what Fellowship Meetings were scheduled for the following Saturday. Next, the same brother would read out any Letters of Commendation for Brethren visitors present that week. Then the Morning Meeting would start. There was no script or written plan, but there was 'a general understanding', my father wrote, 'that things moved in a particular order. Brothers gave out hymns or got to their feet to pray as they were moved by the Spirit to do so. Brethren sisters were not permitted to speak though they could join in the hymns.'

After the first hymn, a brother walked to the table, broke the bread into pieces and passed it round, just as we did twenty years or so later. Everyone took a piece and ate it slowly. When the basket of bread was back on the table, the brother prayed a second time before passing the goblet of wine around. Then the collection box was circulated, a small wicker basket with a green baize lining and a hole in the top for the money.

In the forties, Brethren children were expected to ask to start breaking bread at the age of around twelve. As soon as senior ministering brothers had interviewed the child and confirmed that a conversion had taken place, the child would be declared to be 'in the Spirit'. Teenage children who weren't 'in the Spirit' were considered to be a disgrace to their parents. If you hadn't been converted, my father wrote, or if you doubted any of the doctrine, it was better to pretend to be 'in the Spirit' rather than shame your family or risk getting withdrawn from. Eventually you forgot how to put up any resistance. Or you were just too fearful.

*Better to pretend.* So my father had muddled through then, just as I had done. He'd been baffled too, and he'd found ways to keep quiet and pretend he wasn't. If he and I had been Brethren kids sitting on a fence together outside the Iron Room, could we have found a way of saying how strange it all was? I doubt it. I would still have been 'just a girl' to him. He wouldn't have told me about the secret games he played during the scripture readings. I wouldn't have told him about the hold of the ark that I walked through inside my head when I was supposed to be praying.

'Unless you were "in the Spirit",' my father wrote, 'the afternoon Bible reading was usually not very interesting.' At the age of seven he'd worked out a game to make the time pass more quickly. He'd choose a letter of the alphabet and start counting all the times it appeared in the chapter of the Bible they were reading that day. Soon he discovered that there were more E's than any other letter. So he'd give E a less popular partner, like K or U, to slow it down. The total score of these two paired letters had to beat a combination of two other letters, usually S and N.

'When I'd completed the chapter,' my father wrote, 'I'd move on to neighbouring chapters, noting the scores down in the back of my Bible. The results were often quite close. A word like "possessions" at the end of the chapter could tip the balance just in time. For some reason the SN team seemed to do better in the Old Testament. My mother,' he added, 'never worked out what I was doing, but as long as I was quiet and apparently reading my Bible she was content.'

Was this game an early sign of his gambling? Did my father learn to gamble to stave off his boredom in Scripture Meetings? Even as a seven-year-old, he was racing letters and keeping scores. He would still be keeping tallies on his deathbed – of calories, fruit flies, gambling winnings, and diabetes counts.

My father was smart. When his teachers tested his IQ at grammar school several years later, his score was the highest they'd ever seen by a pupil. I heard people describe him as having a photographic memory. He could memorise whole poems in a few minutes.

His obsession with numbers plagued me and my siblings. He was a compulsive keeper of scores. Later, when we had families of our own and he came to visit, the first thing he'd do – *every time* – would be to explain to everyone gathered at the dinner table how he had shaved three or four minutes off his previous record for the distance he had just driven. He'd produce tattered pieces of paper covered with dates and times and distances, his face flushed with pride.

'The Preaching came at half past six on the Lord's Day,' my father remembered. 'It was always a familiar mixture of the tough and the mawkish: threats of Judgement and Hell on the one hand and sentimental appeals on the other. The general idea was that all humans were hopelessly bad: "*The heart of man is deceitful and desperately wicked*" and that unless we repented and believed in Jesus and the saving power of His blood we'd be judged at The Great White Throne and put into The Lake of Fire. There were variations but the basic theme was always the same. To be fair,' he added, 'the Brethren didn't go on about Hell as much as some people. They talked about the Day of Judgement more.'

'Apart from the Lake of Fire,' he wrote, 'there was the certainty of being Eaten by Worms. There was also going to be a lot of Weeping and Gnashing of Teeth.' He'd tried gnashing his teeth, he wrote, and it hurt. The image of Hell that impressed him most was the Bottomless Pit. The idea of falling down a hole forever frightened him more than any of the other descriptions: 'I used to imagine that endless lonely falling as I lay in bed at night. It made me feel dizzy.'

Edmund Gosse, when he put together his notes for *Father and Son*, remembered something similar happening in his dreams as a boy – an intense sense of vertigo, of being spun through time and space, his heart racing. I didn't have falling dreams. Mine had rain and floods, earthquakes and tidal waves in them. It was, I suppose, just a different kind of vertigo.

'If a visiting ministering brother was preaching,' my father remembered, 'he'd corner you after the Meeting to ask if you loved the Lord or if you'd put your faith in the Blood of the Lamb. I never knew what to say. I didn't blame the preachers, though,' he added. 'They were expected to do that. It was their job.'

His empathy took me by surprise, but then I remembered that later, when he began to preach, my father had to corner children himself, so it was perhaps no wonder he was defensive. I'd watch him rounding on a child after Meeting and asking the same thing: 'Have you put your faith in the Lord?', or 'Have you taken the Lord into your heart?' I'd get asked those questions too, as I stood in my Best Dress clasping my stuffed rabbit. But come to think of it, I don't remember my father asking me about the Lord being in my heart. It was always the Brethren sisters who asked about that.

I worried a lot about that taking-the-Lord-into-your-heart question when I was a very small child. Sometimes I'd be sure he was in there. I'd welcomed him in. I could relax my efforts. I'd be glad he was there. Joyous even. But mostly just relieved. Then a day or so later he'd be gone again. Sometimes his disappearance would coincide with me doing something naughty, sometimes not. I'd have to do the taking-in ritual – praying, confessing, making myself subject – all over again. But the questions that vexed me – was the Lord supposed to wander off like that? Was that normal? – were not the kinds of questions I'd dare to ask. I was supposed to take the Lord Jesus *in*, and he was supposed to take me *up* when the Rapture came. I wasn't sure how all of that worked either. You had to make sense of it in whatever way you could, without help from the grown-ups.

My father's closest friend in the Brethren – I'll call him William to protect his identity – now in his seventies, told me that it was often the little things that kept you obedient, that kept you from running away. He'd had an uncle who'd been withdrawn from for some misdemeanour or other. When, at the age of eight, my father's friend asked his father what had happened to the uncle he'd adored – why he'd disappeared, whether they'd ever see him again – his father had simply said, 'Outside those doors, son, there is *darkness*.' He'd developed an idea in his head, he said, of his beloved uncle groping about in some 'murky, dark horror'. 'I grew up terrified of the dark,' he added.

Now I began to wonder if my fear of the dark came from the same place that William's had. We'd both grown up believing that the darkness beyond our small circle of light was full of scuttling monsters waiting to snatch us. Most children, I guess, feel a dread of what they can't see. Few children are told that they are right to be terrified, that their imaginary monsters are real devils sent by Satan, or that they might even be Satan himself.

# 12

In the 1940s my travelling salesman grandfather became one of the most important ministering brothers at the Iron Room in Kenilworth. At home he was strict, my father wrote. He'd make his children drop to their knees to pray at the slightest transgression. He was often angry or getting angry. His rages would come from nowhere.

His father had had a quick temper, my grandfather would tell people by way of apology or explanation, when he caught himself. David Fairbairn Stott had been a disciplinarian. He'd bullied his children. With Brethren women and children expected to show unconditional compliance and subjection, Brethren men had absolute power in their homes. Their anger must often have gone unchecked. Bullying of women and children must have been common even among otherwise good men.

When my father wrote about my grandfather he described him as a monster who raged and ranted: 'I was afraid of my father,' he wrote. 'He was prone to terrible rages. They came suddenly, like thunderstorms. "Why on *airth* did you do that?" he'd say. "What on *airth* were you thinking about?"

'Sometimes he'd lose control of himself for ten minutes or so, roaring at the top of his voice and beating his fists on the table. He wasn't roaring *at* anyone, he was just roaring. Once he roared on the lower part of the Kenilworth staircase, beating his fists against one of the steps. Afterwards he was exhausted and tearful. It was as if he had been taken ill.

'He was never violent towards my mother. That was something outside his range. He punished us, sometimes with a ruler across the palm of the hand, or if we'd been especially bad he'd use a belt. Sometimes he'd just slap us hard on the side of the head. "By," he would say heavily when he was angry, "By." Not "by" anything, just "By", and he'd draw a deep breath. His anger was always much worse than the physical blows.

'My father's rage hung in the air as a dreadful possibility. "You'll set me off," he'd say when we tried to justify or explain. If one of us misbehaved when he was preaching in The Iron Room he'd stop speaking and frown at us. Other Brethren would turn and look at us. "I'll stop the Meeting," he'd say to us at home. "If I see you doing that again, I'll stop the Meeting."'

My father described my grandfather as having a nervous tic when he was on edge, a kind of winking with his left eye that took the left-hand side of his mouth up with it. 'When this started,' my father wrote, 'it was better to apologise and propitiate, even if the matter under investigation had been an accident. Even then you couldn't always stop the rage; sometimes there was no stopping it whatever one said. Justice did not come into it. If something had been broken or spilt, someone must be to blame. Anger hung in the air, waiting to discharge itself. It was like living on a fault line or the slopes of a volcano. When I read Shakespeare years later, I understood the final roarings and the stricken, exhausted peace at the end of *Hamlet, Othello, Macbeth* and *Lear*. The only durable calm, I already knew, was the one that came after cataclysmic events. You braced yourself and braced yourself and then the terror came and you lived through it and then it blew itself out and you were exhausted and shaking but everything was all right again.'

I thought of my grandmother, raised in a big house by her kindly aunt, or playing out in the Australian backwoods with her sister and cousin, now living out a life of constant appeasement in rainy suburban Britain, stepping between her husband and her children, making peace or trying to keep it, praying for it, smoothing feathers.

The rage wasn't just in the men, or only in the Stott branch of the family: my grandmother's mother, the hauntingly mournful-looking Ada-Louise, my great-grandmother, had been a legendary fury. She'd once thrown one of her daughters across the room and broken her arm. I found that hard to believe when I looked at the picture my father had given me.

Ada-Louise had a strong Huguenot jaw, the long family face. She looked like my two dark-haired brothers. She looked like me. She looked like my son. There are a few black-and-white photographs of Ada-Louise in her twenties – striking, mournful and laced up to the neck – and then photographs of her in her sixties, white-haired, blank-eyed, smiling, propped up by others. In the forty or so in-between years she'd lived in an asylum where they didn't take photographs.

My great-grandfather Hugh Wasson, the boy who'd run away from his home in Northern Ireland to take a boat to Australia at the age of thirteen, sent his beautiful, troublesome wife Ada-Louise, away to an asylum soon after his two daughters had started school. She wasn't mad – she had epilepsy. *Grand mal* seizures. And she was wilful. Medical experts thought an institution was the best place for her. Epileptics were considered loose, untrustworthy and maniacal in Australia at that time. In 1901 the country's most eminent epileptic specialist had decided to gather all of Australia's epileptic women together in an asylum at Ballarat, where they could look after each other and not breed or infect others. One third of those women died in the first seventeen years of the experiment.[12]

Ada-Louise at around twenty

When my grandmother talked about her mother, she usually described her as dressed in white. She remembered her having a seizure at the school gates wearing a white dress. A male stranger had lifted her unconscious body up in his arms and carried her home, daughters in tow, clutching schoolbooks. My grandmother remembered her mother disappearing to Ballarat, then brief visits to the grand asylum building. She remembered the upset and shame, the fear and grief of it all. She remembered seeing her mother in a white straitjacket in a padded cell.

'My mother was wilful,' my grandmother would say when I was ten or so and the two of us were cutting those crosses together into the stalks of Brussels sprouts in her kitchen. Not just ill, but *wilful*. If there were other Brethren women around the kitchen table they'd nod when my grandmother told that story. Wilful women need locking up. Wilful women have husbands who sign papers, doctors who prescribe lobotomies and ECT. They get sent away and they don't return for forty years.

You didn't want anyone to be using the word wilful about you.

Rage was in my father's blood too, but although he wrote about his father's temper in his memoir, he did not describe his own. We, his children, grew up under its shadow, the marks of it on the walls and doors. My first memories of my father are of the walking-on-eggshells kind. He was big, he was volatile, and though he was often affectionate and funny, his affection sometimes had a sharp edge.

We learned to avoid him when he was in certain moods. He'd warn my mother not to set him off. He'd warn us. When something did set him off my mother would shepherd us quickly into the sitting room and lock the door behind her. Then the kicking and shouting would begin.

When I was three or four years old, I've been told, my father came home after a grilling from one of the senior ministering brothers to find me sitting in a corner of the kitchen taking great gasping breaths after a long sobbing spell. He shouted at me to be quiet. This made me start crying harder. All of a sudden he lost control, flew across the room and hit me hard around the head and face. Disgusted at himself, he fled the house.

My face swelled up black and blue. Within hours I couldn't open my eyes. My face had to be covered in foundation and talcum powder to mask the bruises. I had to be hidden for a week from the eyes of visitors so that other Brethren wouldn't see what my father had done.

It was probably one of the reasons he doted on me later, I was told. He'd never forgiven himself. But I don't have any memory of the blows. And he never talked to me about it.

When I told my father's friend William this story, forty-five years after it happened, his eyes welled up with tears, not just for me but for my father, my mother, and for himself.

'We were under terrible pressure,' he said. 'Those were the Jim Taylor Junior years. We were all sleepless, anxious, trapped. We were being watched all the time. We were all living on the edge of a volcano.'

# 13

B ut I'm jumping ahead. All of that shouting and kicking of doors came later, in the 1960s. My father grew up in the 1940s, when the Brethren were strict, fanatical even, but not yet maniacal. It was my grandfather who was doing the shouting back then. My father was still a child, adding up his E scores in his Bible and hoping no one could see what he was doing.

My father won the school English prize in 1946 and brought home Arthur Mee's *Book of Everlasting Things*, an anthology of extracts from great literary works. He was seven. My grandfather must have been proud of the award but wary of the prize. Only certain books were allowed in Brethren homes. He examined the heavy, expensively bound volume, and pronounced it acceptable. 'This was a serious mistake,' my father recalled. 'I knew there was a world outside the Brethren, but I'd seen nothing like this. The Brethren line was that literature, sculpture, painting, and secular music – even human imagination itself – were all mischievous, frivolous, and seductive distractions from the scriptures. When Paul came to Athens and saw all the ancient beauty there he dismissed it as "*idolatrous … the graven forms of man's art and imagination*". The only important thing to God, we were told, was your reborn self in the Spirit.'

To my father's surprise, sin, repentance and being born again weren't mentioned in the *Book of Everlasting Things*. 'A gap began to open up in the wall that had been built between me and "the world",' he wrote. 'I slipped through it.'

My grandparents, seeing my father's pleasure in the book, bought him Mee's companion volumes for subsequent birthdays: *One Thousand Famous Things* and *One Thousand Beautiful Things*. They ordered a set of the *Children's Encyclopaedia*. When the crate containing the volumes arrived, my grandfather summoned the family to watch as he selected the D volume and with a razor blade cut out the entry for Charles Darwin, then threw the excised pages in the fire. Darwin's ideas, he told them, were wrong and wicked and against scripture.

I have my father's copies of Mee's books on my bookshelves. They smell musty and the pages have yellowed. The *Book of Everlasting Things*, 352 pages long, contains extracts from great literature and art. The American Declaration of Independence sits next to Matthew Arnold, Henry Vaughan next to George Eliot. Later in the book there's the best part of *The Ancient Mariner*, twelve pages of *In Memoriam*, nine pages of *Samson Agonistes*, Gray's 'Elegy', five pages each of Milton's *Areopagitica* and *Paradise Lost*, Shelley's 'To a Skylark' and *Adonaïs* – 'in which I almost drowned', my father wrote – a long passage from *Robinson Crusoe*, Keats's 'Ode to a Nightingale', whole speeches by Demosthenes and Pericles, eight pages from *The Odyssey*, Cicero's 'Essay on Old Age', Plato's account of the death of Socrates, Edward FitzGerald's translation of *The Rubaiyat of Omar Khayyám*, eleven of Shakespeare's sonnets and several passages from his plays.

What was my Brethren grandfather thinking in allowing such worldly books into the house? My father, seven years old, was enthralled. He memorised the Shakespeare speeches, rehearsing them in his bedroom when his parents were out – *Julius Caesar*'s 'This was the noblest Roman of them all', *Twelfth Night*'s 'Make me a willow cabin at your gate', 'Tomorrow, and tomorrow, and tomorrow' from *Macbeth*, and 'Come, let's away to prison' from *King Lear*. He fell in love with Emily Brontë, he told me, his eyes full of tears. He took his magnifying glass to the pictures in the *Book of Everlasting Things* – paintings by Raphael, Holbein, Giovanni Bellini, Velázquez and Rembrandt, and photographs of ancient sculptures from Egypt, Greece and Rome.

'The words of remarkable men and women,' he wrote, 'began to swarm inside my head. Other feelings, other judgements, other passionate beliefs, a different seriousness and an unfamiliar gaiety opened up to me as I read.' He then quoted the lines from Keats's 'On First Looking into Chapman's Homer', as he would do again many years later to me during our car journeys, often weeping: '*Then felt I like some watcher of the skies/When a new planet swims into his ken*'.

'Soon I had a small library of pieces in my head,' he wrote. 'I could go there at any time, even when I was in a Meeting. I had a secret, non-Brethren compartment inside my head.'

I thought of the salty ark I'd made for myself, the secret, non-Brethren room inside my own head. I wondered where all the other Brethren children went to in those long hours of

Meeting. Did they have private rooms too? Had the women daydreamed? What about William? Had anyone – other than a small group of the men – really been listening to all that angels-on-a-pinhead exegesis?

# 14

My father was ten when doctors found an abscess in his mother's womb and rushed her to the Queen Elizabeth Hospital in Birmingham. They did not expect her to survive. My father and his brother were sent to stay with their Auntie Bessie and her husband on their farm in Kent. The prayers for his mother at the Kent Meeting Room were urgent and serious, my father remembered. Her father and grandfather were 'famous' ministering brothers in Australia, so my grandmother's illness was much discussed, much whispered about. Weeks passed. The news was not good. The Kent Brethren redoubled their prayers; my father and his brother fended off the sympathetic embraces of the elderly Brethren sisters.

And then, just as the doctors and my grandfather had given up hope, the abscess had suddenly burst. 'A wave of relief and gratitude swept through the Brethren Meeting Rooms in Kenilworth and Kent,' my father wrote. 'In Brethren terms, my mother's recovery was a high-profile event. A miracle. To me,' he added, 'it was proof that God existed.'

When my grandmother returned home from the hospital she told my father about a recurring vision she'd had through the last ten days of her illness. Sometimes, she said, she'd surface from her dreams to find doctors or nurses bending over her, or my grandfather sitting holding her hand, but most of the time in her mind she was walking across a winter landscape, looking up at a network of bare branches silhouetted against a red and gold sky while a heavy bell tolled somewhere close.

She'd been in a prolonged struggle with the Lord, she told my ten-year-old father. She couldn't die, she told God. How would Robert manage? And the children needed her. In answer to her pleas a simple phrase repeated itself, remotely, impersonally, against the steady tolling of the bell: '*One will in the universe,*' the voice said. '*One will in the universe.*'

My grandmother lived like this, slipping between the physical world and the metaphysical sunset, for more than a week. And then one day she capitulated, she told my father. She gave herself up to God's will. '*Thy will be done,*' she'd said finally. '*Thy will be done … Not what I will but what Thou wilt.*' Within twelve hours the poisonous abscess inside her broke and dissipated. My grandmother had told my father this story, I guess, because she wanted him to give up his will too. Give up everything, let the Lord direct your ways. That was the Brethren way.

For months after she returned home, my grandmother would walk to the back door of their Kenilworth house at sunset to gaze at the pattern of winter trees against the sky. 'Sometimes,' she said to my father years later, 'I could hardly breathe when I looked up at them.' He must have felt the same way when he looked at her.

# 15

In the year that my grandmother nearly died, 1948, James Taylor, the Brethren world leader, the man we called JT, a Sligo-born New York linen merchant, received 'new light' from the Lord about worshipping the Holy Spirit.

'New light' was important. You could tell the Rapture was close because the Lord would start to send lots of it. New light meant new instructions, new truths, revealed only to the Brethren's leader, the 'Man of God'. But this particular new light about the Spirit upset people. John Nelson Darby had always taught that Brethren should worship the Lord and the Father, not the Spirit by itself. Now JT was telling them that the Lord wanted them to worship the Spirit equally with God and the Lord. Was he right?

Some senior ministering brothers expressed their concern privately. There was too much stress, they said, being placed on the ministry of Brethren leaders – from Darby to James Taylor. People were putting more emphasis on ministries than on the scriptures. Surely that was wrong. Many of the doubters, however, were wary of saying such things publicly for fear of being withdrawn from. Most did as Brethren usually did – they decided to wait, keep their counsel and see how things played out.

'The Morning Meeting now had to be changed,' my father wrote. 'Everything had to be rearranged. We worshipped the Lord at the beginning, then after the passing round of the bread and wine and the moneybox, everything was about Christ and The Assembly. Then we worshipped the Spirit, then the Father, then the Trinity. There had to be a revision of the Brethren hymnbook so that there were hymns addressed to the Spirit. All the Brethren that fancied themselves as hymn writers got busy writing new hymns.'

JT's teaching in the late forties and early fifties was complex and increasingly esoteric. 'We were the children of Israel fleeing from Egypt through the wilderness to the promised land,' my father wrote, remembering the sense of adventure and risk that those stories excited in them all. 'We thought of ourselves as a community of refugees, travelling across the Jordanian desert, exposed to danger from all directions.

'Egypt,' he wrote, 'was supposed to be the World System we'd left behind, where we'd been in bondage. We'd escaped all the way to the Red Sea. The Red Sea was supposed to be the Gospel, Salvation through the death of Christ, God parting the waters and letting the Brethren through on dry land. That took us into the Wilderness. We were following the Ark of the Covenant which was Christ through the Wilderness and we were being fed by the manna which was also Christ.'

When my father talked or wrote about the manna – the mysterious food that God provided for the Israelites in the desert – he'd always quote the lines from the Bible: *and it was like coriander seed, white, and the taste of it was like cake with honey*. I thought of the boy in the Meeting Room thinking about honey cake and coriander seed, just as I had pressed the bread between my four-year-old fingers to see if it tasted or smelled better squashed, relishing the smell of yeast that lingered on my fingers.

'At the other end of the wilderness,' my father wrote, 'was the river Jordan. The Ark of the Covenant went ahead of you down into the river bed and we were supposed to follow it. This was Christ's death *in you*, a painful experience. Then you came up on the other side and began your life in the new land. On the other side we'd still have to fight encroaching tribes and get things built and established. But this landscape was heavenly – we were now on God's territory, not man's.'

Just to make things more complicated, JT told them that all these things were happening at the same time. 'Spiritually,' my father wrote, 'you'd be leaving Egypt through the Red Sea, learning the lessons of the wilderness, going down into the Jordan and living your life in the land on the other side, *simultaneously*.'

It was a lot to keep in mind, particularly if you were ten years old. My father seems to have struggled not just with the metaphysics of the flight from Jordan story but also with the geography. He was vexed by the fact that the children of Israel were supposed to have taken forty years to travel a distance that should have taken a few weeks. He'd asked his primary school teacher about the exact distance during a scripture lesson.

When he'd quoted the answer at home, his mother wrote to the school and had him 'excused' from scripture lessons. Enraged, he'd waited for his mother to go shopping, then taken down his father's atlas and used the scale and a ruler to confirm the distance his teacher had given him. *Sixty-five miles*. Had it really taken them forty years to walk sixty-five miles? This meant that the children of Israel's average speed through the wilderness had been about eight yards a day, he told me years later. 'And they were supposed to be travelling *day and night*. It made no sense. How could people walk that slowly?'

# 16

The miracle of his mother's recovery in 1948 had made my father resolve to be a better Brethren boy. He'd been deeply affected by the story she'd told him about giving up her will to God. But there was another event in his life in the same year that changed everything.

That summer the Stott clan travelled down together to the great international gathering of Brethren clans that took place annually at Central Hall, Westminster. They called it the 'universal gathering'. Although women, children and non-ministering Brethren men were not allowed into the Meetings during the day, they could attend the evening addresses. Admission was by numbered ticket, checked at the door.

For these Meetings the Brethren rented Central Hall from the Methodists. It was the only non-conformist religious hall in London big enough to seat all the thousands of Brethren who congregated from around the world. That it was just a few yards from the House of Commons must have added to the sense of occasion and of dissenting power. Compared to the usual Brethren Meeting Rooms the décor – polished wood and red damask – must have seemed both disturbingly ornate and very impressive.

At the age of ten, my father had never seen so many people all in one place, nor seated in such a way that made the Brethren hierarchy so immediately visible. On a raised dais just below the huge organ about a hundred men were seated around JT.

'I could see that if you made it into that section of a hundred men,' my father wrote, 'you were getting somewhere. JT was in

Central Hall, Westminster

the front row. In the middle. It was a little bit like those May Day Parades in Moscow, when the Soviet leaders stood in a particular order around Stalin and you could see at a glance who was in and who was out of favour that year. In the JT era these placements only changed slowly. Later, it would be different. At this stage, in 1948, my father was still in the body of the hall, but he was in the part from which you took off into the top hundred. My grandfather sat in the second row just behind JT. I looked on him with a new respect.'

I'm looking for excuses for him now. How could the ten-year-old Brethren boy, already nearly as tall as his own short and stocky father, indoctrinated by the patriarchal begats of the Bible and the family business, not have been moved by this visual display of male power? In that noisy red hall he discovered that his father, the dictator of his domestic world, had little status and was seated only in the stalls. But his grandfather was up there on the raised dais, seated just behind JT, the Brethren leader.

My father was impressed. Of course he was. I would have been impressed too, if I'd been there. All that red carpet and polished wood. The great organ, a hundred feet high. All that noise; all those choruses of Amen. Maybe it was all the red in my father's memory that made him think of the Soviet May Day parades when he tried to describe it. It was making me think of the Nuremberg rallies – Hitler with all his henchmen behind him on the stage. Did my father decide that day that someday he'd be up there on that platform too? That he'd get even closer to the Brethren leader than his grandfather?

'After the Meeting,' he wrote, 'I was with my mother in the crowds outside the hall when JT came past. My mother knew him a little (he was very fond of her father) and she introduced me to him and I shook his hand. I was embarrassed but my mother said that in future years it might mean a lot to me that I had met JT. And she seemed to feel that some of his spirituality might rub off on me at the same time. JT spoke to me gravely and seriously as if I was a grown-up.'

I'd watched my father preach when I was growing up. Not just in our little Meeting Room in Edward Avenue but in the much bigger one in Vale Avenue, with the steeply raked circular seating around the central platform. I'd sit up at the back with my mother and siblings, looking down through the hats and bodies, studying the way he paced the floor when he preached, how he gestured with his hands, how he'd make his sentences curl, rise and fall.

I particularly admired the length of his silences. All Brethren men knew how to pause and hold a silence – it showed that they were waiting for the Lord to guide them – but my father would pause right in the middle of a sentence, and stretch out that silence so much longer than everyone else. I'd press my fingers into the soft leather of my Bible in suspense as I counted out the seconds.

There was one particular line I'd listen out for in my father's preaching, a line that had especially beautiful rhythms. An important Brethren sister from the early Ireland days had once said, 'Let us put away our playthings for the world is in flames' – and that line, dark and poetic, had been passed down among

Brethren over the years. My father loved it. He wouldn't just use it once; he'd repeat it for effect. When I was six years old I watched him repeat it five times. I whispered each of the words along with him under my breath, anticipating where he was going to put the next stress, or the next long pause, keeping a close eye on my grandfather down in the front row opposite me to see, from his expression, if my father would get away with it.

A few years ago I found myself absentmindedly mouthing that sentence, with my father's inflections, as I approached the podium of a vast hall in Heidelberg where I was about to give a lecture on Aristotle and early ideas about evolution. My words must have been picked up by the powerful microphone pinned to my lapel, but thankfully they were drowned out by the audience's applause. After I had pulled up the first slide – a striking photograph of the lagoon on Lesbos where Aristotle had once studied fishes and birds – I held the silence for as long as I dared, until I could see people leaning forward in their seats. I am my father's daughter, I thought as I began to speak, unable to suppress a smile. Had I, I wondered, worked all those years to become a writer and scholar so I could take the microphone, like my father and grandfather, and claim my place up on the platform too?

# 17

Nineteen forty-eight, the year of my grandmother's near-death vision, the year that JT changed the rules about the Holy Spirit, the year that my father shook hands with JT, was also the year that my great-grandmother Ada-Louise was finally released from the Ballarat asylum. Now that new drugs were controlling her epileptic fits, Brethren relatives told my great-grandfather Hugh Wasson, it was un-Christian to keep her there. Ada-Louise, sixty-nine years old, finally came out of the asylum to live in her husband's house in Adelaide. His nomadic, studious, independent missionary life came to an end. After forty years in an asylum, Ada-Louise was difficult; she talked incessantly, and sang hymns at the top of her voice. It was impossible for my great-grandfather to read the Bible quietly as he had been used to doing. His health began to suffer.

His married daughters Kathleen and Betty, now living in England, read his many airmailed letters and decided it was time they 'shared the burden' of their mother. They persuaded their father to move to England and buy a large house in Brighton, where he could live with Robert and Kathleen and their three children. It would be big enough for him and Ada-Louise to have their own wing, but connected enough for Kathleen to help look after her mother.

When the unhappy couple arrived at Tilbury Docks in

mid-July 1953, having been cooped up for weeks reading their Bibles on the SS *Orcades*, their two daughters and their families were on the quay to meet them. Ada-Louise had not seen Kathleen or Betty for nearly forty years, nor had she met her grandchildren, though she'd memorised their names and life histories. My father, then fourteen years old, was fascinated and embarrassed by his grandmother's emotional intemperance. They all were.

'She seemed to be in a kind of ecstasy,' he wrote. 'She kept murmuring and sighing and stroking our faces.' Then, grandly, she introduced them all to her husband, forgetting that he'd been to stay in England many times.

'Rather you than us,' my father's cousin hissed at my father from behind her gloved hand.

Ada-Louise and Hugh Wasson in the 1950s

In my mind's eye my bespectacled, snow-white-haired great-grandmother, wearing a black dress and matching jacket with silver embroidery, stands on the quay in a new country, surrounded by strangers, like a Russian dowager in exile. She is sixty-nine but looks ten years older. Her face, strikingly beautiful in pre-asylum photographs, is now deeply lined, but she still appears wilful. Her face is still a little like mine.

What had she been doing all those years? What had she been allowed to read or see in that grand asylum? I like to think there might have been a garden, or at least a pretty view from her window, and a piano, and someone to listen to her sing hymns sometimes without mocking her. I try not to think of her in that padded cell my grandmother remembered. I like to think that, had I been standing on the quay that day, I might have stroked *her* face or kissed her hand. But I'd probably just have been embarrassed too.

Hugh bought Ada-Louise a second-hand pedal organ that they assembled in the rear drawing room of the huge Brighton house that they and my grandparents had bought with joint funds. For four hours or more every day she played and sang the hymns she'd been taught as a child – most often 'Nearer, my God, to Thee' and 'Almost Persuaded'. She'd sing slowly and with deep feeling, my father remembered, her voice wavering and breaking from time to time as the words and music overwhelmed her. Tipping her head back like a wolf, she would aim the hymn towards the ceiling. She insisted on having the door open so the rest of the house could hear her perform. My father and his siblings would try to shut it without her hearing, but she'd always open it again.

Sometimes she'd be so overcome by her own playing that she'd trot out of the room and grab any passing child, or my grandmother, or the cleaning lady. 'Just come and listen to *this*,' she'd say, forcing her prey into the chair next to the organ. With an audience present she'd weep through the hymn, and then, on finishing, stand, bow and wave royally. 'Then,' my father wrote, 'you had to say the right things and escape as quickly as possible before she started the next one.' When visitors began to prepare to leave she'd run to the piano and sing 'God be with you till we meet again.'

Family dinners were tense, my father told me. His father sensed disapproval from his father-in-law over domestic and Brethren matters. They'd both been used to absolute authority in their homes. Tensions between them increased when Brethren visitors came to stay. And there was his grandmother's unpredictability. She'd wait for openings in the conversation and then tell long stories that embarrassed everyone. Her two teenage grandsons enraged and disgusted her. She told them they ate too much and too quickly, and grumbled incessantly about their 'big feet under the table'. When they asked for second helpings, she'd lean her head to one side and intone:

'To bed, to bed,' said Sleepy Head,
'Tarry a while,' said Slow,
'Put on the pot,' said Greedy Gut,
'We'll sup before we go.'

When she was not playing the organ she'd be listening for the bell at the front door or the side door, the one they called 'the tradesmen's entrance'. As soon as she heard it, my father recalled, she'd scuttle to answer it. Sometimes she'd get there before anyone could stop her. She'd begin by challenging the caller about the state of their soul. Did they know that they were a sinner in the sight of God? Had they put their faith in the blood of the Lamb? Had they taken the Lord into their heart? Sometimes she'd break out into a hymn.

One Friday she answered the door to the fishmonger. Ada-Louise loathed fish and the Roman Catholic Church in equal measure. In her long years at the Ballarat asylum they'd always served fish on a Friday, and as she knew this was a Catholic tradition, she'd considered it idolatrous. My grand-mother arrived at the door to hear her mother, in a righteous passion, haranguing the stupefied fishmonger about the Virgin Mary, the Pope, and the Whore-of-Babylon Vatican. My grand-mother asked him politely to wait while she steered her hyper-ventilating mother back to her room and to the organ.

I had a framed portrait of a young Ada-Louise up on my sitting-room wall until a few years ago. Visitors would some-times say I looked like her, and my daughters would explain that she was Mummy's great-grandmother and her name was Ada-Louise and she'd been locked up because she had epilepsy. 'Ask Mummy,' they'd say when the visitors' questions multi-plied. Then I'd have to find a way of telling them just enough to satisfy their curiosity without going into the entire Brethren story. If I went there I knew we'd be discussing cults for hours.

But that wasn't the only reason I'd taken down the portrait.

'She just made me feel sad,' I told my daughter Hannah when she asked where the picture of her great-great-grand-mother had gone.

In truth, Ada-Louise's face had come to stand for all those women who'd been shut up or locked up. Not just Brethren women, but all women who'd been bullied or belted by men who'd been allowed too much power in their homes. Her face haunted me. One day when my daughters were a bit older, I told myself, I'd talk to them about that, about patriarchy and how dangerous unchecked male power can be. I'd talk to them about Ada-Louise.

A decade later, a long-running story on *The Archers* finally prompted that conversation. Heavily pregnant Helen Archer had stabbed her controlling husband with a kitchen knife after years of isolation and mental abuse. She was arrested. The audience for the show grew by millions. There were chatrooms devoted to the storyline, and money was raised for support groups for victims of abuse. The whole country, including my daughters, then in their early twenties, seemed to be tuning in. But my daughters didn't need me to do any explaining when the subject came up.

'It's called coercive control, Mum,' Kez said. 'They've passed a law about it.'

'Took them decades to listen to the campaigners, though,' Hannah said, her eyes bright with anger. 'Did you know that the law didn't even recognise rape inside marriage until the nineteen-*seventies*? Un-bel-iev-ab-le.'

'I know,' I said, trying to be positive. 'But things are better for women now.'

'Mum, you've read *The Handmaid's Tale*,' Kez said. 'You know we can't ever take feminist progress for granted. They'll take our freedom away again unless we protect it.'

'Look at what's happening in Poland over abortion,' said Hannah. 'Thousands of women had to take to the streets to make the politicians scrap that Bill.'

I knew. I'd been teaching feminist theory and writing for years. I'd given my daughters copies of Margaret Atwood's *The Handmaid's Tale* as birthday presents during their teens. We'd groaned together about sexist adverts on the television, talked about equal pay and equal rights, and agreed about how important it was to stand up and make a noise when you thought something was unfair. Now they were bringing me articles to read and telling me about documentaries to watch by women of their generation. I was learning from them.

I haven't put that photo of Ada-Louise back on my wall, though, despite the hope my daughters and their friends give me about a more fair and just future. My great-grandmother's face still makes me feel sad.

# 18

By the time he turned fifteen in 1953, my father recalled, he was living an entirely divided life. When his closest school friend referred to his father as 'a religious maniac', he did not challenge him. He was not an unbeliever, he insisted when I pressed him, but his relationship with God had become a mere insurance policy, just in case it was all true.

Often the insurance policy did not work.

One winter day, when he was around ten or eleven, he returned home from school to find the house empty. This was

My father, at about ten

unusual. He had no key of his own, so he climbed over the back fence into the garden of a school friend and the two of them played with the boy's new cap gun. When he returned to the house half an hour later, his hands and clothes smelling of gunpowder from the caps, there was still no one there. He stood on the front steps wondering what to do.

'As I looked up at the golden scatter of clouds in the sunset,' he wrote, 'a horror crept up on me. The Lord had come. The Rapture had happened. I'd been left behind. The whole world seemed to be trembling,' he recalled, remembering the wind in the garden trees. All the real Christians had gone, and now the Tribulation would start. How soon? How long did he have? Should he warn the neighbours' boy? Run? Soon there'd be beasts and false prophets everywhere. Where could he hide? He was finding it difficult to breathe.

When he told me this story years later, he claimed he'd passed out on the steps leading up to the tradesmen's entrance. I sympathised. I breathed Brethren air for a much shorter time than my father, but I still find myself suppressing a shudder sometimes when I see a particularly lurid sunset, or television footage of flooding, or days of rain forecast on the evening news. A friend once referred to those fear-struck days of mine as my Old Testament Days, but if anything they were fire-and-brimstone days, wormwood days, Book of Revelation days – not Old Testament at all. These were the days of rain Ezekiel had written about when he described strange creatures, with multiple human and animal heads, that he'd seen in the clouds. Even rainbows were supposed to remind us that the Lord had for some reason postponed the wrath that was going to be unleashed on us all. We were always living on borrowed time, waiting, and studying the skies.

When my father's mother, grandmother and sister came back from their impromptu shopping expedition, my father wrote, he recovered himself. He said nothing to them about what had happened. They had their tea just as usual, and he did his homework, with Grandma across the hall singing to the ceiling again. It had been a warning from God, he told himself. A warning of what was to come if he continued his secret dissenting and disobedient life.

# 19

'When you were a teenager,' I asked my father in those last weeks of his life, 'did you rebel? Did you try and run away?'

'It wasn't as tough back in the forties and fifties,' he said, trying to find a comfortable position in the reclining chair. 'Life in the Brethren was a good way of life, provided you were prepared to accept the privations. Very few people came in from outside. We'd *all* grown up as Brethren. It was the only life we knew. Brethren looked after you and were supportive if people were in trouble. The idea of being out in the world was frightening. You had the feeling that if you went outside the Brethren there'd be no morals at all. People would cheat you and trick you, because the world outside is under the control of Satan. You'd run back into the Brethren to be safe.'

I remember that terror when I was growing up too. I was constantly watching – or listening – for Satan, hearing the tapping of his hooves on the cobblestones in the streets of Brighton, looking at the children in the primary school playground and imagining the scale of the wickedness in their homes.

When I took the little path through the wood behind our house to visit my grandparents, I wouldn't be watching out for suspicious strangers, I'd be listening for Satan. I made deals with the Lord Jesus to get me to the end of the path, to the gate that led back onto the street. Usually I promised to keep looking straight ahead, rather than behind – a token of my faith – in return for protection. When I broke that promise, turning my head at the sound of a snapped twig or a bird or dog rustling through the undergrowth, I'd run, terrified, towards the gate before a slavering, horned Satan stepped out from behind a tree to catch me. He couldn't get me once I was back across the threshold of a Brethren house. That was the only place you were really safe.

'If you went to a family wedding which was not a Brethren wedding,' my father continued, '– it was discouraged, but it did happen sometimes in the fifties – you'd feel at a loss. You wouldn't know how to behave, and you'd feel exposed and you'd be grateful to get back amongst Brethren.'

'Didn't it just seem like everyone at the non-Brethren wedding was having a better time?' I asked him. I was haunted by the phrase he'd used: *at a loss*.

'If you talked to a Christian from outside they'd use words that would jar with you,' he said. 'Brethren have a vocabulary and a way of talking about things that becomes the truth to you. It's been worked out over many years. So if somebody else comes in and starts talking about Jesus in a way that's off-key, it makes you feel ill at ease and out of place, so you're actually quite grateful to get away from that worldly wedding and back amongst people who speak the same language as you.'

'What kind of off-key?' I asked, though I knew exactly what he meant. People still seem off-key to me out here in the world, even though I've lived among non-Brethren more than five times longer than I lived among Brethren. It often feels as if the words I've learned to speak since then don't stretch far enough, don't describe the things I feel or imagine well enough. The things that crowd the dark, for instance, or flicker at the edges of my vision, have no name.

'It wasn't just phrases or ways of speaking,' my father said. 'It was ways of dressing and behaving as well. If an interloper got in, say a journalist passing himself off as a Brethren visitor, he'd break subtle rules and codes of conduct so that people would know he wasn't a proper member of the Brethren immediately. There was a real tribal sensitivity. My father used to say that when he was driving to a Meeting in a strange town, he could spot the Brethren sisters walking along the road. He'd say it was the Spirit telling him, but I always used to think it was their hats.'

# 20

When my father began to study A-Level English he became even more disorientated. He read *Hamlet*, *Coriolanus*, *Much Ado About Nothing*, Wordsworth, Keats, Housman, Coleridge, Dylan Thomas, *To the Lighthouse*, *Howards End* and T.S. Eliot. And then one day his teacher gave them Yeats's 'The Wild Swans at Coole'. My father was utterly bewitched.

When my father's teacher told my grandfather in 1957 that my father was uniquely talented and should be studying for Oxbridge, my grandfather, impressed and proud, agreed to let him sit the entrance exams. In the fifties, Brethren young men were still allowed to go to university, though in 1961 it would be banned. More than fifty years later, the Brethren still have a ban on higher education. 'It takes our people away from the Lord,' a Brethren priest told a journalist in a rare interview in 2003.

Now my father's lies escalated. To study for the Cambridge exams, he had to lie to both his father and his teacher. When his teacher arranged a summer camp at Stratford to see the Royal Shakespeare Company, my father made excuses not to

My father aged around sixteen

go. When he was offered the lead in the annual school Shakespeare production he had to find a reason to refuse. But he also went to his teacher's house in the evenings for extra tutorials with other members of his class, despite his parents' disapproval. He lied to his parents when he made his first visit to the theatre to see Paul Scofield playing Hamlet. Fifty years later, he could still remember the names of the entire cast.

He heard Brethren voices perpetually as he read, he told me in a lowered voice, and then he'd summon them to show me what he heard, what surfaced in his resting mind every day, every minute. 'There were the father voices,' he said, 'they were harsh and judgemental':

*The mind of the flesh is death ... the mind of the flesh is enmity against God ... it is not subject to the law of God, neither indeed can it be ... He that is a friend to the world is constituted an enemy of God.*

But there were also the kinder mother voices, which came on the other side of his head:

*When Israel was a child, then I loved him, and out of Egypt have I called my son …*

*Take my yoke upon you, and learn from me, for I am meek and lowly in heart, and ye shall have rest to your souls …*

*How often would I have gathered you, as a hen gathers her chickens under her wing …*

*Come, for night is gathering quickly o'er this world's fast fleeting day, If you linger in the darkness you will surely miss your way.*

Fifty years later he could still quote those lines from scriptures and from hymns. 'Those voices,' he told me, 'never gave up.'

I heard voices too as a child, sometimes when my head tipped to a particular angle, or when I was falling asleep or had just woken: loud, soft, haranguing, enticing, sometimes in English, sometimes in a language I did not recognise. They were very similar to the voices my father described, though he seems to have heard primarily Brethren mantras and scriptures. Eventually, of course, my father would recite those same words himself when he preached. Repetition of simplified mantras and maxims, social psychologists have proved, is one of the key methods of indoctrination; it affects the physiology of neurological pathways, particularly in teenagers, whose brains are still growing.[13] It's a powerful form of brainwashing. And of course my father's exceptional IQ and photographic memory made it very hard to silence those voices once they got in his head.

In the sixth form my father's Brethren voices were telling him that Yeats and Shakespeare were a frivolous waste of time, that all the apparent vistas that were opening to him were carnal and corrupt, *'the pleasures of sin for a season'*. He veered from one way of seeing to the other. 'One was graven on stone,' he wrote, 'the other rippled like water. One asserted, the other side sang and whispered, beguiled, suggested, asked questions, claimed nothing, resonated.'

# 21

It wasn't all prohibition and exegesis in the Brethren in the 1950s. Before 1959 Brethren were allowed to take holidays. Brethren families converged on St Ives in Cornwall every summer. It was where many Brethren young men selected their future wives, or had them selected for them. St Ives is where my father met my mother.

'If you looked down on Porthminster Beach from the road above on any day except the Lord's Day,' my father wrote, 'you'd see the holidaying Brethren immediately. There'd be a huge semicircle of perhaps sixty or seventy deckchairs set close together. The chairs kept them closed off from the rest of the beach; the area they made was bounded by the sea on its open side. "Worldly" families were scattered over the rest of the beach, but the Brethren had no contact with them.

'Within the semicircle the older Brethren men – some of them quite distinguished in Brethren terms – spent their days on the beach discussing "the Truth". They had their Bibles open on their laps and they'd talk for hours. The sisters talked about their children, and some of them knitted or sewed. Some of the respected spinsters and elder wives took part in the Bible discussions, but they were restrained and tentative; most of what they said was framed as questions. Paul had said: "*I do not suffer a woman to teach, nor to exercise authority over a man.*" So Brethren women were expected to keep their opinions to themselves. Small children played in the sand within the semicircle. Teenagers swam in the bay and played cricket or rounders. There was also tennis on the hard courts above the beach.

'On non-Meeting nights, Brethren teenagers were allowed to gather together after their hotel and boarding house dinners. They met at a coffee bar called "The Picnic Box". They drank

Brethren women at the beach

coffee and sometimes ordered the speciality of the house, a very large circular plate of biscuits and exotic cheeses. Afterwards, they walked together along the cliffs. Sometimes they swam at Porthminster Beach after dark. Sometimes during the week Brethren families went to Prah Sands and Perranporth in a convoy of cars to play cricket.

'There was no swimming or beach-going on the Lord's Day. On the Lord's Day evenings, after the Gospel in the Meeting Room, some of the Brethren gathered on the quay and several brothers preached to the passers-by. They'd have to compete with other evangelical groups – get themselves heard above the sound of the Salvation Army band. Then the teenagers would walk along the cliffs to Porthmeor beach and sing hymns above the breaking waves at sunset. We'd usually finish with "*How sweet the Name of Jesus sounds*" to the tune of Crimond,' he remembered, 'so that we could practise the descant.'

Later he said that he could remember very little about the hotels they stayed in, or the interior of the St Ives Meeting Room. But he remembered the beach – the golden colour of the sand and the sound of the cricket ball hitting the bat, the texture of browned and bare skin, and the white of a particular swimming costume gleaming in the dark.

My father, now very tall and athletic, not exactly handsome but more than usually eloquent for a seventeen-year-old, stood out from the crowd of Brethren young men. He'd fallen in love – not with my mother, but with the girl of the white swimming costume. She had slipped her hand into his during one of the evening walks. She was three years older than he was, twenty to his seventeen, and the assistant matron at a boys' public school. They had four days together before she'd had to leave. She walked with her toes turned out a little, the way dancers sometimes do, so he'd called her 'Penguin'. They swam out to the anchored raft off Porthminster Beach after dark one night and lay kissing on the fibre matting under the moon and stars.

She left St Ives by train the following day, the same day that my mother arrived with her sister and parents. She and my father were introduced on the beach, but he'd been too heartbroken to talk much. He exchanged letters with the Penguin every day for months. Her letters arrived with a small penguin drawn on the back of the envelope. After Christmas she wrote to say that as they lived so far apart and their ages did not match, she thought they should 'discontinue' their 'friendship' – and, she added, 'My parents wish it.' The penguin on the back of this particular envelope lay flat on its back and had an arrow in its stomach.

When my father expressed interest in my mother, the girl he'd met fleetingly at St Ives, another Brethren girl invited them both to her birthday party. He was seventeen, my mother twenty-one. They met again at a Brethren wedding. My father invited my mother to watch the University Boat Race from Putney in March. He'd won a place at Fitzwilliam College, Cambridge, he told her. He'd be starting in September, and was going to try for the rowing team.

He remembers walking along the Thames. He remembers swans and weeping willows and my mother's coat, which had a fine herringbone pattern and a large, soft collar that she turned up behind her head. When she laughed and turned towards him, he told me, the darkness of her hair, thickly plaited and pinned up around her head, took his breath away. They talked about Jane Austen, Charlotte Brontë and Yeats, he said – but I know he would have done almost all of the talking. Cambridge won the Boat Race. It rained. On the train afterwards they ordered tea and toast and talked, my father said, as if they were already engaged to be married.

He arranged to go to Salisbury for a weekend to stay with her and her parents. It was a disaster. Head in a book, he missed the train and turned up very late. She had to cancel the restaurant booking she'd made. The following day he borrowed her father's car, a Rover that was polished every week, and took a turn too tightly, scraping and denting the car all along the left-hand side. It was a sign, my mother told me decades later, that she should have taken notice of. He was going to go on crashing cars for the rest of his life.

# 22

My father's first letters home from Cambridge were all about rowing and the problems he'd had getting his rowing kit washed and dried in time for the next outing. His college crew were out on the river at dawn every day, training in the early-morning mist.

He was going to lectures, writing essays, talking to the other undergraduates on his corridor and on his crew. In comparison to life at home, he must have felt very much in the world, and he clearly relished it; but he also knew, as all Brethren undergraduates did, that the local Brethren were keeping a close eye on him, and would be writing to his parents with regular reports. He was expected to attend Cambridge Meeting most days of the week, and several times on the Lord's Day.

My father messed up his first year at university, his cousin told me. Reports from the Cambridge Brethren arrived claiming that he'd gone off the rails, that he was backsliding morally. 'Backsliding' was a word I'd often heard used about Brethren young men. It seemed to cover a multitude of sins. I suspect my father's worst crimes were that he missed some Meetings and had been seen going to the cinema and socialising with non-Brethren. It probably also meant he'd begun to ask questions about doctrinal matters.

Everyone back home was holding their breath. The family honour and reputation were at stake. My great-grandfather Hugh Wasson now decreed that no other young Stotts were to go to university, or into any other form of higher education. My father had been corrupted and muddled, he declared. He wasn't going to risk that happening to any of his other grandchildren.

In his second year of university my father began to attend lectures by C.S. Lewis. He read his way through all Lewis's books, but it was the final page of *Mere Christianity* that brought him to his knees one night, both metaphorically and literally, in his small rooms in Willis Road. The conversion was so violent that, years later, the details of the room, the wallpaper, the light through the window, the scattered pattern of the papers on his desk, had seared themselves like a scorchmark onto his memory.

'Submit to death,' Lewis wrote, '... submit with every fibre of your being, and you will have eternal life. Keep back nothing ... Look for yourself, and you will find in the long run only hatred, loneliness, despair, rage, ruin, and decay. But look for Christ and you will find Him, and with Him everything else thrown in.'

'The words,' my father wrote, 'leapt off the page. Here was the most powerful of my new literary apostles reinforcing all the old Brethren arguments.' His defences collapsed suddenly, 'like the walls of a sandcastle swept by an incoming tide'. There was that sea metaphor he so often used. He'd been engulfed again. He knelt and prayed. It was, he wrote, a 'halting, painful prayer'.

'I look back on that young man and his capitulation,' he continued – confirming in that one word, 'capitulation', the degree of exhaustion I'd sensed in him – 'I look back on that young man in that small lonely bedroom with affection and sympathy. I didn't have a chance.'

It's the empathy that surprises me. The empathy he has for his remembered, capitulating self. And mine for him.

'I didn't have a chance.'

A chance to do what, though? To get away? To not believe? But he had made a *choice*. He had chosen to follow Lewis's kindly, pleasure-taking God instead of his father's punitive one.

'I'd been brought up to believe in a transcendent God. Now, with Lewis and Donne, I began to think about an *immanent* one.' He quoted lines from Gerard Manley Hopkins: *the world is charged with the grandeur of God. It will flame out, like shining from shook foil.* This new God loved the world rather than shunned it.

Under Lewis's spell he went to see *Look Back in Anger* and *Waiting for Godot* at the Cambridge Arts Theatre. He watched Bergman's *The Seventh Seal* and *Wild Strawberries* at the Arts Cinema.

'Cinema stopped being furtive entertainment,' he wrote; 'it contained both moral instruction and metaphysical power.' In Brighton during a vacation he saw Laurence Olivier in *The Entertainer*. He had 'chosen' a complicated, spine-contorting middle way: he'd stay in the Brethren, and bring this other world into it.

# 23

My parents look happy in the black-and-white photographs I have of them from the 1950s. Among those packs of young Brethren at St Ives in the apparently halcyon summers before 1959, I can see them moving gradually closer together. In the early ones they stand far apart, two figures among a big group, he leaning against a seaside railing, she with her stylish collar turned up against the wind; then there's a picture of them closer together, in a group of four or five cousins. The women are conservatively dressed; some wear headscarves. They wear no make-up. The men look a bit geeky, but otherwise, if you'd been on the promenade in St Ives that day, you wouldn't have known they were any different from anyone else.

Many ex-Brethren I've talked to describe the fifties as a golden age in Brethren life. It was only when Jim Taylor Junior took over as Man of God in 1959 that things went wrong. He ruined it all, they imply. He was an aberration, a monster. He

St Ives, 1956. My father is on the right

made good people do unspeakable things. But even in the fifties, I can see, there were already serious prohibitions in place:

No cinemas, theatres, circuses, music halls.

No sports halls.

No radios or television sets.

Friendships with non-Brethren – tolerated but not encouraged.

No trade unions.

No sex before marriage.

No trousers for women or short skirts.

No fashionable clothes.

No tabloid newspapers.

No thrillers or modern novels.

No short hair.

Within five years the prohibition list would have grown to four or five times this length. Within ten years it would be at least twenty times as long.

Around this time, in the late fifties, my father remembered, he and my mother, now engaged, discussed whether or not they should stay in the Brethren. With the rules getting stricter, many young people were leaving. My mother suggested they put the decision to the Lord. What she meant by this was that they should look for an answer in the scriptural verse on the Day Dawn calendar for that particular day. It's what many Brethren did. If you were going to let the Lord direct your ways, you had to be confident that you could read the signs he sent. The Day Dawn calendar was one of the ways the Lord directed the Brethren. You might as well have rolled dice, I wanted to protest, or read tea leaves, or spun the roulette wheel.

My father couldn't remember the exact scriptural text on the Day Dawn calendar that day, he told me, though he thought it had been about walking in the light. He and my mother decided it meant they should stay in the Brethren.

But I'm pretty certain they'd have stayed even without consulting the Day Dawn calendar. They were optimistic and happy. They didn't know what was ahead. And anyway, how could they have left? If they had left the Brethren in 1959 they would never have seen their parents, siblings, uncles, aunts or friends again. They would have orphaned themselves.

# 24

'We're in 1959,' I said, looking back over my notes. I'd just seen that sense of urgency creep up on him again. He wanted to watch the cricket; he wanted to sleep. But he knew he was running out of time. He was an eyewitness to this strange piece of history. Very few people had seen what he had seen. He *had* to make a record before he died.

I went to fetch the tape recorder.

'Why didn't we see it coming?' he asked.

'It's easy to see it with hindsight,' I said. 'I'm not sure I would have guessed what was going on either. Maybe even JT Junior didn't know.'

I adjusted his chair so he could sit up a little. My brothers had gone for a walk; my stepmother was taking a nap.

'Just half an hour,' I said. 'You need to conserve your energy.' I closed the door. Something had made me want to draw the curtains. There'd been more snow flurries outside overnight.

'You should see the soil,' I said. 'The snow's dusting it like icing sugar. It's very pretty. I can see twenty or thirty lapwings from here, too. Twice as many as this time last year. They'll be nesting in a month or so.'

But he wasn't to be distracted. He was already back in 1959.

'That was the year that JT Junior seized power,' he said after I'd pressed the record button. 'It was a seismic shift in Brethren history. Seismic.'

All ex-Brethren describe 1959 with similarly dramatic metaphors. Sometimes they call it a coup. Whatever comparisons they use, geological or military, they mean that nothing would be the same again. There was no going back.

'It took JT Junior ten years,' my father said, 'to completely transform the Brethren into a cult. It didn't happen all at once. But when he seized power it was violent and sudden. The rest was a kind of ten-year lava flow.'

My parents were out of the country when the coup happened. They'd married quickly so my mother could accompany my father to South Africa. He'd been offered a three-month summer internship with Wall's ice cream in Johannesburg; they'd be staying with Brethren families, and he'd be preaching. In June 1959 they flew into a South Africa deeply scarred by a decade of apartheid. The Brethren coup took place in Central Hall, London, a month later.

Ever since James Taylor died in 1953, the 100,000 Brethren around the world had been waiting for the new 'Man of God' to emerge. For six years the leadership rotated between four men, one of whom was the rather erratic JT Junior, James Taylor's son. Each July, people half expected one of the four to take the upper hand at the annual three-day Central Hall conference, but summer after summer things had gone on much the same. Until 1959, that is. My grandfather was at the gathering, but he wasn't amongst the top brass up on the stage

Brethren photographed at Central Hall in 1959. Gerald Cowell is at the podium, JT Junior immediately to his right

in the photo that one of the ex-Brethren sent me. He'd only been a trustee of the Brethren publishing house they called the Depot for five years, so perhaps he wasn't important enough yet; or perhaps they'd had to ration the seats. Had he minded not being up there?

It was the usual vast gathering. Senior ministering brothers from South Africa, New Zealand, Australia, America, South America, even Iran, had flown to London. My grandfather described the events to my grandmother. She wrote about them to my father in Johannesburg.

'The question of professional associations came up again,' my father said.

I was struggling to keep up. I couldn't see how any of this was important. Yet remembering the details of that 1959 gathering seemed to be agitating my father more than anything else in the story he was trying to tell me.

'Professional associations?' I said. 'Why did that matter?'

'James Taylor had banned union membership ten years before,' he explained, with obvious impatience. 'Now Brethren were saying that if blue-collar workers weren't allowed to belong to unions, then white-collar workers – Brethren doctors, architects, chemists and lawyers – should leave their professional associations too. But that was going to be a problem, because many of them would lose their jobs.'

'Someone had to decide,' I said, feeling my way.

'Yes, exactly. One of the four leaders, Gerald Cowell, took the microphone and began to make the case for a slow, staggered withdrawal from the associations. He even suggested that someone might write to the government and get some kind of special dispensation.'

He asked me to adjust his pillows so he could sit upright.

'Now at this point,' he continued, his eyes brighter than I'd seen them for days, 'at this point, JT Junior intervened in a way that was very un-Brethrenlike indeed. He came in very abruptly and said, "Are you saying we shouldn't get out immediately?" Cowell was slightly taken aback, but he repeated his proposal.

'Taylor quoted the New Testament at him: "Come out from among them and be separate," he said. "That's what it says. It doesn't say *go slowly*. Come out from among them and *be separate*. That's what it says."

'JT Junior just kept hammering on about this. There were awkward pauses and a very un-Brethrenlike contretemps went on, and JT Junior made this sort of howl of *Come out, come out*.'

'*Howl?*' I said. 'What kind of howl? Was that normal?'

'Taylor was unpredictable,' he said. 'He could be aggressive. It wasn't the Brethren way, but suddenly here he was, openly defying Cowell, goading him, then howling: *Come out, come out*. Once he'd shouted down Cowell like that, everyone knew JT Junior was the new leader.'

Had JT Junior planned to take over the leadership? Several ex-Brethren who lived through that period, some of whom were at Central Hall in July 1959, have told me since my father died that they think Bruce Hales, an Australian accountant and JT Junior's right-hand man, had been behind the coup in some way. He was the uncle of the most recent Brethren leader, who was also called Bruce Hales. The older Bruce had married JT Junior's daughter Consuela only a year before the coup. Had he begun to work on JT Junior over family suppers? Had he stoked up JT Junior's impatience with the pace of Brethren decision-making processes? The timing certainly looks right. When my parents flew back from South Africa that August, JT Junior was already putting draconian new rules in place. Neither of them knew the scale of the storm they were about to enter.

# DURING

# I

Three weeks before my father died there'd been a lunar eclipse. A blood-red moon had hung low in the sky above the Mill, silvering the fields and the river. He'd staggered outside to the riverbank, leaning on my younger brother, and they had stood there watching the moon turn black. Two tall men, father and youngest son, their arms around each other, gazing at the sky.

Now, the following day, laid out in the middle of the room under a moth-eaten gold velvet throw, he was fighting the effects of the morphine, and though he was impatient to get on with our interview, he was easily distracted. He wanted the door closed before we began. He seemed to think there might be someone out there listening. 'Is that noise coming from in here?' he whispered when the whirr of the tape recorder started up.

I hadn't expected his story to be full of the minutiae of Brethren leadership conflicts. Through all the hours I recorded him that week, my father kept to a ruthlessly straight chronological line, describing each new Brethren edict, each new struggle for power, month by month, excommunication by excommunication. We both knew he was running out of time, that he couldn't afford to meander. But he only got to 1963, the year before my birth, before he was too tired to continue. He was still only twenty-five then, tall and lanky, a fledgling preacher, and already the father of a son.

'But how did you feel?' I'd interrupt. 'What did my mother think about that? Wasn't that the month that Chris was born? Didn't you cut his umbilical cord?'

I kept trying to get him to step sideways, out from amid the Brethren patriarchy and their closed rooms and doctrinal disputes. I wanted him to tell me about the family home, where my mother was having babies and sterilising bottles, that detached, four-bedroom, mock-Tudor, half-timbered house opposite Hove Park, with the lilac tree in the garden, and the bush with the white berries that you squashed between your fingers, and where our tricycles made tracks in the morning dew.

We'd lived through those dark years too, after all, and had been marked by them. But it wasn't just that I wanted to be in this story of his. It was that I was increasingly certain that the full picture, the one he couldn't bear to look at, had to include our day-to-day family life and our private dreams as well as the dramas played out in the Brethren corridors of power. It had to include the women and children as well as the men. It would only be half a story without them.

But my father had only one objective in the hours I recorded him: he wanted to understand how he and the other Brethren men of his generation had been bewitched, turned from decent, earnest, promising young people into brutal Brownshirts. He had to understand that before he could be ready to die. It struck me that even after we'd recorded five hours of that interview, he was getting the facts down, but still not really understanding what they meant. I think he knew that too.

It wasn't just me he was talking to. When he woke in the night in those last days he'd open up his laptop to write to a group of eighty or so ex-Exclusive Brethren all over the world on an online forum called PEEBS.net. The name came from a word outsiders had often used to describe the Plymouth Brethren: Peebs, or the PBs. The site had been set up by ex-Brethren to provide a place for escapees to get support and to talk about their experiences. It had a flashing red 'Rescue' button on its home page. My father had been talking to the PEEB community for six years, sometimes every day. He seemed to have become an important presence there. It was where he'd met my stepmother.

Now that they knew he was dying, these ex-Brethren from Australia, London and America had gathered online to listen and to console. *They* hadn't kept interrupting with the wrong questions. They knew what to say, and what language to use.

One of the first things I had to do after my father died was to write to these people to tell them that he'd gone; that yes, that *was* what his silence meant. I told them about the owl that had come for him. I told them he had died a good death with his family around him. I thanked them.

In January 2013 PEEBS.net mysteriously disappeared. The ex-Brethren webhost, Tim Twinam, who ran the site from a log cabin in Vermont, and who'd been wrestling with Brethren legal action for five years or more, suddenly wasn't answering his emails or his phone. People were saying the Brethren had either paid him off or threatened him. His seriously ill wife, they said, had just had expensive hospital treatment, more expensive than they could have afforded without outside help.[1] Even now, no one really knows what happened to make Tim Twinam shut down the site.

But all those conversations and exchanges and words my father had left on the PEEB site hadn't disappeared. A member of the community sent me a transcript of everything my father had posted, retrieved from a data dump somewhere. It ran to hundreds of pages. More ex-Brethren websites and blogs sprung up after PEEBS.net had been closed down, my informant told me. 'That's the thing about the internet,' he said. 'You can close down one part and another part will grow somewhere else.'

As I read the to-and-fro of daily banter in the transcripts, my father's conversations with ex-Brethren from New Zealand and Australia, Germany and South Africa, I was struck by how many different voices there were. Some were irascible, others grief-stricken or furious; many were still devout Christians, while others were zealous atheists. They teased him; they sent him poetry; they wrote to tell him about what the Brethren were doing now; they told him about someone who'd escaped and was being sheltered, about what had happened in their houses in the sixties and seventies, and sometimes about what was still happening.

The PEEB community must have been, it seems to me now, like a Greek chorus in the chambers of my father's mind as he slipped away. All through those last weeks, while I had been asking my clumsy questions, long after he could no longer reach for his laptop, these people were in the house, in his head, attending, a hushed, respectful presence. They helped him to face his death, but they had also helped him to remember. They reminded him that his story was their story too.

# 2

My parents flew back to Britain from South Africa in September 1959 for the final year of my father's Cambridge English literature degree. They rented part of a house close to the Cambridge Meeting Room. My father went back to his rowing, his classes, his books and essays, his Brethren undergraduate friends. My mother bought second-hand furniture, sewed curtains, washed his rowing kit, and cycled two miles every day to her new full-time job as an accountant for Spillers flour mill up near the station. They broke bread with the Cambridge Brethren at the Mawson Road Meeting Room on the Lord's Day.

They wouldn't have had much time alone. Every night my father's friends came to the house and sat up talking late as they'd always done, except now they talked about the Brethren families who were leaving.

My father was studying *The Faerie Queene*, a long Protestant allegorical poem written by Edmund Spenser in the late sixteenth century. He'd composed it, Spenser wrote, 'to fashion a gentleman of noble person in virtuous and gentle discipline'. The gentle knight of the story, the Red Cross knight – named for the red cross emblazoned on his shield, like the knights of the Crusades – goes through a series of ordeals and trials. It must have been perfect reading for my father.

When I looked at the annotations in his hardback copy, shelved next to Arthur Mee's *Book of Everlasting Things*, I was struck by how he'd turned the poem into a theological thinking ground for himself, by how many scriptural references he'd added in the margins, many distilled down to mere numerical references: *Tim* 2:2; *Cor* 3:5; and so on. 'Can you explain the difference between the Solomonic and the Davidic codes?' my father's friend William remembers him asking one night that winter. William couldn't, but my father could. He seems to have been sharpening his rhetorical tools and gathering ammunition. He was preparing to enter the ring as a Brethren combatant. He knew he'd have to know his scriptures inside out if he was going to win against the older Brethren.

JT Junior, sixty years old, was also preparing himself for a fight. He'd been waiting in the wings for thirty or forty years, biting his tongue, furious about the way his father's 'new light' on the Holy Spirit had been ignored. Now that he'd assumed leadership he wasted no time in asserting his authority. He had some things to prove.

In the spring of 1960, only months after he'd taken the leadership, JT Junior placed an absolute ban on membership of professional associations. 'If you're not with me,' he told the Brethren, 'you're against me.'

Thousands of Brethren white-collar workers around the world 'unyoked' and resigned from their professional associations. Many lost their jobs. The Brethren were now in the news. They'd be in the papers most months throughout the 1960s.

Although many Brethren were now leaving the fellowship in protest against the new hardline edicts, JT Junior remained defiant. The great winnowing had begun, he declared. It was, he said, a clear sign that the Rapture was close.

'You either had to commit yourself or get out,' my father said years later when he was interviewed for a BBC documentary about the Brethren. 'It became a bit of a crusade ... Before, it had been a bit flabby and inconclusive. Now it was something that you could either accept or reject, something very clear-cut. People were suffering for it – giving up professional associations and losing their jobs, and giving up jobs that involved entertaining clients, and so on. This is why I said there was a spirit of a crusade.'[2]

JT Junior spoke about the Brethren as his ranks; together, he promised, they would rout Satan on his own battleground. 'We must keep in mind,' he wrote, 'that the Lord is a man of war.'[3] And by the time he flew to the UK from his home in New York in late July 1960, ready to drive his new hardline militaristic separatism home, he was in full war mode. The timing was good. Cold War tensions were running high. There were new charismatic leaders on the world stage too: Billy Graham was rallying millions to his evangelical crusades; JFK had just been nominated as US presidential candidate.

JT Junior had won the battle over professional associations. Now it was time to step up another gear and clean up all the Brethren households once and for all. Brethren had no business eating with non-Brethren, he declared. It was time to build some walls.

JT Junior gave an address at Park Street, Islington, in July 1960, entitled 'The King and his Men', a speech designed to rally a new generation to his crusade against Satan. My father was in the auditorium that day; his father, as a trustee of the Depot, was now sitting up on the platform.

In a series of notes I found in one of my father's files, he described the 'King and his Men' speech as the principal turning point in his own radicalisation. I can see why. He was twenty-two and newly married, head of his household. He'd spent his life up to then cowed by his own father's absolute authority. He'd been following the Red Cross knight through *The Faerie Queene*. He was ready to become a leader, and he wanted a place up on that platform for himself.

JT Junior took as his scripture that day the story of King David capturing Jerusalem in 2 *Samuel* 5: 6–10. The Lord wanted the Brethren to go to war, he told his audience, to become David's men, to take risks on the battlefield, to capture Jerusalem. Now was the time. But although he could see that the young men in Britain were ready to fight, he told them, the older Brethren were holding back, hesitating, because they were self-important, stuffy and stuck in their ways. They didn't have the stomach for the fight. They'd have to be barred from the house, he said, if they didn't commit. The young bloods – the Davids – would show them what was what. They shouldn't put up with these dithering old men any more.

It was a clever move. JT Junior was marshalling the young against the patriarchs. It was the 1960s, and he was using the spirit of revolution and revolt that was already in the air to promote an extremely right-wing puritan crusade in which the young would take the lead.[4]

For my father, imagining himself as a knight taking on the corrupt forces of Roman Catholicism, as a soldier in David's army defeating the Jebusites against all the odds, or as David himself taking on Goliath, that address, as he put it, 'reset the agenda'. It stirred his blood. He may have been sitting down in the auditorium with his Brethren friends, while his father was up on the platform, but nothing was set in stone.

'Now,' he wrote in his notes, 'a sizeable, and powerful, number of young Brethren began to rise up and make themselves heard … Driving the traditional brethrenistic element in Britain on to the back foot, making them feel defensive, that was a very important part of the whole campaign … JT Junior persuaded us young Brethren that we'd inherited a radical tradition but the old people had turned it into a comfortable establishment. It was our job to stir them up to radicalism again.'

'A great sifting is going on,' JT Junior kept repeating; sometimes he'd call it a 'spewing'. This must mean, he'd tell them again, that the Rapture was close. The Lord was moving quickly: 'The Lord is cleansing his temple.' Time was running out. For the next eight years, every time things got difficult JT Junior would tell the Brethren it was a sure sign that Satan was ramping up his assault – and that, in turn, was a sure sign that the Rapture was getting ever closer.

# 3

When I read the transcript of JT Junior's 'The King and his Men' speech, the rhythms of the language took me straight back into Meeting, where as a very small child I listened to my father's and grandfather's voices as they rose and fell, incanting and descanting. Satan was close, they'd preach; he was a trickster, always looking out for opportunities to use a wayward brother or sister to get himself inside our closed circle. The Brethren had all grown up thinking of themselves as besieged by Satan's forces, who were rallying outside the walls of the Meeting Room, so JT Junior's new rhetoric of attack rather than defence must have stirred their blood.

As a child I struggled to think of all those stocky men in their suits and hats going to war. It was even more difficult to imagine the sisters, in their hats and headscarves, whooshing up into the air when the Rapture came. I was always worried about how they'd keep their hats on and their skirts down.

But despite the apparent blandness of our suburban lives, according to those preachings and addresses, spectacular dramas and showdowns were always happening. JT Junior persuaded the Brethren that personal suffering and subjection to his absolute leadership were the only ways to fight back against Satan's growing power. The mini-skirted sexual decadence of the 1960s, and the sheer number of Satan's new converts out there, were, he claimed, sure proof that the Rapture was fast approaching. The Lord was sending the Brethren more and more powerful signs in order to keep his precious people walking in the light when everyone else was disappearing into Satan's darkness.

So although my father was already primed for battle in 1960 by that heady collision of C.S. Lewis's lyricism, Edmund Spenser's Calvinism, and the bower-of-bliss-smashing Red Cross knight's and JT Junior's calls to arms, when his closest Brethren friend began to consider leaving, and then died suddenly, he persuaded himself it was a personal warning from the Lord.

'A fortnight before his death,' my shocked father wrote to his mother just after his friend Christopher Tydeman's funeral in the summer of 1960, 'Christopher was here [in Cambridge] for a weekend. He came at his own invitation. His last words to me were, "I'll see you in a fortnight's time if I'm still in fellowship." He was upset and puzzled by recent happenings and when he came here he was full of questions. We talked very late both Friday and Saturday evenings. I wasn't able to answer his objections, his mind was always more acute and analytical than mine, but I think we both became impressed as the discussion

A group of my father's Brethren undergraduate friends.
Christopher Tydeman is second from the left

went on with the stress that is laid on action ("he that hears My words and does them"). I say we were both impressed because I don't want to give the impression that he was the questioner and I the answerer. That was not so. We helped each other on Saturday night, I think.'

Christopher, still considering whether to leave, had gone to hear my father preach the following day. When my father drove him to the station, Christopher's goodbye had been enigmatic: 'Thank you very much for the weekend,' he said. 'I got my answer and it wasn't what I expected.' My father wrote to his mother that he'd been searching for an explanation of those words ever since his friend's death.

Christopher wrote to my father a few days later. He'd come to a decision, he said, but he still did not reveal what it was.

Then two weeks later, down in St Ives, he slipped on a rock pool, hit his head, and died.

At the funeral, Christopher's Brethren father had taken his son's undergraduate friends aside and told them that he was certain the death was 'not an accident'. Did he mean that Christopher had killed himself? Jumped? Or worse: was Christopher's father telling those young men that his wavering son had been singled out by God, struck down and made an example of?[5]

Whatever it meant, my father changed. His letters were now full of crusading metaphors. Gone was the pleasure-loving, hesitant young man of the Cambridge years, and in his place there was a zealot, or at least the performance of one.

A few weeks ago I found a tiny newspaper clipping among my father's papers entitled 'Man Falls 100 Feet'. The man was Christopher Tydeman. He'd fallen from a cliff and died of his injuries, not slipped on a rock, as my father had been told. Was this the beginning of a larger pattern of cover-ups, secrets and lies around the increasing number of Brethren mental breakdowns and suicides?

# 4

In the spring of 1960, while he was finishing his last year at Cambridge, my father went for an interview in Birmingham for a job with 3M, the Minnesota Mining and Manufacturing Company. 3M had been manufacturing products like masking tape and sandpaper in America since early in the century, and were expanding into global markets with new products, including surgical and audio tape. Their success, they told my father over lunch after the interview, was rooted in treating their employees as one big family. They were looking for bright, talented ideas people who could sell their products and help expand 3M's place in the UK market.

Six foot four in height, affable, well-built, Cambridge-educated, and soberly dressed, my father must have looked and sounded impressive. He came, he told his interviewers, from a long line of travelling salespeople: his father had been a salesman for Dubarry and Roger et Gallet, and he himself had worked in South Africa as the assistant sales manager for the brand-new sales team of Wall's ice cream. The job would be perfect for him, he told my mother when he was offered the position, as 3M wouldn't require him to join a union or a professional association.

But by the time, six months later, that he put on his suit and took himself off to 3M's UK head office in Birmingham, JT Junior had proclaimed that Brethren should no longer eat with non-Brethren, because eating together was 'an act of fellowship'. The charter once again pointed to Paul's letters, 1 *Corinthians* 5: 9–11 this time: 'I have written to you in the epistle not to mix with fornicators,' Paul wrote; 'not altogether with the fornicators of the world, or with the avaricious and rapacious, or idolators; since then you should go out of the world. But now I have written to you, if any one called brother be fornicator or avaricious, or idolator, or abusive, or a drunkard, or rapacious, not to mix with him; *with such a one not even to eat.*'

The Brethren fishermen who sailed in mixed crews up at Eyemouth, Port Seton and Peterhead now either had to find ways of eating separately from their fellow crew members on tiny boats with a single cabin, or had to leave the crew. Understandably, they caused offence. Non-Brethren sailors began to refuse to sail with Brethren sailors.

When my father told his new employers he could not eat or drink with his work colleagues or clients, they accused him of hypocrisy. He'd eaten with them during his job interview, they said. Why not now, only a few months later? He tried to explain that this was a new rule in his Church; that he was simply following orders. He even tried to quote the passage from 1 *Corinthians* 5, but no one was interested.

It is difficult to convey the scale of the devastation that the 'eating rule' caused, not just in the workplace but in Brethren homes around the world. If a Brethren husband was living with a non-Brethren wife, he could no longer eat at the same table with her. If a Brethren daughter had taken her elderly non-Brethren mother to live with her and her family, the mother would have to eat in a separate room. If a Brethren teenager did not want to join the Brethren, he or she would have to eat in another room. Brethren children had to come home from school, or eat at a separate table in the school canteen, to avoid being contaminated by non-Brethren children. My mother picked us all up from school at lunchtime and gave us a meal at home. When we drank the bottles of milk the school provided, the teachers had to usher us into a different part of the room from the other children. No one explained why. I suspect no one really knew how to.

Many ex-Brethren told me stories about how difficult it had been at work once the eating rule was imposed, how lonely and isolating it was. My father's closest friend during the sixties, William, agreed to meet me for lunch with his wife in a restaurant on the Essex marshes forty years after we'd last seen each other. I couldn't help feeling we were meeting out there, miles from anywhere, in an almost empty restaurant, because we needed to be sure we would not be overheard. Outside, the halyards of sailing boats clanged against their masts.

In 1960, William told me, when my twenty-two-year-old father was selling tape in Birmingham, William was working in a raincoat factory as a sales representative. He was also in his early twenties, also newly married. He was doing well at work, gaining trust, establishing his place in the team. But with the new eating prohibition, suddenly he could no longer socialise with his colleagues. He had to eat at a different table in the canteen, and explain that this was a religious rule. He didn't dare break it in case someone saw and reported him.

His colleagues were offended and baffled, he told me. He became increasingly isolated. Every day he felt he was walking on knives, that he might be sacked at any moment. He dreaded lunch and coffee breaks, and would search for excuses to get out of the office. It was impossible to concentrate on work. Soon, he said, he was lurching constantly between anxiety, insomnia, frustration and rage. My father, working amongst the bright, ambitious young men of 3M, must have felt the same.

William knew that what was going on was wrong, but neither he nor his wife had ever lived outside the Brethren; they could not imagine doing that. They were frightened. He'd broken Brethren rules as a young child, just as I had done, just as my father had done. He'd hidden Brethren-banned books like *Biggles* in the saddlebag of his bike under Brethren-approved books about birdwatching and astronomy. He'd even considered leaving altogether when he was older, but when he'd tried to talk to his mother about his doubts, she'd said sternly, 'Something's wrong with you, William,' and he'd started to wonder if perhaps she was right. When he expressed his concerns about the eating issue in a letter to a family friend, and told her he was thinking about leaving the fellowship altogether, the friend had written back, 'Are you really prepared to kill your mother?'

A cousin introduced me to an ex-Brethren woman she knew who lived near me in London. I asked her to dinner. 'Ruth'

– she didn't want me to use her real name either – was seventy. She and her parents had lived through the JT Junior years. I asked what had happened in her family as a result of the eating rules. She still found it difficult to talk about, she said. Even fifty-five years later, it was painful for her to remember.

She'd been the only child of a Brethren father and a non-Brethren mother. Before 1960 that hadn't been too much of a problem, she said. She attended Sunday Meetings with her father and uncle and aunts; her mother didn't. In 1960, when JT Junior began to enforce the new separation rules, her uncle, struggling to keep his job and to comply with the new Brethren rules about professional associations, committed suicide. Ruth was fourteen. Only weeks after her uncle's death, the local Brethren told her father that if her mother didn't join the fellowship he'd either have to leave her or leave the Brethren.

Late one evening, two of the local Brethren priests came to their north London home. Ruth watched the whole episode from the top of the stairs. Their home was unclean, the priests said; it would contaminate the local assembly. Was Ruth's mother now ready to join the Brethren? When her mother told them she wasn't going to join, they turned to her father. Was he now going to leave his wife? When he said no, that he wasn't going to leave her, they told him he'd have to leave the Brethren. The two priests then left.

Ruth went to bed as she was told, but the house had 'an atmosphere of unbearable tension'. She was woken up some time later by frightening sounds from downstairs. She ran down the stairs just in time to rescue her mother from being strangled by her father. He had her on the floor with his hands around her neck. Ruth had to use all her force to pull him off.

'When he turned towards me,' she said, 'it was with an unrecognising, wild look in his eyes unlike anything I'd seen before.'

The next morning a doctor referred her father for psychiatric treatment. Soon after, with her mother still refusing to join the Brethren, the three of them left the fellowship altogether, leaving behind all her father's family, who would not be able to speak to them again. Her parents stayed together, Ruth said, but their marriage never really recovered.

Everywhere this new hardline separatism was making life difficult for Brethren – sometimes unbearably so – but as my father would tell the BBC interviewer sixteen years later, there was also something exhilarating about that collective suffering. JT Junior kept on telling them that suffering was 'The Thing'. Consider Christ's suffering on the cross, he'd roar at them. And you think you have it bad?

I found a picture of my father in the years he worked for 3M. He was dressed in a good suit, well-cut. He looked handsome. There were several pens lined up in his top pocket. He was standing alone in some kind of conservatory, looking not down over that great view, but up, as if he were about to preach, and was waiting for inspiration. He looked lonely, lost in his thoughts. A single hook hung from the wooden window frame. It made me shudder. It looked ominous, hanging out there in the void of his future, as if he were snagged on it, or a puppet

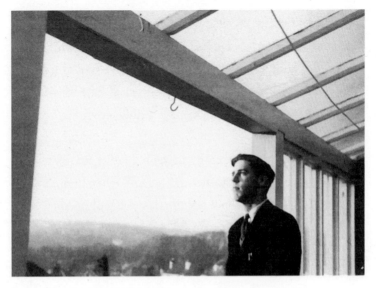

My father, photographed around 1960

to it. I wondered if my mother had taken that picture. Had she seen the hook too?

The choice of jobs for young Brethren men like my father narrowed dramatically in the early sixties. Almost every line of professional work was now out of reach for most of them: bankers, architects, engineers, pharmacists, teachers, engineers – they all had professional associations. Most employers would not take on an employee who refused to eat with his colleagues or clients or to join a union. Married Brethren women were not allowed to work now at all.

Next, JT Junior banned university attendance. Being a member of a university, he declared, was like being a member of a union. Education corrupted; it nurtured the natural mind rather than the spiritual mind, and it took young people away from the home and the watchful eye of their parents and other Brethren. All Brethren young men and women enrolled in degree programmes now had to either leave their universities or leave the Brethren. My father had just slipped through. He'd be one of the very last Brethren to have graduated.

JT Junior's extreme rules of separation in the early sixties forced thousands of young men either to join Brethren businesses or to start up their own. They must have been relieved to leave non-Brethren jobs after all the social isolation and anxiety that the eating rule had caused. This generation of Brethren young men were enterprising and resourceful. A group of cousins in Sussex set up a company that imported wood to make matchboxes decorated with Sussex scenes. Others sold fudge or honey, hardwood flooring or handcrafted kitchens. Older Brethren were expected to provide loans for these new businesses and to keep them afloat if they ran into trouble. Most flourished.

JT Junior, guided and advised by his son-in-law Bruce Hales, and Bruce's brother John, now set about creating a global infrastructure for wealth-creation and accumulation, all under the direct management of Brethren leaders. Later, they'd work out ever more inventive ways to avoid paying taxes, including using gift aid and trusts, and campaigning for charitable status. Soon the Brethren would be very rich indeed.

# 5

'A ruthless gestapo had been set up to enforce Big Jim's new rules,' my father told me.

'Gestapo?' I said. 'Isn't that a bit extreme? Nothing in the Brethren story compares to the scale of what the Nazis did.'

He'd been reading *The Rise and Fall of the Third Reich* again – I'd seen it open on his study desk.

'It's not the *scale* of what happened,' he insisted, 'it's the pattern. There's always a charismatic leader and a group of people who are cut off from the world. They're slowly brainwashed into thinking they're the chosen ones; that they're surrounded by evil and that if they want to save themselves they have to do exactly what they're told. It's the same pattern every time.'

Later, once I'd started reading books on the social psychology of cults, I could see he was right. 'Totalist systems', as experts called them – and that could mean the whole Maoist regime or a cult like the Exclusive Brethren – did have common patterns. They all depended, for instance, on a network of enforcers and interrogators to operate effectively.

He and other young Brethren men, my father said, had hauled themselves up onto their hind legs to turn themselves into the two-legged thug pigs of George Orwell's *Animal Farm*.

But what did that *mean*? What had he and William – and other men like them – actually done in the sixties that was so bad?

My father had not been able to face writing that part of his life story. He'd died trying to face it. So I wrote to William to ask, as carefully as I could, if he had interrogated other Brethren, or if he remembered anything my father had told him about all of that.

It was just too painful to remember, William replied a few days later. Too shameful. It made him shudder. But he would try.

'Unlike your father,' he wrote, 'I was only involved with three cases. They were all men. It was normal for two Brethren to conduct the questioning. Usually it took place in the sitting room, but with the understanding that we were not to be disturbed.'

I thought of fourteen-year-old Ruth watching from the top of the stairs as the black-coated priests interrogated her parents. It was easy to feel for her. Now, for the first time, I was beginning to imagine what it might have been like to have been one of those priests, knocking on doors late at night, embarrassed and ashamed but not able to show it, making older men confess to having had sexual thoughts, humiliating them.

'If a confession was finally made,' William wrote, 'it was something quite innocuous or trivial, usually about [unfulfilled] sexual desires, at least in all the cases I was involved in. The sessions could last for two to three hours; sometimes they'd go on till quite late at night. I used to go home feeling that I was probably more guilty than the person we had humiliated.'

Although there may have been many Brethren priests in the sixties who were confident that they were routing Satan, there were also men like William who felt very uncomfortable with what they were doing. I'd seen this discomfort in the body language of three Brethren priests interviewed in a documentary the BBC made in 2003; the Brethren were doing everything they could at the time to counteract bad publicity. Those three men, dressed in perfectly pressed white or pale-blue short-sleeved cotton shirts, sat on one side of a table clutching their Bibles and answering the interviewer's questions.

They looked like rabbits caught in headlights, I thought, as I watched the interview, paused it, and played it back in slow motion. Each time I replayed the scene and saw how nervous they were, the sight of them there behind the table scared me a little less. The youngest of the three, in his late thirties, seated in the middle, had talked, with an attempted assurance, about how he'd been lost to the darkness but had returned to the light. But every time he tried to defend Brethren expulsions, or the way they shut people up, he stuttered, hesitated, and stuttered again. His eyes darted from side to side, looking for guidance from the two older men.

When the producer of the documentary gave an interview to the *Guardian*, he said the priests had threatened him: 'We're rich,' they'd said. 'We'll take you to the cleaners.' One of them had told him, 'The devil's here. I can see him behind you.'[6]

But what had it been like for my father, I wondered. How had he felt about making these visits that William described? I wrote to the PEEB community. What was it like, I asked, to be visited by Brethren 'interrogators' back in the sixties? Did anyone remember? And did anyone remember what it was like to be a priest?

Ten or eleven people replied to my request for information. Some wrote just a few lines, some several pages. Everyone seemed angry or upset by what they remembered. Many of them, I noticed, had replied in the early hours of the morning. 'You've opened up a real can of worms here,' one wrote. The memories, she said, had made her shake.

The answers I received were all about having been interrogated. No one wrote about doing the interrogating. Their stories were shocking, and remarkably similar. The men were called 'priests', not 'interrogators' or 'exactors', they said. Their visits were called 'Priestly Visits', or just – rather chillingly – 'Priestlies', or 'PVs'. The interrogation might last two hours or more; it always took place in the family sitting room; no one ate or drank anything – the priests would be contaminated if they did – and no one else was allowed in the room, even when the priests were questioning a teenage girl.

Sometimes the priests would be satisfied with a simple confession, and there'd be prayers and tears and 'restoration'. But if there was resistance or denial, or if the sin was particularly grave, the priests would have to recommend to the 'Care Meeting' that the sinner be 'shut up' or placed 'under discipline'. This meant consigning them to solitary confinement in a room in their family home, with no contact with any other family member, their meals left on a tray outside the door, for an unspecified period of time. The priests would continue to 'visit' every few days, sometimes for weeks or months, until they felt the sinner had 'come right' or was 'in the clear'. The priests didn't use the language of exorcism, my informants told me when I pressed them on this, but to me it seemed implicit in what they were doing. 'Smell out the enemy,' JT Junior had preached, 'chase after him and kick him.'[7]

Most of the people who replied to my questions had been teenagers in the sixties. The misdemeanours they'd been questioned about ranged from acts that the Brethren considered very serious – such as falling in love with someone outside the Brethren, or being seen going into a cinema, smoking, or even having a cup of tea with someone who wasn't Brethren – to imagined acts or thoughts. Licentious thoughts had to be confessed to as well.

No wonder William had shuddered. No wonder he'd described Priestly Visits as a process of humiliation. And, as he had pointed out, if my father had done more Priestly Visits than most of these young men, it wasn't surprising that he had not been able to talk or write about it.

It struck me that a system of surveillance and forced confession like this must have been very effective. Even when the sinner had been absolved and allowed back into the fold, all the priests would now know their secrets, and would have seen them deeply humiliated. And, of course, every priest would have been terrified that at any moment the tables might be turned on him. Everyone was petrified into compliance.

Sometimes when a Brethren teenager had been put under discipline, the whole family would be engulfed in the punishment. 'Rachel' described how, when she and her two brothers were teenagers in the 1960s, they'd been 'shut up' numerous times, meaning they were confined to the house and prohibited from contact with anyone. On one occasion she and her brothers had been made to leave the family home for a month, but usually the whole family were excluded at home together. When her youngest brother, then sixteen, had gone to see three Brethren priests to seek counsel about something private that worried him, they'd circulated details about what he'd disclosed. He'd been taunted by his Brethren peers, and suffered a nervous breakdown. Soon afterwards, the three siblings had been made to attend a Brethren Meeting in which their father was told he was 'not repentant enough', and they were all made to leave and be 'shut up' again.

'Our Priestly Visits took place mainly in the evening,' she wrote, 'sometimes just with my dad, my parents, or all of us together, sometimes in the lounge, sometimes around the dining room table.' No one drank anything, because the priests weren't allowed to eat or drink with Brethren under discipline. 'At one stage,' she wrote, 'my dad was required to write a list of all the sins he had committed before the next visit. When he handed them the list, he was told it "wasn't good enough" and he had to try harder to remember things he may have done!'[8]

Even if people did find some way to leave the Brethren, the priests could still knock on their door at any time. Several of the people who wrote to me described finding a pair of priests waiting outside their workplace, intent on getting them to come back into fellowship.

'They used to wait until my staff had gone home and show up at the business,' 'Philip' wrote. 'Luckily I had a front vestibule in which visitors had to ring and wait for the door to be unlocked. I would just freeze in my office chair and not move or make a noise. I would hear a low rumbling of voices until they left.'⁹

The priests were, like my father, family men, raising their children, minding their grandchildren, cutting the lawn or washing the car on Saturdays. My father would come home late at night, and lie in bed next to my mother with his head full of the remembered tears and sobs and wails from the evening's confession. Worse still, he may have lain there planning new ways to extract the confession he'd failed to get. And when the last years of the sixties rolled round, I'd have been sleeping in the next room, or lying awake clutching my stuffed rabbit. In the morning he'd be planning his next preaching over breakfast, while my brothers and I quarrelled about which of us was to have the cream at the top of the milk bottle. He'd be searching for a scripture to support a new disciplinary procedure while my mother would be clearing away the dishes or brushing out and plaiting my long and unruly hair.

No wonder he lost his temper so often, and no wonder my mother had to hurry us into the sitting room so many times and lock the door. There must have been so many things he couldn't talk about. Was this why he'd beaten me so badly at the age of three? And it wasn't just my family living in a state of anxiety and terror, nor was it just my father enforcing the rules. 'Priestly Visits' and 'Care Meetings' were going on not just in our little seaside town, but in Brethren households all around the world. They are *still* going on.

There were more suicides. On Hayling Island in 1961 a couple told their twenty-year-old son, a travelling car salesman who wasn't in fellowship, that he could no longer eat with them or his sister, or even come to the house. After spending several months in exile, distraught about the shame and distress he was inflicting on his parents, and the prospect of never seeing them again, he gassed himself to death.

Elsie and Winnie Rhodes, two elderly unmarried Brethren sisters, ran a small egg farm at Watling Street in Staffordshire. In 1961, local Brethren told them that under the new rules they'd have to leave the Egg Marketing Board or be withdrawn from. The small red stamp of the Marketing Board was, Brethren told them, the sign of Satan's system. Deprived of their livelihood, the sisters quickly fell into debt. A cousin, concerned that she had not heard from them for some time, drove to the farm, but Elsie and Winnie didn't open the door. 'We were shocked by what we found,' the cousin told a journalist. The farm, once a prosperous family business, had been horribly neglected. 'The hen pens hadn't been cleaned out and the gates were hanging on their hinges.'[10] In June 1962, forced to sell their smallholding and terrified of the consequences, Elsie and Winnie walked together into a local lake and drowned themselves.

# 6

At around the same time as the Rhodes sisters' deaths, Stanley Milgram, a distinguished psychologist at Yale, began a famous series of experiments about obedience. He'd read the reports of Adolf Eichmann's trial in Jerusalem the year before. 'Could it be,' he asked himself, 'that Eichmann and his million accomplices in the Holocaust were just following orders?' Were Germans more than usually obedient towards authority figures? How far would a study group of Americans go in obeying an instruction if it involved harming someone else?

Milgram took forty volunteers individually into a closed laboratory room. Each was told by men in white coats to inflict electric shocks on a paired 'learner' in another room every time that learner made a mistake. What the volunteers didn't know was that the 'learner' was being played by an actor.

Even Milgram was shaken by the results. Sixty-five per cent of participants continued obeying orders, believing that they were inflicting shocks to the very highest level – 450 volts – even when they heard screams of pain, and even when they knew they could kill the learner with voltages of that level. Every one of the participants continued to 300 volts. The experiment has since been replicated by other teams, and the results have been roughly the same.

People obey, Milgram concluded, not just if they recognise the authority of the instructor as morally right or legally based (the white coats and the laboratory conditions of his experiment), but because that authority relieves them of responsibility for what they do. We learn this kind of unthinking obedience, he pointed out, in the family, the school and the workplace. He did not add churches to this list, though he should have.[11]

Why had those decent young Brethren men turned into bullies? Because closed, rule-bound, discipline-focused totalist systems like the one we lived through made dissent virtually impossible. It paralysed people. Even if men like my father knew that what they were doing was wrong, they didn't know how to oppose it. Even if they refused to comply, they couldn't stop the bullying, because they'd simply be expelled, and someone else would step forward to take their place.

# 7

I knew there was money being made from JT Junior's system, but it took me some time to realise just how much, or how the system actually worked. When JT Junior and Bruce Hales put the vast Brethren revenue-collecting system in place in the sixties, they began by setting up tax-free payments described as gifts; they channelled these through the Brethren publishing house we called the Depot.

When I was growing up, my family was always talking about the Depot. Grandpa was at the Depot again. Something or other was a Depot matter. Someone had telephoned from the Depot. I knew that the Depot had something to do with the ministries, the rows of colour-coded Brethren books that lined the shelves in our sitting room. I was taken to its offices once as a small child. I remember a small brick building, windowless corridors, piles of boxes, and an untidy room with desks and typewriters. It reminded me of the Stott and Sons warehouse with its secret rooms and back staircases. I wanted to play there, but Grandpa Stott would never have allowed that. He left me in a small side office with a Bible while he attended to Depot business in another room.

Since 1931, the Stow Hill Bible and Tract Depot had published volumes of Brethren ministries, the Day Dawn calendar, Darby's Bible, and various Brethren magazines, first from a shop in Wales and then from premises in Kingston upon Thames. Until the 1950s it had been a bit of a wing-and-a-prayer operation, run by four part-time trustees, with various Brethren and non-Brethren employees and a Brethren manager who liked to do the editing, and some censorship, himself.

The manager's idiosyncrasies had become a thorn in the side of JT, especially when he'd been trying to press the new Holy Spirit line in the 1950s, and the manager kept editing those sections out of his printed ministries. JT resolved to be patient, but the cuts infuriated his son. In the last years of his father's life, JT Junior spent hours counting the number of cuts the Depot manager had made to his father's addresses.

He couldn't understand why his father put up with this insubordination.

Immediately after JT's death in 1954, my grandfather was appointed to one of the four prestigious Depot trustee positions. Within weeks the Depot manager had been sacked, no doubt by my grandfather acting under JT Junior's orders.

Soon after his appointment, my grandfather began to assemble an anthology of the new harder-line ideology, designed for Brethren boys. He called it *The Way Everlasting*. It was first published in 1958, when my father was nineteen. My grandfather must have had his own sons in mind when he planned it. It contained extracts from thirty-four Brethren senior ministering brothers, from John Nelson Darby to JT, including three by himself, one by my great-grandfather Hugh Wasson, and five by Gerald Cowell. The book warned of the dangers of worldly literature, advanced education, trade unions, and all other Christians. It was an immediate success, selling 18,000 copies in its first year, almost twice as many as the volumes of JT's ministry the Depot sold over the same period. Like Mao's *Little Red Book*, published six years later, it was small enough to be carried in the pocket. My father's friend William, in his late teens when the anthology came out, remembers hearing it lampooned by another Brethren boy as 'Bob Stott's Bumper Book for Brethren Boys'.[12]

If my grandfather had seen what was coming, he'd have kept his pen dry and his head down. A year after the book came out, JT Junior took the leadership position. He excommunicated Gerald Cowell and all his supporters a few months later. When the Depot's four trustees met in the summer of 1960, JT Junior decreed that all Cowell's writing was to be excised from Brethren printed ministries. From now on, the Depot would print approved ministries only; there'd be no more magazines, Day Dawn calendars, or books for young people. There were to be no more reprints of *The Way Everlasting*. In front of 2,000 Brethren assembled in Central Hall that summer, my grandfather was forced to confess that his book had been based on a 'revival of the Sunday School principle', and been judged wrong. This was the first of what would become a wave of public confessions.

Excommunicated husbands and wives, fathers and mothers were now bringing court cases against the Brethren and writing to their MPs. The Methodist leaders realised that the Exclusive Brethren, who rented their Central Hall every summer, were a cult that split families, and cancelled their contract with them. More suicides reached the press. The story of the Methodists throwing out the Brethren made it into the newspapers too.

The 1962 three-day Meeting took place in one of the conference halls of Alexandra Palace in north London. The proceedings were taped, transcribed and published. Kez found a copy I'd overlooked among my father's papers.[13] When I opened it, the cadences of the men's voices and the phrases they used struck me as so familiar that I began to sweat. *I'm a girl. I'm not allowed in here. I'll get caught.* I remembered all the times I'd been ushered out of our sitting room when the Brethren men came to consult with my father. My mother caught me once with my ear pressed up against the closed door, and waved me out into the garden. But I wasn't going to miss the chance of listening in this time. I read on.

According to the transcript, hundreds of Brethren men had gathered in Alexandra Palace as usual. They'd flown in from all over the world – from Sweden, New Zealand, South Africa, France, Germany, Jamaica. I tried to reconstruct the auditorium in my mind. I knew their hats would be hanging on hooks somewhere. They'd have their Bibles on their laps. My father would be somewhere in the auditorium and my grandfather up on the stage, sitting with the three other Depot trustees, right next to the Man of God and his clever businessman son-in-law Bruce Hales, his new right-hand man. It was only a year since my grandfather's public confession. He'd be trying to keep a low profile.

Alfred Gardiner, the longest-serving Depot trustee, took the microphone. They were making good progress in reprinting the hymnbooks, ministries and translations, he told the men in the hall, but the work was slow. Mr Hales had devised a new system that would make it possible to bring The Truth to Brethren all around the world much more quickly. Gardiner explained how it was going to work: there would be a new hardbound and numbered set of full ministries. From now on every Brethren house would be required to own a full set. It would cost £10 a year for the new volumes, and £60 for a complete set. Local enforcement officers would check that all households had them. Brethren were to start paying immediately.

Bruce Hales took the microphone. Reasonable, eloquent, matter-of-fact, he explained that the Brethren had been running a successful prepayment system in Australia for a while now. It made everything so much *easier*. If every household had a full set of ministries, all Brethren, especially the young, would receive the word of the Lord as it unfolded, as it *happened*.

I do the calculations. With an estimated 100,000 Brethren around the world in 1959, even allowing for 20,000 defections, there must have been at least 10,000 households remaining. The vast majority were in English-speaking countries – America, Australia, New Zealand – but even if you allow for the fact that some were non-English-speaking, that's still at least £600,000 coming into Brethren coffers immediately, with £100,000 a year to follow.

In 1962, £1 was equivalent to roughly £20 at today's values. That means that in this one-hour Meeting the Brethren agreed to pay the current equivalent of about £12 million up front, with £2 million in annual income to follow.

One of the young Brethren administrators who worked in the Depot general office during the 1960s told me about the impact of Hales's prepayment system. He didn't want me to use his name, so I'll call him Frank. 'The effect on the finances of the Depot was dramatic. I remember going to the bank with large amounts, many tens of thousands of pounds on one occasion (about £80k).'[14]

When I asked my father in those last days about how the Brethren's money system worked, he was defensive. He was close to the end. His lucid moments lasted only twenty minutes at most. I should have been distracting him with music and poetry, I told myself, not pestering him with questions about the Brethren's finances, but he'd been so insistent about this record of his, so anxious to get it down. There were so many questions I wanted to ask.

'By 1962,' I said, going back over my notes, 'the ministries seem to have become more important than the scriptures. How did they get everyone to agree to pay so much for them?'

'We didn't see it like that,' he said slowly, without even opening his eyes. 'We were getting the truth straight from the Lord. We didn't mind about the money. The Lord was working fast. He was on his way.'

'The Rapture was coming, you mean?' I asked. 'You really thought it was *that* close?'

But he'd gone again, down into the morphine.

# 8

It became difficult to sleep at the Mill in my father's last days. With death so close, we were all wired. I took snatches of sleep in the afternoon, drifting off in front of a Bergman film or when the cricket lagged. I'd judder awake, frightened, certain there was something in the room, something watching. I couldn't shake off the feeling that my father and I were in trouble, that someone had been listening in, someone had reported back.

At night when the old mill creaked, I'd look out across the fields where the moon lit up the snow to the glow on the

horizon where the Polish night labourers were digging up pota-
toes under portable strip lighting. Once a pair of red eyes – fox,
rabbit, weasel – flashed back at me and then were gone.

On those sleepless nights, if my brother was taking the night
watch I'd roam my father's study, looking for photographs. The
tall bookshelves were piled three or four deep with dusty books;
the cheap shelving sagged alarmingly under their weight. After
I'd spent a few hours rummaging, my hands would be coated
in a layer of grey dust.

One night I found three rows of colour-coded Brethren
ministries hidden on a low shelf beneath a set of Toni Morrison's
novels, some volumes of poetry, and a hardback copy of Richard
Dawkins' *The God Delusion*, its spine broken by the number of
index-card notes my father had tucked inside. It struck me that
in this chaos of books and papers, the ministries were the only
books he'd arranged in any order. He hadn't been able to throw
them away, or even box them up and store them in the attic;
he'd just buried them under other books. He had used them, I
remembered, to plan his preachings back in the sixties, in the
days when he worked hard to practise his JT Junior voice.

I spotted an old volume of JT Junior's letters on that bottom
shelf, letters the Man of God had written through the sixties to
Brethren round the world. I remembered the New York vernac-
ular JT Junior used, his deliberately provocative and brash
tone, and my father's look of intense concentration, the way he
always seemed to speed up when JT Junior's recorded voice was
playing on a tape in the car. JT Junior's private letter-writing
voice was just as aggressive as his spoken one. At two in the

morning he seemed to be shouting in my father's darkened study just as loudly as his recorded voice had once boomed out in the car. It still made me flinch.

In the letters JT Junior had written in 1962 he was furious that British Brethren were being so slow to get their houses clean. How could Brethren still be living in the same house with aged aunts who were not in fellowship, he ranted, or teenagers who wouldn't break bread? It was insufferable. The local compliance officers he'd appointed were not being nearly tough enough.

In July 1963 he was preaching in Bournemouth, hammering home his new edicts about 'natural relations'. Brethren, he insisted, needed to cauterise their family feelings. He ranted about 'circumcision'. He wanted Brethren to cut off their family members as if they were bits of surplus unclean flesh. It was time to put the Lord before family relations, he wrote, time to get those houses really *clean*. But what he really seemed to be saying was that he wanted all those thousands of Brethren to put him before everyone else.

'Have you cut off the flesh?' he asked. 'Have you still the flesh in the house? Have you cut off your relatives if they are out of fellowship? That is the suffering point ...'[15]

Reading JT Junior's letters in the Mill in the early hours of the morning, I was hearing not just his American intonations, but the voices of all those other ranting men too: my father, my grandfather, thumping the table, their voices rising and falling in a confused cacophony, competing to trump each other with Biblical references. The women, on the other hand, those women who always sat quietly next to me in the back row of the Meeting, their soft hands folded over their Bibles, were *still* not saying anything.

By 1964, the year I was born, JT Junior had implemented scores of new rules about homes and family life. Brethren could no longer live in the same house as non-Brethren members. Husbands had to leave non-Brethren wives. Wives had to leave non-Brethren husbands. Small assemblies were to be merged with larger ones to form 'city positions' with a designated leader. Brethren could no longer work with anyone who had been 'put out of fellowship'. Brethren could not live in flats unless they had a separate entrance. No televisions or wirelesses were allowed in Brethren houses. All young children were now expected – 'encouraged' – to break bread.

All around the world Brethren compliance officers held 'Care Meetings' to identify and take action against the unclean households in their assemblies. Frank sent me a transcript of a set of notes he'd taken of the disciplinary decisions made in six hundred separate Meetings he attended in the sixties. The notes were concise, but the stories they revealed were chilling.

Under the heading 'North Finchley, 1962', one note read:

Miss Parks in a house nearly fully divided.

Miss Paynter has broken communion with her sister.

Mrs Rook and daughter are still in the same house. All three
    cases are a great concern. Dr Rook is nearly an invalid. He
    has the wireless. There is no work of God in him.

What this meant, I realised, was that poor Miss Parks had been 'shut up' and was now receiving 'Priestly Visits'. She would not be allowed to return to Meeting until the priests had confirmed that she had 'fully divided' from the non-Brethren family members she shared her home with – almost certainly one or both of her elderly parents. Even then the priests would not be happy until they moved her out of that unclean house completely.

Miss Paynter was doing better than Miss Parks. She was no longer in contact with her non-Brethren sister, but was still under close surveillance and 'under discipline'. She wasn't out of the woods yet.

Mrs Rook and her daughter were still living with the invalid and radio-listening Dr Rook. It wasn't looking good. The two women would almost certainly have to be withdrawn from unless they left that unclean house once and for all.

So many elderly women carers were being bullied into absolute compliance. And this was just the picture I could see from the notes for a single London 'Care Meeting'. How many more thousands were there under discipline all around Britain and the world? What was to become of these poor women, tormented as they were by the fear of having to live alone, and unprotected, in Satan's system?

According to another of Frank's notes, on 2 February 1963 – eleven days before my older brother was born – Miss Paynter was in trouble again. Her name comes up under the title 'Cases of Concern, re unclean accommodation and other – North Finchley':

Miss Paynter. She has come to the preachings only. She knows very little and needs teaching. The resistance has gone. She has sat behind separately all the time. She wears the token. The matter has gone on for many months. She loves the brethren in a small way. There is a piece of an ear.[16]

That 'piece of an ear' is a reference to *Amos* 3:12: 'Like as the shepherd rescueth out of the jaw of the lion two legs, or a piece of an ear; so shall the children of Israel be rescued that sit in Samaria in the corner of a couch, and upon the damask of a bed.'

It's very difficult to grasp exactly what verses like this actually mean, but the senior Brethren ministering brothers always insisted that they knew. In this case 'a piece of an ear' was code for 'We haven't given up; we'll get her clean yet.'

'The resistance has gone' was the sentence that haunted me most of all. It reminded me of the fate of my mournful great-grandmother, the wilful Ada-Louise, and those blank eyes of hers.

# 9

My brother was born on 13 February 1963. My father delivered him and cut his umbilical cord. My parents named him Christopher, after Christopher Tydeman.

When, in his dying days, I interviewed my father about life in the Brethren, he showed no interest in describing how it had felt to become a father. He'd struggled against the morphine to record the tiniest details of the new edicts that were coming in during the sixties, but he seemed entirely indifferent to what was going on with his wife and children at home.

'February 1963? Wasn't that the month that Chris was born?' I asked.

'Yes, yes, it was, yes,' he replied. 'But the point is that you can't understand the eating issue unless you understand the direction JT Junior's ministry was taking in February 1963.'

How had my brothers and I learned to walk, talk, run and read in this strained, highly scrutinised and discipline-obsessed world?

I was born twenty months after my brother, on 24 September 1964. After four years of JT Junior's fierce edicts, Brethren were now almost completely isolated from the world, and knew little about what was going on in it. JT Junior, convinced that the Rapture was now only weeks or months away, was obsessed with getting Brethren houses clean in time. In February 1964 he prohibited meals in restaurants, cafés, canteens and trains.

The following month he banned non-Brethren cleaners or mothers' helpers. Brethren were no longer allowed to sit on juries. Meetings were now expected to be held every day. As part of his campaign for clean houses, he banned all pets. Brethren had to either find alternative homes for their animals, or have them put down. Thousands of parents had to find ways of explaining to their distressed children where their beloved pets had disappeared to.

In June 1964, JT Junior decreed that Brethren should be employed by fellow Brethren whenever possible. This would reduce their contact with the outside world even further. My father, who had been working as a sales rep for Chivers jams in Cambridge, gave up his job to become a partner in Stott and Sons, my grandfather's wholesale grocers in Brighton. My parents moved from Cambridge into my grandparents' house. The move must have put pressure on my already exhausted mother. As a young Brethren wife and mother, she'd also have to attend Meeting every day with her two young children, help my grandmother to keep the peace at home, and to feed the many Brethren visitors who came from all over the world.

My father and grandfather would have had a good deal to discuss, because in 1964 the Brethren had come under attack. Gresham Cooke, the Conservative MP for Twickenham, appalled by the stories his ex-Brethren constituents were telling him about broken families, suicides and excommunications, had put a Bill to Parliament called the Family Preservation Bill. He wanted to make it illegal for family members to be separated in this way, and told newspaper reporters that he wanted to ban the leader of this destructive cult from entering the country.

When JT Junior arrived at Meeting Rooms on his usual summer tour of the UK in 1965, he was jeered by large crowds of protesters and cross-questioned by journalists camped outside. At Dorking, he was jostled and forced to stop preaching because he couldn't make himself heard above the chants of the protesters. He cancelled an arranged meeting with Gresham Cooke and flew back to New York furious and shocked by what he described as press harassment. When the *Sunday Times* ran an article called 'Big Jim and his Profits', he threatened the paper with a libel suit. In September there were rumours that he'd been admitted to hospital.

With JT Junior in and out of hospital and being hounded by the press, Bruce Hales and his brother John took the reins. A new, business-obsessed era began. Bruce Hales was in his mid-thirties, an engineer and a charismatic management consultant. The brothers stepped up the pace of the money-production machine by organising invitation-only seminars to groom young Brethren businessmen like my father to train others to set in place methods and procedures for tax avoidance, gift aid and trust funds. Just like JT Junior, the Hales brothers were often rude and sarcastic to the older members of the Brethren. They quickly garnered a large following from young members like my father as a result. Meanwhile they told Brethren that JT Junior was very ill, worn out, and 'suffering for the testimony'.[17]

In JT Junior's absence, the Hales brothers consolidated Brethren assets, amalgamated small assemblies into larger ones, and ordered a programme of building new Meeting Rooms to their own designs. These windowless buildings looked more like bunkers or bank vaults than places of religious worship. The brothers ordered Brethren who owned rental properties to liquidate these assets to provide money for the new Meeting Rooms or to provide mortgages to young couples like my parents looking to buy their first home. An elderly Brethren woman helped my parents buy a four-bedroomed detached house near the Hove Meeting Room, overlooking Hove Park. The more young Brethren families like ours became financially dependent on other Brethren, of course, the less likely it was that they'd be able to leave.

My father became one of the Hales brothers' young acolytes. He enjoyed the status and the attention. He'd been helped to buy a house. Now that he was working alongside his father in the family business, the Hales brothers were treating him, not his father, as the special one. All Brethren businesses had been placed under close supervision. He and his father had to fill in forms detailing profits, budgets, targets and timesheets. He and other young businessmen would be 'whisked off', he wrote on PEEBS.net, to business seminars in a private house in London, conducted by the Hales brothers 'wearing collar mikes'. 'Then in the evening, we would sweep into Park Street to a Meeting that Bruce Hales was taking and feel like we had inside knowledge because we had been with him all day. We were a sort of embryonic mafia.'

No wonder he didn't remember much about what was going on at home. He couldn't have been there much at all. And there must have been tensions with his father about the direction the business was taking. My grandfather must have hated being overlooked and overruled, but he would have had to hold his tongue.

There were mutterings against the Hales brothers throughout the winter. Two men who worked at the Depot were interviewed, sacked, and withdrawn from for criticising them. A group of ministering brothers taped one of the business seminars and took it to JT Junior, complaining that the new 'commercial system' the brothers were promoting was against scripture.

Then something extraordinary happened: news reached down to the Brethren networks in October 1965 that JT Junior had *withdrawn* from the Hales brothers for 'bringing commerce into the assembly'. This event must have struck terror into Brethren around the world. If, like my father, they'd been acolytes, even lowly ones, they must have expected trouble. But they also knew that if they denounced the brothers, it might be even worse for them. Brethren fathers and sons, like my grandfather and father, would have been set against each other again.

A spell of expulsions of the Haleses' supporters began, followed by another wave of confessions. These group confessions had been taking place for several years. Frank described seeing people queuing up to get hold of a microphone to confess in the Park Street Meeting on the night of 1 October 1964 – just one week after I was born. It was a 'frenzy' he wrote.

They were still queuing at 11 p.m. Now the group confessions largely concerned the Hales brothers.

Rumours circulated that Bruce and his wife Consuela, JT Junior's daughter, had retired to a farm in the Australian outback, and that Consuela had had a nervous breakdown. The old guard were back in power. The terrified young bloods steeled themselves for punishment or expulsion.[18]

Single elderly women continued to bear the brunt of the power lurchings and disciplinary decisions. John and Bruce Hales had two unmarried aunts called Rhina and Eva. They'd lived together for fourteen years in a suburb of Melbourne. Eva had disagreed with Exclusive Brethren separation rules, and so, despite her devotion to her sister, she'd joined the Open Brethren. When Eva had gone into hospital for an operation, local Exclusive Brethren had taken Rhina to live with them. After Eva was discharged a few months later, Rhina was not allowed to go home to her sister, or to have any contact with her. A few days after Eva returned to her empty house, in November 1965, only a month after Bruce and John had been deposed, relatives broke into the house and found her body on the kitchen floor. She'd gassed herself to death.

Why had the Hales brothers fallen from power so spectacularly? No one I've spoken to knows for sure. There's no evidence to prove one theory or another, and whichever way you look at it, there was very little 'of God' in this struggle for power. And that's what my Christian ex-Brethren relatives always say when the Taylor decade comes up in conversation. 'Man is corrupt,' they say sadly. 'This was Man's doing.'

By the summer of 1966, JT Junior had restored the Hales brothers. Was he satisfied that he'd made his point, clipped their wings, or was this all just part of a plot he'd devised with them? Perhaps it was a way of showing the Brethren, particularly the Hales acolytes, that no one was safe, that even JT Junior's right-hand men were dispensable. Whatever the explanation, he had secured the terrified allegiance of all the Brethren young men who'd once followed the Haleses. Now he began a campaign to denounce anyone who had spoken against the brothers. A new wave of public confessions followed. Across the world Brethren were forced to admit that they had been guilty of vindictiveness towards the brothers during the period of their expulsion.

# IO

I was, I am told, the baby who cried; the baby who refused to sleep. My mother followed the instructions given to young mothers in the 1960s, which were to leave a baby to cry itself to sleep. Sometimes, she said with admiration, I'd take more than an hour to 'go off', and she interpreted from this, as most mothers certainly did at that time, that my will needed to be broken.

One of my very first memories is of lying in a bed in a darkened room in our house in Goldstone Crescent in Hove. I am three or four years old. In that memory I can't see the shape of the room or any of the furniture, but there's a patch of wallpaper next to the bed that has come loose. I am pulling and tugging at it, curious about the colour of the wall underneath and trying not to think about the voices I am hearing.

Most nights I heard voices when I was close to falling asleep. They were near to my ear. Some muttered and heckled and harangued; others were sweet as honey. I had no control over them.

Forty-five years later, in a Cambridge college courtyard under a dark winter sky, Oliver Sacks asked me to describe them. We'd had dinner together at King's College and had shared stories about the LSD hallucinations we'd had; we'd talked about Darwin and ghosts and about the drug-induced vision of cobalt blue Sacks had once seen. Now, at the end of the evening, I remembered the things I had seen as a child, the voices I'd heard and the monsters I saw. It always happened, I told him, when I was falling asleep or waking up.

'Patterned and repeating shapes?' he asked. 'People standing by your bed? Voices with strong patterning – very distinct in sound and texture?'

'They spoke in different languages entirely sometimes,' I said. 'I didn't understand some of them.'

'Hypnagogic and hypnopompic,' he said, as if he diagnosed the conditions of dinner companions like this all the time. 'They're hallucinations that happen when you are falling asleep – hypnagogic – and when you wake up – hypnopompic.' He'd had them too, he told me. And so had Vladimir Nabokov. He urged me to read Nabokov's description of them in his memoir, *Speak, Memory*.

It's difficult in truth to separate out the visual from the auditory hallucinations I had as I fell asleep. I saw and heard things that my brothers and parents did not seem to experience. And according to my mother, I saw things during the daytime too. She remembers rushing into the sitting room or the kitchen to find me wild-eyed and screaming, pointing at tiny bits of fluff on the floor, as if in fear of my life, as if there were monsters approaching. My howls of alarm and despair were a complete mystery to her. I don't remember what scared me about the carpet-fluff, but I do remember the voices and the monsters I saw on the curtains in my bedroom. I can still see them very clearly. I still see things. But they don't frighten me so much now that I know I'm not the only one to have them, and that there is a physiological explanation.

I remember lying in bed listening to my parents' muffled conversation in a distant room, their voices rising and falling, and seeing Satan – or my idea of Satan, all horns and scales and a flashing, grinning mouth – projected on the darkened surfaces of the curtains. It was always the same set of six or seven voices I could hear talking to me, not always in a language I recognised. When I was older they'd reappear in my dreams as The Committee.

By the age of three or four I had developed a perfectly workaday, familial relationship with my God. He was an older-brother God rather than a father God. He could be appealed to and he could concede, but he was unpredictable, and not always to be trusted. If you do this, I'd say, I'll do that. Sometimes he complied, other times he didn't.

I managed the terrors of my small domestic space by negotiating with this God in what I called prayers. I appreciated the company late at night, when my father's snores grew gradually louder in my parents' bedroom next door, and I could hear the creaks and groans of the house as the radiators turned themselves off.

Occasionally, if the voices terrified me more than I could bear, I'd call out to my parents and my father would come in, sometimes on all fours, pretending to be a bear. I dared not tell him what I saw projected there on the curtains – the monsters with wings and claws and hooves, that were both male and female, human and animal. If my father was in a good mood, he'd tell me stories and make me laugh. If he was in a bad mood, he'd shout. My mother gathered talismans to protect me from the dark: she crocheted me a comfort blanket from soft blue and green wool, and gave me a stuffed toy rabbit with long ears. I discovered that if I tucked one of the rabbit's ears between my little toe and the next toe along of my right foot, the voices would stop. Eventually I'd fall asleep. And the day would begin again.

# II

When I was four, my parents, alarmed at my sleeplessness and loss of weight, took me to see a doctor. Although we were not supposed to have contact with non-Brethren, doctors were an exception. Later, when the separation rules stepped up again, I'd be taken to see my Brethren doctor uncle, my father's sister's husband. Mostly we were not sick and we did not see doctors. But on this occasion my parents must have been alarmed. The doctor insisted that I see a specialist.

I claimed to see things at night, my parents told him. I rarely fell asleep before midnight. When my parents had been banished to the waiting room and the doctor pressed me to confide in him, I told him I saw Satan, and that when I concentrated very hard I could make the angels appear. He seemed to think the angels were good, but I explained that even among the angels you had to work out the good ones from the bad, and that some of them had both wings and hooves. The bad ones said terrible things, I told him; they talked just like Satan. It was very hard to tell the difference. He asked the nurse to collect a urine sample; he took notes; he ordered more tests. He did not ask my parents where I might have got such strange ideas from.

Whether these visions were hypnagogic or hypnopompic hallucinations, or a form of sleep paralysis, I like to think I was dreaming the whole household's tormented dreams, that I was the lightning rod through which all my family's imaginary voices and nightmares passed.

And now I think about my mother, stuck at home with tiny children, not allowed to work, having to cook for all those Brethren visitors and to get her own brood up at dawn on the Lord's Day and get us washed and changed, ready for breaking bread, then come home and vacuum – again. She had a double burden: she was expected to keep both dirt and Satan out of her home. What was happening in *her* dream world?

William, my father's closest Brethren friend, remembers my mother as both a great beauty and as the woman who hoovered. In the early days of my parents' marriage, Brethren men would stay late to discuss assembly matters over several glasses of whisky.

'Your mother,' he told me, 'would get rid of us by getting the Hoover out.' Of course she did. She wasn't allowed to express opinions, complain, pray aloud, or preach. She'd never win an argument against my father. She'd just set him off. With the Hoover on its highest setting, it could do her roaring for her.

My mother was houseproud by nature, but she was also expected to be. There was a daily routine of vacuuming, laundering, dusting, scouring and polishing. Different rooms and cupboards in our house smelled of different cleaning and polishing products: Pledge, Brasso, Dettol, coal-tar soap and Vim. As a Brethren girl I was expected to be my mother's helper. I'd shake out wet sheets with her, fold dry sheets, sweep down the staircase, scour the bath with Vim, tip the powdered Smash and the measured water into the food mixer and stare down into the grey-white gloop until all the lumps had mixed in. But though I was happy to do all this because I loved my mother, I resented the fact that my brothers did not help, and that my mother did not ask them to. Brethren boys did not do housework. That was women's work.

Why would only my brothers inherit the family business? Why was it Stott and *Sons*, and not Stott and *Daughters*? Why didn't the Spirit speak through women? Why didn't my brothers have to sweep the stairs? Why did Brethren preachers have to be men? Where in the Bible did it say that the Lord only spoke through men? It wasn't fair. Nothing was fair. I studied the Brethren women around me to see if any of them were angry too, but it was impossible to tell.

I'd heard my adored grandmother talking about her mother's wilfulness, heard her talk to other women about wilful wives, or about how so-and-so should remember to be proud to be flesh of her husband's flesh, proud to subdue her will to his. I knew the women would never back me if I spoke out. They'd be shamed by any insurrection of mine. It would be the work of Satan in me. If the Lord wanted me to be silent and obedient like that for the rest of my life, just because I was a girl, then I wasn't sure I liked the Lord.

I'd have howled with fury if I could, but I knew there was no persuading anyone or making any difference. Years later, a male cousin who'd been raised in the Brethren but run away at the age of twenty-four asked me why I supposed that out of all his ten siblings he was the only one who'd refused to believe in the Taylor system. Like me, he'd had to nurse his outrage silently and secretly. Speaking out never brought change, he told me, only trouble. 'You're just a girl,' my brothers would say. *Just a girl.* But it wasn't easy for the boys either.

Brethren women and girls were not supposed to have their hair cut, because women's hair, JT Junior had decreed, was their 'glory'. My brothers had short hair, and little combs in their back pockets to keep it tidy. My hair had never been cut, so by the time I was three or four, it stretched down to my waist when it was wet. Thick, heavy and curly, it had to be combed and plaited constantly. My mother would tug the comb through the endless knots.

Friday nights were hair-washing and nail-cutting nights, a family grooming that prepared us for the five or six weekend

Brethren Meetings, including the compulsory 6 a.m. Meeting on the Lord's Day. My brothers and I would sit on the landing outside the bathroom, waiting to be called in to have our hair washed over the sink. While I was waiting for my turn I'd untangle my long plaits and run my fingers through the knots. My brothers would be in and out of the bathroom and back playing in the garden in a few minutes. It took ten times as long to wash and rinse my hair.

It was too long and thick for the sink, so I'd kneel over the edge of the bath with my hair coiling down onto the white enamel. My mother used a watering can to rinse the soap out. My hair was like her own: both a glory and a burden. Hers was pinned up, mine perpetually pulled back into tight plaits. Later, when JT Junior decided that Brethren women should display their 'glory', she'd have to take her hair out from the braided coil she wore on the top of her head, brush it out, and wear it down her back under a headscarf.

I was surprised not to find any pictures of me from this period wearing a headscarf or a hat, but there are very few family photographs at all taken during the Taylor years. 'Cameras were considered as worldly, and a distraction from the Lord's work,' a cousin explained. 'None of us have many pictures from that time.'

When I took the kitchen scissors to my three dolls, cut off their hair and painted their lips with red felt pen, I like to think I did it for all of the put-upon, subjected Brethren women I saw around me. My parents sent me to my room as punishment. My grandparents questioned me closely about it. I was 'such a sweet and good child', I heard my grandmother say. 'What could have got into her?'

Exhausted by having to get us up and dressed for dawn Meetings, my mother would take afternoon naps, particularly when an elderly Brethren baker and his wife took my younger brother out in their shiny grey Morris Minor to give her a break. They'd return him a few hours later with cake tins full of still-warm fairy cakes and scones. Before taking her nap, my mother would check that the front and back doors were locked, get out some bricks or other favourite toys of ours, and draw the curtains. She would then sit in an armchair and close her eyes. *Just for a few minutes*, she'd say. *I'm just going to close my eyes for a few minutes.* My older brother and I would play quietly in the same room until she woke up.

In the cine films my father made in the sixties and seventies, we children are always dashing about in that strange, slightly-speeded-up way: running, climbing, kicking balls, riding tricycles in rich, flickering Technicolor. We are never more than a few inches away from each other. But while my brothers are usually intent on each other or the football they're chasing, and my mother is doing her best to avoid the camera, I'm gazing up at my very tall father behind the camera. My eyes glitter with pleasure at whatever he is saying. *Gub-bey, over here*, he calls to me, using my nickname, always with the emphasis on the second syllable. I turn and smile up at him. I cover my face and uncover it. My father himself is never visible, but the sun casts him as a long shadow here and there on a

A still from one of my father's cine films from around 1971

lawn or carpet, and from time to time I can see him reflected back in my own eyes.

# 12

I remember my childhood as a sequence of dimly-lit Meetings interspersed with short bursts of noise and light when we rode tricycles or scrambled over climbing frames with other children in the bright green of Brethren gardens. But how much time did my brothers and I actually spend in Meeting? I examine my father's documents and the list of JT Junior edicts that he'd collected. In the mid-1960s, JT Junior, apparently ever more certain that the Rapture was only weeks or months away, had decreed that Brethren babies should be baptised at eight days old, attend Meeting immediately, and be offered the bread and wine as soon as they were weaned. If they reached out for the bread dangled in front of them as they sat on their mother's knee, this was proof that they were ready to join.

It's not just the nonsense and the trickery that alarms me now – after all, how can a six-month-old baby reaching for bread be *choosing* anything but food? – but the number of hours we Brethren children spent listening to the men talk. My brothers and I – and thousands of other small Brethren children of our age around the world – attended nine one-hour Meetings a week before 1968, and eleven a week between 1968 and 1970. That makes a total of just over 3,000 hours I spent sitting absolutely still, listening to a small group of men, including my father and grandfather, preaching obscure Biblical exegesis and prophecy, in voices that rose and fell and paused in strange incantatory cadences, before I was six years old. No wonder I heard voices. No wonder they never stopped.

Brethren children were expected to be quiet and well-mannered in Meeting. We'd sit in the back row with our mothers, clothes pressed, faces scrubbed, shoes polished, hair tightly plaited or pinned back with clips, Bibles on laps.

While the Brethren ministering brothers talked of the nature of grace, the coming of the Lord, wells and springs, Lot and his salty wife, Sodom and Gomorrah, the Corinthians, the Pharisees and the Laodiceans, I daydreamed as I had taught myself to do in the warehouse, imagined scenarios, turned the men and women in the room into my puppets, made them do remarkable, astonishing things. I'd have the Brethren brothers and sisters fly – headscarved, suited or hatted – across the room; sometimes I'd have the flying bodies crash into each other. I'd have them all taken up into that mansion of a thousand rooms, set them off up there together like a human cannon, and then snatch them straight back down again.

The metaphysical questions and imaginings that vexed me, just as they had vexed my father at the same age, came from my attempts to apply a child's sense to what I heard in Meeting. I produced tangled things. I'd pick up a few sentences of the men's ministries and Biblical exegeses here and there, recognising sections of the Bible being quoted, and try to translate a meaning for myself. I'd get a foothold for a few seconds, and then slip and slide off again.

Was it the endlessly riddling and incomprehensible nature of Brethren ministry that made me yearn to open doors I was not supposed to open? Or was it all those hours I'd spent running and climbing unsupervised in the dusty and dark warren of the warehouse, all the secret back rooms I'd found there, up staircases that seemed to appear from nowhere?

Between my parents' bedroom and the bathroom in our house in Goldstone Crescent there was a locked door. Sometimes I'd get a glimpse of the dark, gloriously coloured interior of the room when my mother slipped in to fetch something. The curtains were always drawn shut, so the room was dark, but I could make out two beds fitted with rich purple covers, matching heavily-lined floor-to-ceiling curtains, and a kidney-shaped dressing table that stood in the bay window. Whenever my mother went in there, she'd make me wait for her on the landing. After coming out again, she'd check that the handle was firmly closed, then she'd lock the door and slip the key into the large polished copper tea urn that stood on the landing.

When my mother disappeared into hospital for observation in the last month of her fourth pregnancy, taking with her several bundles of sea-green wool so she could knit my dolls new coats, my grandparents, or some other Brethren couple, must have moved in to care for me and my two brothers, to cook and run the house. I remember only the certainty that now I might finally find something interesting. I looked in cupboards, under beds and loose floorboards, not only for the many things I knew my mother hid from us – cakes, marshmallows, fruit, dolls, suitcases of baby clothes – but for darker things too, things I could not imagine or name or know I was looking for.

The first time I slipped the key from the urn, eased it into the keyhole, and nudged the door of the guest room open, a long crack of light slid across the floor like the path the moon made on the sea. I could just make out the shape of an enormous pram with two blue hoods at the far end of the room. Smocked baby clothes gleamed white against the floral purples of the bedcovers. I stood on the threshold, paralysed by the mystery of what I was seeing and by the miracle that I'd not been caught. I didn't dare enter the room, but pulled the door slowly shut, locked it, and replaced the key in the urn.

Soon I was slipping into the darkened room more and more often, closing the door behind me, treading quietly to avoid noisy floorboards, opening drawers in the half light, trying out the handles of the magnificent royal-blue pram hoods to see if the mechanism worked the same as the one on my dolls' pram, or lying on the floor between the beds to watch the inverted pictures of the garden flickering across the ceiling.

One day, when I was finally brave enough to lift the latch on the wardrobe doors built into the far alcove, I thought I saw eyes looking back down at me from a tissue-paper bundle on the top shelf. Something – or somebody – needed rescuing. I knew I'd have to stand on a chair to reach the bundle, but I feared that someone downstairs might hear me. Still, there was no other way. I dragged the chair as quietly as I could across the pink carpet and wedged it between the bed and the cupboard, climbed up onto it, and stretched as high as I could towards the bundle that I was now convinced was an abandoned child. I tugged at the nearest corner, hoping to catch the bundle as it fell. But as I wobbled up there on the chair, the tissue-paper parcel fell past my outstretched fingers and hit the floor with a terrible shattering sound.

I waited, pinned to the spot, for the inevitable running feet on the stairs or stern voice calling my name, but nothing happened. I ducked down out of sight between the bed and the cupboard to unwrap the bundle, dreading what I would find. Inside the white tissue paper I discovered the broken fragments of a porcelain doll's head, her skin as white as eggshells, and with the most delicate pink paint flushed across her cheekbones. A single blue eye rocked inside its broken socket. I rolled the tissue paper back around the lacy body and stuffed the bundle behind the heavy curtains. I was certain that I'd heard it whimper.

When my mother returned home from the hospital a few days later, still heavily pregnant, I lay awake, waiting for the bundle of broken pieces to be found, all through the long night that she howled in labour while my brothers and I lay in our beds, our pillows pulled tight over our heads, all through the sirens and blue lights of the ambulance that came for her. Though I was allowed to touch the fuzzy walnut-brown head of my new baby brother as the paramedics carried my mother down the stairs strapped into a wheelchair, I was in agony. I told myself that that tired and tight smile she'd given me was because she knew about the shattered doll, and was waiting for me to confess and tell her I was sorry and that, yes, I had taken the Lord into my heart.

'I did it!' I wanted to scream at her. 'I did it! I broke the doll. And I stole the key. I'm the one. It was *me*!'

I knew the bundle of tissue paper wrapping the broken doll must have been found, but no one ever spoke to me about it. The whole terrible saga disappeared into the miraculous home-coming of my tiny new twin siblings.

# 13

My brothers and I understood that outside was dangerous. And all the outside people were dangerous. I'd look through my bedroom window across the road into the darkening park beyond the thick fringe of trees and imagine Satan and his people over there, scuttling about, doing wicked things.

The streets outside our Meeting Rooms and Brethren homes were owned by Satan and thronged with Satan's traps and snares: shop windows full of television sets with moving pictures that you tried not to look at but couldn't take your eyes off. Hoardings on newspaper stands; cinemas with giant illuminated letters; adverts for perfume and make-up; women in mini-skirts. There were snatches of music too, from open windows or café doors, rapid drumbeats and seductive melodies. The grown-ups would say all these things were 'worldly', and in the Meeting Room they preached that Satan, the enemy, used them in his battle for our souls.

Someone gave me a notebook and a pencil sharpened to a dusky point. But instead of practising my letters, I took to sitting on the wide bedroom windowsill with my eyes fixed on the bus stop below. I was curious about the worldly people down there, what they were doing, what sins they'd committed, how dangerous they were, what they were going to do with their sin-packed worldly days. With my new pencil and notebook I began to keep detailed records of every person I saw waiting there, noting down times and dates, the buses they took, their hair colour, their height, clothing, even shoe colour. As I became quicker and more accurate at chronicling Satan's people, my spelling improved. Why did my father and I both keep these obsessive records, mine descriptive and his numerical?

'Gub-bey,' my brothers would call. 'Gub-bey, what are you doing up there? Did you get lost?'

'I'm reading,' I'd call back, holding myself very still. 'I'm just reading.'

I was certain that one day the police would come to our house because they'd heard that there was a child there who kept records. I must have confused the police with the Brethren priests, because in my imagination the men who came to the house always wore coats and black hats, not helmets. They would ask my parents if they could speak to me. I would climb the staircase solemnly to my room, slip the notebook out from under my mattress, and carry it down to the sitting room where my parents would be chatting with the two 'police officers', exchanging surprised and admiring looks. They'd find their murderer in my notebook, and they'd shake my hand and thank me.

The grown-ups told us that inside our house and our Meeting Room we were safe, because we were the chosen ones. We'd be protected from all the terrible things that were soon to rise up and engulf all the people outside our fellowship. But I was also frightened inside the house – by my father, by the certainty that I'd be caught looking at things I shouldn't be looking at, or going into rooms I was not supposed to go into. I was frightened by the things I glimpsed in the shadows. More than anything, I was afraid of the increasing certainty I felt that all the horrifying things that were about to happen to all the bad people outside our house and Meeting Room would also engulf my brothers and me – that we'd drown, burn, be hunted down. Because we were not good. We had not separated from iniquity. We didn't seem able to.

I felt like a cuckoo in the nest, an interloper, the child who didn't fit. But then, I was also often certain that none of us fitted. Apart from my mother, we all cheated on Brethren rules. I can't recall a single instance when I'd actually seen my mother transgress, though I can remember times when she failed to denounce my father for *his* many transgressions, as Brethren rules required her to do. There were many times when I'd heard her – or thought I'd heard her – make a quiet tutting noise, but she'd never say anything. I'd seen the radio my father kept hidden in the tyre compartment in the boot of the car. I knew my brothers hid comics under their mattresses, and talked with worldly boys in the park. They knew I told lies. There were secrets and transgressions everywhere in our house, a great webwork of them. Was I supposed to tell on my father, on my brothers? Would I be punished for not telling? Was the Lord keeping a notebook about me?

Cinemas were worldly, part of Satan's system, but in the sixties Brethren were allowed to film home movies and project them onto portable screens or their sitting-room walls. Because my brothers and I had grown up with no television or radio, and very few children's books, these flickering, oversized Technicolor versions of ourselves were especially magical. My father bought a movie camera and filmed us playing in the garden, dressing up at our grandparents' house or picnicking with other Brethren families in public parks.

Fascinated by these moving images of myself, I began to run imaginary film sequences in my head. One of my favourites involved a car screeching to a stop in the street where I was walking with my parents and brothers. A man and a woman would jump out, hardly stopping to close the car doors, and run across the road towards me. The woman would take me in her arms, kneeling on the hard tarmac as if in prayer.

'It's her,' she would sob to her companion. 'I knew we'd find her. Didn't I say, if we just kept looking we'd find her? And here she is.'

There was another version in which a couple would snatch me from under the eyes of my parents as we walked down the street in broad daylight. Before my parents had time to protest, they'd have bundled me into their car. They'd heard of my remarkable abilities, they'd tell me. They wanted me to come and live with them.

Was I scripting meritocratic secular versions of the Rapture? In these car-screeching dramas I'd be chosen, plucked out of grey suburban obscurity, not because I had taken the Lord into my heart, but because I read well, or because I kept scrupulously detailed records of suspected criminals. In these scenarios my parents would lament my disappearance, and chastise themselves for having overlooked me.

Sometimes I found clues that fuelled these cuckoo-in-the-nest fantasies. As well as the key to the guest room, my mother kept blankets inside the copper tea urn that stood on the stair landing. I'd pull over a stool, stand on it, then slip off the lid so I could look down past the strata of coloured blankets into the dark depths of the urn. My mother, I had come to realise, sometimes hid food there, probably to keep it out of sight of my father or my brothers and me, to save it for a special occasion. One day I saw a box of sweets; another time a box of cakes. One Lord's Day I spotted five shiny red apples nested like eggs in a grey blanket. I left them alone, but found myself coming back to lift that lid every time it was safe to do so.

One day when my parents were busy entertaining Brethren visitors in the sitting room and my brothers were playing football in the garden, I thought I saw the edges of what looked like a white box down in the darkness. I stood on the stool and quietly lifted out the blankets one by one, then reached down, listening for the warning sound of doors opening downstairs. Once the box was safely on the landing carpet, I slipped off its cardboard lid, hardly daring to breathe. The box was full of tightly typed documents, but among them were also three letters written in a fine italic hand, one addressed to me and one for each of my two older brothers. I replaced the box under the blankets and slipped the lid back on the urn.

I sat for a long time examining the sealed envelopes, turning them over in my hand. This discovery would reveal the secret of all secrets, I told myself; it would change my brothers' and my lives forever. But I knew I could not take the next dangerous step alone. I could hear my heart thumping in my chest as I walked down the staircase. I found my brothers playing in the garden and brought them, protesting but obedient, up to the landing, where I'd hidden the precious envelopes under the carpet. The three of us sat in a circle around them. The envelopes, I told them, contained letters from our real parents. They'd sent us instructions on how to escape and where they'd meet us. We had to open them. There wasn't much time left.

My brothers, mesmerised, nodded assent. I ripped open the envelopes, tearing across the beautiful italic handwriting. But there was nothing inside. The envelopes were empty. I could not understand why. I wept with fury and disappointment. Why, I asked my brothers, would our parents have taken the trouble to write to us but not have put anything inside the envelopes? I stuffed the torn paper back among the other papers in the box, slipped the lid on, placed it carefully back at the bottom of the urn, and replaced the folded blankets in the order I had found them. I told my brothers never to speak of the box or the letters again.

Years later my father told me that when my mother had found the torn envelopes in the box some months later, she'd been mystified. The envelopes had been a present from a stamp-collecting Brethren brother. He'd bought us all first-day covers to mark the days on which we'd been born. The stamps

I had torn through were collectors' items, intended to be given to us when they had accrued value with time. My mother didn't care for stamps, and the torn envelopes did not much trouble her.

Sigmund Freud, I discovered later, had written about this fantasy of mine. Some children of a particularly neurotic or imaginative sensibility, he wrote, convince themselves that they will be rescued by the 'real' parents from whom they have been stolen or kidnapped. Almost always the fantasy family is of a higher social standing, so the 'rescue' reveals the bastardised nature of the siblings as well as the hollow status of the 'adoptive' parents. The details of the fantasy, Freud wrote, depended on the particular imaginative materials available to the child: a nearby manor house, local aristocracy, books, fables and stories. Mine were made up of the strange experiences life in the Brethren had given me. My rescuers were 'worldly' people.

My fantasy played itself out again and again, not because I did not love my parents, or felt they did not love me, or because I was any more unhappy or lonely or disorientated than most other children my age, but because I was certain my parents were keeping secrets from me. I was probably daydreaming the fantasies of my parents, too. Each of them, I am certain, must have longed to be plucked out of this strange world we'd washed up in.

# 14

Between Meetings, Brethren children played noisily in the manicured shrubberies of large detached houses while their parents talked inside with other Brethren grown-ups. The Brethren children who hosted us in the short breaks between Meetings in neighbouring towns on the Lord's Day – teenagers who seemed impossibly, throat-tighteningly glamorous – played hide-and-seek with us or took our hands and led us down through fruit trees and orchards and kitchen gardens to a musty summerhouse where they had stashed forbidden comics under the floorboards.

One long summer afternoon two or three Brethren teenagers put on a shadow theatre for us in a barn, making characters with their hands behind a screen they'd stitched together from an old sheet. We were not allowed to tell.

Children kept secrets from the grown-ups. Grown-ups kept secrets from the children. We passed around *Beano* comics and looked out for approaching grown-ups, and made up stories that didn't have any Bible people in them. We watched each other's backs. We never talked about the Meetings, or about whether what the grown-ups preached was right or wrong.

Grown-ups, we knew, sometimes broke promises. They were not always to be trusted. When I was five, I came to understand that my father was not to be trusted.

Although large sections of the Bible were a puzzle to me, I was convinced that if I concentrated hard enough I'd be able to figure it out, and that my father's approval would surely follow. I could not work out, for instance, whether the Holy Spirit – then such an important part of our Meetings – was a dove or a ghost, or the ghost of a dead dove. I turned my mind to the problem in Meeting or when I was trying to fall asleep at night.

One day I had an epiphany: if there was an earthly tripartite family made up of Jesus, Mary and Joseph *down here*, there had to be a heavenly tripartite equivalent. This meant that if the son was Jesus *up there*, and God was the father, then the Holy Spirit had to be the *mother* up there. It made a blinding kind of sense to me, given the silent, birdlike, ghostly, self-effacing nature of the Brethren mothers I knew. I felt the exhilaration of intellectual discovery for the first time: the Holy Spirit, I was now certain, was Jesus's heavenly *mother*. It was the early hours of the morning. I heard the grandfather clock in the hall strike two. My brother was snoring in the bunk above me. I was too excited to sleep.

I waited until after the morning Bible reading before I knocked on my father's study door. He was sitting behind his desk in his smart work suit and tie, with his Bible open in front of him. I had a question about the Holy Spirit to ask him, I said. I carefully explained the logic of the pattern I'd uncovered, drawing the diagram on a piece of Stott and Sons headed paper. But when I told him I had been wondering if the Holy Spirit was Jesus's spiritual mother, he laughed. I was being too literal, he said. I was using the wrong part of my mind.

When I found the courage to ask the question that was keeping me awake – who or what, then, *was* the Holy Spirit? – he read me verses from 1 *Corinthians* 2. In this letter, he said, Paul explains to the Corinthians that certain mysteries can only be apprehended with the spiritual mind, and not with the natural mind. I was using my natural mind to think about the Holy Spirit. That wasn't going to get me anywhere.

Embarrassed and disappointed beyond measure, I dared not tell him that he had evaded my question. Instead I asked him to promise not to tell anyone about our conversation. He promised. We prayed. I did not sleep that second night either. I lay in bed looking at the underside of the bunk above me, with its links of interconnected chains, rehearsing follow-up conversations with my father and with God. I could make no sense of it, but I knew I was not stupid.

The next morning, the Lord's Day, my mother bundled all five of her scrubbed children into the car as usual, to go to the Morning Meeting. This austere, high-walled, windowless red-brick Meeting Room on the outskirts of Brighton held five hundred Brethren brothers and sisters. We sat on wooden chairs arranged in a circle, the women and children in the uppermost, outermost circles, the men on the inside. My father, then in his early thirties, had by this time perfected a declamatory, slightly mannered preaching style, and was making a stir as a young ministering brother. People travelled some distance to hear him.

On this particular day he preached to an assembly of two or three hundred south-coast Brethren for twenty minutes on the importance of educating Brethren children about the dangers of the natural mind. His daughter, he told them, had asked a question about the Holy Spirit, and he had explained to her about 1 *Corinthians* 2. We should not leave our children, he intoned, to languish in spiritual ignorance. We must be vigilant. My face burned red, not with embarrassment but with outrage. People turned to smile at me. I bit my lip hard, and tasted blood. I swore I would never forget that act of betrayal.

# 15

My mother taught me to read when I was three years old. I remember the black shapes, dark against the white flashcards she used, the intense pleasure I took in deciphering the word on it before my older brother did. Though I took to reading early, he didn't. I'd snatch the cards when he looked away, and hide them among my toys.

He must have hated me then. I was a little show-off. A little *girl* show-off. I didn't care. I had something to prove. There was a begat system to violate in my house; it was enshrined in the Stott and Sons logo that it sometimes seemed had been stamped onto every surface in our home – on the boxes, on the paperwork, on the key-ring my father carried, on the files my mother stacked on the shelves. Boys inherited. Boys spoke. Boys had power. Girls didn't. I countered that system with will and subterfuge. Eve *stole* the forbidden fruit. If God knew everything, then he must have known she was going to do that. He could have stopped her. But he didn't. And he didn't seem to be stopping me either.

We got our reading practice from the Bible. There were hardly any other books in the house, just the coloured rows of ministry in the sitting room and the volumes of the *Children's Encyclopaedia* arranged underneath.

Every morning my brothers and I gathered around the great iron bed in my parents' bedroom to read the Bible. Each of us would read a chapter. We worked our way through the books, tipping from one story to the next, from Noah's ark to Moses in the bulrushes to Joseph and Potiphar's wife to Ezekiel with the dry bones, the staccato of *Leviticus* giving way to the swells of *Song of Solomon*. Sometimes there would be pockets of iambic beauty that I couldn't get out of my head for days.

*And-God-re-mem-bered-No-ah.*

Job was a particular favourite of mine. Though the story made me furious with the Lord for making Job suffer such terrible things just to prove a point to Satan, the language seemed especially beautiful, especially the bits about the whale.

'His sneezings flash light,' I read from my Bible when my turn came round, 'and his eyes are like the eyelids of the morning. Out of his mouth go forth flames; sparks of fire leap out: Out of his nostrils goeth smoke, as out of a boiling pot and cauldron. His breath kindleth coals, and a flame goeth out of his mouth.'

I itched to correct my brothers when they hesitated over a word or got the rhythms wrong, but I was not allowed to speak after I finished my chapter. The great victory of those mornings was getting to the end of my chapter without stumbling or showing the slightest sign of self-satisfaction. Although I could sometimes see my father's joyful approval, I did not acknowledge it or meet his eye. I was not praised. Praise encouraged spiritual pride. I didn't really understand what my parents meant when they talked about spiritual pride, but I knew it was one of the worst sins of all, one I was especially prone to, it seemed. It was one of the many things I was supposed to be vigilant about.

Despite the fact that only Brethren brothers preached, and sisters were silent and obedient, I imagined a dazzling Brethren future for myself. By the time I'd beaten my elder brother at reading and at the times table, I'd decided that I'd be one of the first Brethren girls to be allowed to preach in the Meeting Room and in three-day Meetings. I was going to be the first of the female preachers. It was my calling.

There were plenty of glorious sons in the Bible, of every shape and size. Sons who inherited. Sons who were rewarded. Sons who were nurtured and recognised. Sons forgiven. Prodigals. And there were all those son sequences: Jacob begat Esau and Esau begat ... Most, if not all, of the daughters in the scriptures, it seemed, by contrast, were traded by their fathers or brothers, or raped or offered as wives or as compensation prizes. There didn't seem to be much to look forward to about being a daughter in the Bible. There were no chains of begats for daughters.

So it made sense to turn myself into the son who overtook all his siblings. I'd be Joseph. And Jacob. The canny, overlooked, improbable sons. The ones who beat everyone while no one was looking. Joseph had been the youngest, the puniest, the least likely, and he still got to be king of Egypt. But I'd have to know the Bible better than my brothers if I was going to get anywhere. I began to memorise whole chapters, and to write lists of all the books of the Bible in the right order, just as my father had done as a child.

When my brothers and I got confused about questions of theology or doctrine, we couldn't untangle them because asking questions was risky. My mother, usually busy preparing food or making curtains or feeding a baby, would say, 'Ask your father.' When we did – if he was home, which he usually wasn't – he would launch into a long lecture that was impossible to follow. So the misunderstandings we made privately from listening to preachings in Meeting turned into muddles.

Things got even more confusing when we went to school. My two older brothers and I were sent to Connaught Road Junior School, a state primary in Hove. There were no Brethren schools in the sixties, though today Brethren children are bussed long distances to expensively equipped 'faith' schools where they are closely supervised, girls are segregated from boys, 'science' is carefully censored, and students are taught that evolution is a false theory.[19] But although we were schooled alongside worldly children, we were supposed to have no contact with them. We came home for lunch to comply with the Brethren eating rule. In fact, there was no danger of our making friends with any worldly children, because we had no idea how to talk to them. We spoke a quaint kind of Brethren-ese – we talked about 'the Lord's Day', 'walking in the light', 'in the arms of the Lord' – and I noticed the effect those phrases had on the other children.

The things that preoccupied and excited me and kept me from sleeping – the precise layout of the great mansion in heaven; where the angels lived in the great city; how transparent the Holy Spirit was; whether a murderer could ever be repentant enough to get taken up in the Rapture – were clearly not things the other children thought about at all. The things we heard them talk about were fascinating, but incomprehensible. None of them thought they needed to explain that *The Banana Splits* and *The Monkees* and *Tom and Jerry* were television programmes, or that 'the Seagulls' were the Brighton and Hove Albion football team. I stood in the playground with my brothers, our backs pressed up against the brick wall, trying to be invisible, watching and listening.

In 1969 all the children were talking about Neil Armstrong and the first moon landing, but I had no idea what it meant. Brethren families like ours, who were forbidden to have newspapers or television sets, would not have seen the pictures of the blue cloud-laced earth from far away, or watched Armstrong take those strange underwater steps on the dusty moon. We were, of course, living on a kind of satellite planet of our own.

# 16

The teachers at Connaught Road were used to Brethren families. They didn't put up a fight when Brethren parents stipulated what their children were permitted to read or study. They probably weren't allowed to – they were expected to respect and accommodate religious differences. And in any case, why would they object? Brethren children were well-behaved, obedient, hard-working, never any trouble. You'd hardly notice they were there, except for the strange clothes they wore.

The teachers banished us from the classroom whenever the lessons strayed into areas that conflicted with Brethren teaching. They took no chances. And in the 1960s and seventies, when the Exclusive Brethren took their totalitarian turn, that meant we spent many of our school hours in the long corridor that ran the length of the Victorian building.

No assembly. No prayers. No classes about poetry or fiction. No science that conflicted with the creation story. No gym. No ballet. No music classes. No sports. No discussion of ethics or philosophy. The teachers handed us worksheets. We had comprehension practice, quizzes, handwriting sheets, maths sheets. We'd be given a stack of them and a high desk and chair out in the hallway.

It was always a relief for me to be in the corridor – it was quiet after the hubbub of the classroom. I'd hear the rest of the school as if through water: fragments of teachers' voices, children singing in choir, or flute music, or the thud of feet in the gym. The air was full of the smell of poster paint and glue.

Sometimes I'd glimpse one or both of my brothers somewhere further up that hallway, their heads bent over their pile of worksheets. I wasn't allowed to call out to them, but if I waited long enough, one of them would sometimes sit up, look around, see me, grin and wave. I'd wave back. The only other people we saw out there were the worldly boys who'd been sent out of class for misbehaving. They'd sit on chairs outside the head teacher's room, fidgeting, waiting to be called in and reprimanded. Sometimes a teacher would come out to make sure I was doing what I was supposed to be doing, but eventually they felt confident that I was entirely obedient, and were content to leave me be.

One day my teacher told me that when I got to the end of a particular worksheet, I could go to the library for independent reading if there was time left before the bell rang. I still don't know if she realised what she was saying. I nearly told her I wasn't allowed in the library, but I swallowed the words. When my classmates had library time, I would sit on a faded red plastic chair in the corridor outside the door. I'd peered in from time to time, and been astonished that there were so many books in the world, that someone had thought to put them all in one room, and that they came in so many shiny colours.

'At home we only have ministries,' I told my teacher once.

Her eyebrow rose just a flicker. 'That's nice,' she said, and turned to another child.

There had been other books in the house once, I discovered later – my mother's adored and beautifully leather-bound Jane Austens, my father's collection of Shakespeare and poetry. But in 1962, when JT Junior ordered all Brethren households to cleanse themselves properly, my father had boxed up all the books and packed them into the boot of the car. Many of them reappeared in the years after we left the Brethren – he must have stashed them somewhere for safekeeping, just as the Romans buried their treasure when they evacuated Britain in the fourth century, or the Catholics hid their relics under floor-boards during the Reformation. But though his books came back, my mother's Jane Austens did not.

God had not exactly said it was all right for me to go into the school library, but he hadn't exactly said it wasn't, either. Usually he sent a sign. I was good at looking for signs – a bird flying one way or another, the wind blowing towards me or away from me, even car numberplates could be signs. He hadn't sent a sign this time. The library door was open. That, I persuaded myself, probably meant it was all right. The Lord must be showing me the way.

I headed for the far corner, where the fiction shelves were. The old floorboards creaked noisily beneath my feet. The bell might ring at any moment. A teacher might usher me out. My brother might glimpse me through the door and tell our parents. But I was already in, and the bell had not yet sounded. I reached up and pulled out a book.

On the cover of *The Secret Island*, a group of four children a few years older than me crouched on a clifftop looking down on a sandy beach where some suspicious-looking grown-ups were unloading a rowing boat. The children looked as if they were in danger, but they also seemed to know what they were doing. *Mike, Peggy and Nora were sitting in the fields, talking together*, I read. *They were very unhappy. Nora was crying, and would not stop. As they sat there, they heard a low call. 'Coo'ee!'*

I read as if turned to stone, breathing in the musty smell of the book, my bare knees marked by the edges of the floorboards. Before this I had only read the Janet and John books with my mother: *John is in the tree. Janet is in the kitchen.* And the Bible, of course. I had read most of it by now, aloud, kneeling on the floor of my parents' bedroom. But there were very few stories about children in the Bible, other than Jesus, and he didn't have any brothers or sisters, or go to school, or play in the fields, or cry. He preferred to talk about the Bible to grown-ups in the temple.

*Why was Nora crying in the field?*

As Peggy and Mike comforted Nora, a scruffy boy called Jack appeared, and asked what was wrong. The children explained that they were being treated as no more than farm slaves by their aunt and uncle, that their real parents had gone missing, that they were very unhappy.

When the bell rang ten minutes later, I stuffed the book underneath a dusty red beanbag in the corner. Brethren children were not allowed to borrow library books. I would have to hide it so no one else could borrow it before I came back.

*Where had the children's parents disappeared to?*
*Could Jack be trusted?*

# 17

Over the next few weeks I read the whole of *The Secret Island* without discovery, punishment or consequence. When the bell rang I'd go to my next lesson, complete my worksheet, and head back to the library, checking over my shoulder to ensure that I hadn't been seen. Would they escape to the secret island after all? Would the leaky boat they'd stolen stay afloat? Where would they sleep? How would they open the tins they'd taken from the larder? What would happen when the food ran out?

Jack now occupied the place in my head where only God and my parents had been before. He was on the right, and they were on the left. It was easier to keep them in separate rooms. I negotiated with God, but sought advice and good sense from Jack. I agreed with Jack when he told the others that sometimes grown-ups could be cruel, unfair, and plain wrong. He was right when he said that under certain circumstances it was all right to steal food. After all, as Jack said, the bad aunt and uncle wouldn't have to provide for the children any more once they'd escaped to the secret island, so stealing a few provisions in the night couldn't exactly be wrong.

Although I read all the books in Enid Blyton's Secret Series, it was *The Secret Island* that I kept coming back to. It made my heart beat faster. I was in love with Jack. He always knew what to do. He'd know how to plan for when the Tribulation came. He'd found the island in the lake that no one knew about. He knew where a boat was hidden. He told the other children that they could all live there together, build a cabin out of willows, and live off the land while they waited for their real parents to come and find them. And their real parents did come and find them.

Years later, when my father recited Yeats's 'Lake Isle of Innisfree' again and again – *I will arise and go now, and go to Innisfree, And a small cabin build there, of clay and wattles made* … – I'd be back in the wood on the island with Jack, tying the willow branches together. *Nine bean-rows will I have there*, my father would declaim, lost in his own imagined refuge, *and a hive for the honey-bee* – and I'd be lighting the candles in the wood with Jack as night fell.

At home I became stealthy. I wrote out a list of the things Jack had told the children they should take on the night they ran away:

Empty tins for storing things in
Saucepan
Axe
A fine sharp knife
Sugar
Knives and forks
Books and papers for reading quietly
Ludo and dominos
A sewing workbasket

Matches

Mixed nails and a hammer

A small magnifying glass for making fire

'On the night before they left,' Blyton wrote, 'they broke into the larder and took: Some tea? Yes! A tin of cocoa from the top shelf. A packet of currants and a tin of rice from the store shelf, too. A big load, a few cakes from the cake-tin!'

By the time my mother gave birth to my twin brother and sister, I had gathered a stash of stolen objects. I'd known for some time that when my parents and all the other Brethren grown-ups disappeared in the Rapture, and we children got left behind, Satan's people would come looking for us. There was nothing in the Bible about what to do when that happened. We wouldn't be able to stay in the house – I'd read about Sodom and Gomorrah and the terrible things that happened there, and guessed that was what would be unleashed when Armageddon started. We'd have to escape to caves in the mountains, or find a boat somewhere and cook over fires we had to start ourselves.

There was a copse with thick woodland and hiding places just behind our house. That's where I planned to spend our first night. But now that there were two new babies in the house, things would be more difficult. I was glad that my father and one of the other Brethren priests had baptised them in the bath when they were a few days old. But I didn't know enough about baby souls to be able to say one way or the other whether my parents would be allowed to take the babies with them in the

Rapture. So I'd have to be ready in case they got left behind too: powdered milk, sterilising equipment, bottles. I made my mother show me the whole routine, and how to check the temperature of the milk by squeezing a few drops onto the back of my hand.

# 18

Something really bad had happened. My parents were talking in hushed voices again. I listened from the back of the car. I set up my dolls in the hallway near the phone so that I could eavesdrop on the long calls my father kept making and receiving. It was the end of July 1970. I was nearly six. We had two tiny wailing babies in the house whose cots had been put in my bedroom, and I wasn't sleeping – not because of the noise they made, but because I couldn't stop looking at them. They were so beautiful and strange. They made my heart ache.

There were five of us now, and the baby routine on top of the usual domestic routines filled up every minute of the day. I bottle-fed my baby brother while my mother fed my sister. The house was thick with the smell of baby sick, sterilising tablets and Dettol. My mother had always used a lot of Dettol, but now my father was bringing home industrial-sized bottles of it from the warehouse. Even through all that noise and smell and excitement I could tell that something important was happening outside the house, because the phone never stopped ringing.

My mother was usually changing one baby or feeding the other or washing nappies, so my brothers and I would answer the front door when my grandfather and the other men arrived to consult with my father that summer. They disappeared into the sitting room. My mother took them biscuits and bottles of whisky or pots of coffee, and when they left, my father would summon her. She would leave me to mind the babies, and would close the door behind her.

Through the hushed talk on the phone, the raised voices behind closed doors and the whispered conversations between my parents, I heard the words *Aberdeen* and *Mrs Ker* repeated again and again. I worked hard to piece together the clues, but when my father glimpsed me trying to listen in while he was on the phone, he kicked the sitting-room door shut. Although I failed at the time to work out what Aberdeen meant, or what Mrs Ker had done, or why everyone was so upset, I did know that it was because of Aberdeen that our lives changed forever. Aberdeen was the reason we left the Brethren and went to live in the outside world. Aberdeen turned everything upside down.

# 19

What had actually happened at Aberdeen only took shape for me years later. I was sixteen. We'd been out of the Brethren for eight years by then, and the circumstances of our leaving had been overlaid by all the dramas that had happened since. It was 1981, the day after my father had been taken to prison for embezzlement and fraud. His landlady had told my mother that if his effects were not removed from his flat by the end of the week she'd be taking them to the dump. So my mother and I had let ourselves in to my father's impossibly messy post-divorce flat, taking Dettol and rubber gloves, and started opening the drawers and looking in the boxes. My mother wanted to find the deeds to the house we lived in. She had to save it from the lawyers and creditors, or we'd all be homeless.

On the table I found an open file filled with yellowing newspaper clippings. The first one I pulled out was from the *Daily Express*. It was dated August 1970. There was something about the photograph under the headline that looked creepy: a very old man was sitting on a sofa with his arm around a pretty young woman. His hand seemed to be very close to her breast. She was smiling in a rather pinched, uncomfortable way. The headline read, '"We are not ashamed," says Big Jim.'

Big Jim, I remembered, was what journalists called JT Junior, the Brethren Man of God. And here – finally – was a picture of the mysterious Mrs Ker. Philip Finn, the New York correspondent for the *Express*, had interviewed JT Junior in his house in New York about a scandal that had just taken place in Aberdeen.

I did not want my mother to see the clipping, or the file I'd opened. Everything was bad enough already. I was upset for her to be seeing my father's dirty and disordered flat. She hadn't found the house deeds, and she was putting everything she could find into the black bin bags and boxes we'd brought with us. I was trying not to inhale the strange smell of off milk, cheap hair oil and the newspapers that had been piled high in every corner. I stuffed the pile of newspaper clippings into my school satchel, and went to look through the boxes my mother had left for me to search through.

Later, after we'd gone home and my mother had gone out to work, I closed my bedroom door and nudged the chest of drawers in front of it. I tipped all the cuttings from my satchel onto the floor, found the *Daily Express* piece, and read it through slowly.

Philip Finn had turned this scandal into an episode from Benny Hill, all nudges, winks and smirks. He was making it seem silly – but it wasn't silly, it was terrible and epic. *This* was *Aberdeen*. This was what my parents had been talking about eleven years earlier. This was what they'd been trying to make sense of. *This was why we left*. Finn wrote:

Big Jim Taylor put his arm round dark haired Mrs. Madeline Ker at his Brooklyn, New York, home tonight, kissed her lightly on the cheek and said: 'I don't care what people say. She is a very, very pure person.'

Then the balding, silver haired leader of the Close Brethren said: 'We have never at any time done anything improper.'

Resting on his lap was a large leather-bound Bible, and in his right hand he held a tumbler half full of Scotch.

As we talked in the upstairs sitting room of his large detached house 32-year-old Mrs. Ker, mother of four, from Harrow, Middlesex, smiled up at him.

When I arrived at his home, Big Jim was sitting in an armchair wearing only underpants.

He said: 'I suppose I had better put my pants on. But, quite honestly, I find it more comfortable just sitting in my underpants.'

Big Jim seemed quite at ease, and quite oblivious of the sensation surrounding him and Mrs. Ker and her husband during their recent visit to Nigg, Aberdeenshire.

Then it was claimed that Mrs. Ker had been found in bed with him when other members of the sect walked in.

It led to a furious row among members of the sect, and today Big Jim was busy sending off up to 8,000 letters 'explaining' the events in Scotland.

Mrs. K and her husband Alan, a research chemist are staying with Big Jim and his wife Irene (60).

Today Mr. Ker was not at the house, and Mr. Taylor and Mrs. Ker explained that [he] had gone to Washington on business and would be back later.

Mr. Taylor, who claims that his hold on the leadership of the Brethren is still unchallenged, said: 'Absolutely nothing happened in that bedroom that Mrs. Ker and I are ashamed about.

'It is true she was laying under the sheet on the same bed as myself. But I was on one side of the bed, and she was on the other.'

Whose clothes were on the floor?

Said he: 'Some of the clothes were mine. I don't know who the other clothes belonged to.' 'I didn't ask her to lie under the sheet. Mrs. K chose to lie under it of her own free will. Certainly nothing improper happened, and it is wrong to say that she was naked.'[20]

It read like the Janet and John books. Where is John? John is in the tree. Where is Janet? Janet is in the bedroom. Her clothes are on the floor. Whose clothes were on the floor? Mrs Ker's clothes were on the floor.

None of it rang true to me. The underpants. The photograph. The stupid, lecherous preacher. By then I was taking drugs, going to concerts, reading E.M. Forster and memorising soliloquies from Shakespeare so I could impress my father. But I still distrusted newspapers. I regarded them as worldly and corrupting, full of lies, Satan's way of brainwashing people. And Philip Finn wasn't helping. JT Junior's 'bedroom dealings', as Finn had called them, were grubby and embarrassing, but he had no idea how much damage they were going to inflict on so many Brethren families like mine.

# 20

It was another thirty years or so before I discovered the full story of Aberdeen, the distressing details that lay behind the version Philip Finn had written for the *Daily Express*.

Kez found a pamphlet among my father's papers called *If We Walk in the Light*. My father and grandfather had written it to help Brethren assemblies decide how to act after the scandal broke. It included scores of witness statements, and a transcript made by my father of JT Junior's last, foul-mouthed, rambling preachings, given in between climbing in and out of bed with Mrs Ker. We found other witness letters archived online. There were no sly sexual innuendos and winks here. This was deadly serious.[21]

In July 1970, JT Junior, seventy-one years old, Brethren Man of God, had flown to Britain from New York for the annual summer three-day Meeting and to do his usual round of preachings up and down the country. On the morning of 23 July he arrived in Aberdeen by plane, and was driven from the airport to a large blue-and-white-painted bungalow called AiryLea, in Nigg, a southern suburb of the city next to a golf course. A local senior ministering brother called James Gardiner had been given the honour of hosting him. There were several other guests, according to the witness statements: 'Dr. and Mrs. Robert Gardiner of Perth, Mr. and Mrs. Jim Gray of Edinburgh,

Mr. and Mrs. Edward Steedman of Falkirk and Miss Anne Gibb of Falkirk.'

One of them, Ted Steedman, recorded some of the events of that first day:

We arrived at James Gardiner's house on Thursday evening. Mr. Taylor was in bed resting and joined us about 7 p.m. He very soon paid a great deal of attention to the sisters, spoke in a crude way of their having had relations with men and constantly asked different ones when the results would be '... when is the delivery?' He made reference to women's bras and seemed obsessed with the sisters' breasts. He made one sister after another sit on his knee, with one especially he kissed her for minutes at a time, putting his mouth over hers and sucking her in a most peculiar way, all the time fondling and caressing her body, making her husband look out the window while doing so. His tactics with other sisters he wanted was to say that they didn't like his ministry, were not with him, and so on, until they came to him. This went on till the Kers came about 9 p.m. They should not have been there, but Jim insisted they stay, so that James Gardiner and his wife had to sleep in most difficult circumstances. When he had gone off to bed we found the first sister he had handled was very upset. We found in the morning she was nearly hysterical through the night.[22]

The Kers, a young Brethren couple with four children, were from London. They'd flown to Aberdeen to hear JT Junior, and were due to stay with other Brethren a few miles away, but had been invited to break their journey at Nigg. There's no mention of the Ker children. Presumably they'd been left at home with family in London.

By 9 p.m. JT Junior appears to have been drunk, aroused, and frustrated by an evening of groping those poor women. And then in walked pretty Mrs Ker. Something had been going on between them for a while, some people told me. 'William' had seen JT Junior groping Mrs Ker's breasts in a car park outside a Meeting a few weeks earlier when he'd first arrived in Britain.

JT Junior insisted that the Kers stay in the Gardiners' bungalow rather than in the accommodation that had been arranged for them nearby. The Gardiners had to give up their bedroom and make up a bed for themselves on the floor.

According to James Gardiner, later that evening Alan Ker 'led his wife', barefooted and in her dressing gown, through the kitchen, dining room and living room, to the room in which JT Junior was staying at the back of the house. He returned to his bedroom alone. The following morning, Mrs Gardiner saw Mrs Ker leaving JT Junior's bedroom. All through the day, Mrs Ker went back to the bedroom between Meetings. JT Junior was almost an hour late for the afternoon session. James Gardiner knocked on the door of his room, but got no response. Twenty minutes later Mrs Ker came out, saying she had had to wait until she was 'released'.[23] Her husband led her to JT

Junior's bedroom again that night, again returning to his own room alone.

So far Mrs Ker had been described as compliant. While the other female guests had become upset by all the groping, some even 'hysterical', Madeline Ker in her dressing gown and bare feet had allowed herself to be calmly led back and forth to JT Junior's bedroom by her husband. She was behaving in a completely *subject* way, as Brethren women were supposed to do. But, one of the witnesses said, when she'd been prevented from going to JT Junior, she'd become 'impudent'. When James Gardiner reminded her that he was the head of the house, and responsible for what happened in it, she'd said to him, 'I don't accept you as head of this house.'

I was surprised how much Mrs Ker's behaviour shocked me. It was so un-Brethrenlike. Here was a Brethren woman standing up to the Brethren men, but just so she could go back to that lecher's bed. I'd give my right arm, I thought, to be given an hour to ask Mrs Ker what was going on, why she'd let herself be led like that. But no one was asking Madeline Ker anything. They were just calling her names.

The following day, Saturday, Mr Gardiner barricaded the route to JT Junior's bedroom, to stop the Kers from getting through. Mr and Mrs Ker tried to break down the door, cracking a glass panel. Later in the day, Mrs Ker managed to slip into the room, staying there alone with JT Junior for some time, so that they were again late for the afternoon Meetings. When she came out of the room she told her host that JT Junior wanted him to know that he was a 'son of a bitch and a bastard'.

'It is hard,' Ted Steedman wrote, 'to put on paper the atmosphere of madness.'[24] When JT Junior woke the next day, Steedman wrote, he was calm, and presumably sober. He gave a good address in the morning Meeting. But he started drinking again at lunchtime, and Steedman recorded: 'his demeanour changed, as though something came over his mind. He became nasty, almost animal like and his conversation unclean.'[25]

What kind of monster was this, sitting at his hosts' dinner table and making the women sit on his lap in turn so he could grope their breasts and suck at their mouths in front of their husbands? These were people my parents knew. People who had been to stay in our house, slept in our spare room. Good people. Eminent Brethren men. What would my father have done if he'd been there and JT Junior had tried to touch my mother like that?

# 21

J T Junior wasn't just climbing into bed with Mrs Ker. He was also preaching. In the Aberdeen Meeting Room, where hundreds of Brethren men and women had gathered to hear him, the Jekyll and Hyde of the AiryLea bungalow had turned into the spitting mouth of Samuel Beckett's *Not I*. You can take almost any page of the forty-page transcript of his

Aberdeen preaching at random and JT Junior's words and obsessions are pretty much the same, only arranged in a different order. What he says is shocking enough – the words of a man suffering from alcoholic dementia – but so too is the mood of collective hysteria in the Meeting Room. Could the Brethren gathered there that day really have thought that the Holy Spirit was speaking through this man? And what was my father thinking as he transcribed this madness, which would eventually appear in the whistle-blowing pamphlet he and my grandfather put together?

[Loud laughter and stamping.]

**JT Junior:** Now we must get on with this meeting here and the next address: Now we have Mr. George Terries. The next address. You never had it so good. You big boob, you. And then, the next is what? Because we're still producing [not clear]. We had the hell of a time in our house just a few minutes ago – 'ell of a life. That so-and-so. But it's No. 2 now. We got No 1. That's No. 1, that's George Terries. Anybody know him? Anybody know George Terries? We're going to have the 'ell of a time here. I want to tell you my purpose that he's a very good factory. I'm still looking for that. George is No. 1 … No. 2 is coming but it comes slow. She's in terrific pain. You bastard! You bastard! We need a doctor here. Go to sleep Stanley, go to sleep. We have plenty of hymns, to hell with you. We're having a very good time. You bum, you. You big bum. Scott! Bum! Scott! Bum! Scott!

Bum! Scott! Bum! Scott! Bum! Now you have it. You never have it. You never had it so good. You never had it like this, you nut, you.

[40 seconds pause with bursts of laughter] [Shouting]

**JT Jnr:** You stinking bum! You stink! Why didn't you bring some toilet paper with you. Very fine meetings.

**MBT** [identity unknown]: Yes, first class.

[Pause with indistinct remarks and laughter then shouts of laughter with cheering, whistling, and stamping.]

**MBT:** What I would like to know, Mr. Taylor – is this to be the pattern for all meetings?

**JT Jnr:** Look at that son of a bitch there.

[Pause culminating again in laughter, stamping and whistling.]

**JT Jnr:** You never had it like this before. You bastard, you.

[Loud laughter, stamping, and whistling.][26]

I wanted to hear what the 'loud laughter' sounded like. When I found the audio recording of the Meeting that someone from PEEB had put online, that laughter didn't sound anxious or hysterical, as I had expected. People were guffawing. JT Junior must have been miming and gesturing and playing the clown, because the audience sometimes laughed in the long pauses when no one was saying anything. Sometimes the laughter and whistling went on for half a minute or more.

Had they all gone mad? Was this a kind of collective hysteria, like what had happened at the Salem witch trials? Did they think that God actually sounded like this?

JT Junior goaded the older men in the Meeting with jokes about faeces, constipation and purging. His preoccupation with spiritual cleanliness – a lifetime of using words like 'spewing' and 'purging' – had turned into a sequence of grubby jokes about bums.

**JT Jnr:** David, where the hell you been? Thank God for you. I thank God for you every time. You been stinking somewhere. What you been doing at?

**DJD** [identity unknown]: In Hell.

**JT Jnr:** You haven't had any privilege to do that. You feeling better? Thank God for that. You feeling better, David? Thank God for that. You feeling better, David? Thank God for that. Are you feeling better, David? Thank God for that. The whole thing, too. What about your intestines? Was that the trouble? To hell with them! 'ell with them. 'ell with them. You hear that George? George! You st … George! Did you hear? Yes. You st … 'ell with the other one! 'ell with the other one! Stay awake, you boob! What do you think, we're going to get on with all these songs from Detroit? To hell with them, 'ell with them, I said. 'ell with them! You big bum you. You never had it so good. And don't you think, don't you think you're going to go away with this stuff. You here, what's your name? Son of a bitch.

**JG:** John Gaskin.

**JT Jnr:** Get up. You look like nothing. Sit down! You never had it like this before. Eric! Awake? You awake there? Well, get up and perform Eric, get up. Get up, Eric. Get up! Eric, get up. Sit down. You never had it like this before. You stupid people here, what do you think I am? I'm a professor. Here you, I'm not finished with you yet. You nut! Get up. I'm not finished with you yet. Well, I'll tell you this. Don't you mention any cars any more, remember? So what the hell are you? Skunk. You never had it like this before. That son of a bitch. I was very careful using the word son-of-a-bitch because I wouldn't know. I wouldn't know you have to be careful about it. Is everything alright with your bowels? You never had it so good. Stand up, Mr. Gardiner. I would like to introduce you to Nicodemus. And will you answer the question that I ask you Nicodemus? You couldn't. Who are you? Who are you?[27]

# 22

According to the witness reports, after this extraordinary afternoon Meeting, JT Junior and Mrs Ker disappeared off into the bedroom again. Stanley McCallum arrived for dinner. He was one of the Brethren top brass, one of JT Junior's right-hand men. No one dared tell him what was going on. Someone asked Mr Ker where his wife was. He told them she was resting. An hour or two passed. Someone asked when Mrs Ker and JT Junior were going to appear. They carried on waiting. Eventually McCallum said, 'There is something wrong in this house,' and the older men said, 'Yes, there is.'

James Gardiner went through to JT Junior's bedroom and opened the door. He found Mrs Ker undressed and in bed with JT Junior, who was wearing his pyjama top, which was open at the front. Gardiner called Mr Ker and told him to get his wife out, and summoned McCallum to the bedroom to witness the scene. When McCallum reprimanded JT Junior, JT Junior brazened it out: 'The devil is in you,' he roared, 'and I have to get him out. You've been wrong all your life.'

Gardiner pointed at Mrs Ker's clothes lying on the floor, but JT Junior said, 'You can't prove they are her clothes.' When Gardiner demanded that the Kers leave his house, JT Junior roared, 'She's my woman.' He tried to leave with the Kers, but was prevented. Though it was long past midnight, Gardiner called a doctor who had been attending JT Junior for several weeks. He gave JT Junior a sedative injection which sent him to sleep. The following morning, JT Junior's son, James the Third, flew his father back to New York, heavily sedated.

By the time Stanley McCallum got back to the USA himself, JT Junior's spin doctors had told his local assembly that he'd plotted JT Junior's overthrow, and that he was a homosexual, a sodomite, and had a criminal record.

In Aberdeen, Gardiner and the other shell-shocked bungalow witnesses put together their witness accounts and sent them to the New York assembly.

In New York, JT Junior's supporters, concerned about the press attention the story was getting, rang Philip Finn and offered him an interview in JT Junior's house, with the Kers present. It did not go well, what with the underpants and the whisky and all. JT Junior had not done himself any favours. If he wanted sex, he told Finn, would he have spent a thousand dollars and gone all the way to *Aberdeen*? 'Brooklyn,' he joked, 'would have been cheaper.'

JT Junior, backed by his supporters and the Hales brothers, now spun a new defence. Over the following weeks, the story of a plot gave way to a more sophisticated and nuanced narrative: Aberdeen, Brethren were told, had been a deliberate test of loyalty, devised, designed and orchestrated by the Lord himself to identify and expel interlopers as the Rapture approached. Even the Kers were repeating this story. They'd keep doing so for decades.[28]

In a few weeks Brethren spin doctors had turned JT Junior from a lecherous alcoholic bully to a martyr, prepared to jeopardise his personal honour for the Lord's Truth and to ensure a final necessary purge before the Rapture began. But then, just three months after Aberdeen, JT Junior died of an alcohol-related disease.

When I made my promise to my father on his deathbed that I would try to finish his book, complete the part of the story he had not been able to face, chronicle the Nazi decade he'd talked about, I started off thinking of myself as a detective solving a crime. Now that I could finally see the full, abject picture of those ten years, I wasn't gathering the details just for my father any more. I wanted to explain all of this to the child in the red cardigan I'd once been, the girl who'd done her best to understand the deranged world she was born into, but who just ended up furious and confused. I wanted to tell her that someone would put the pieces of the puzzle together. I'd done that, I realised – for her, for me.

But once I assembled the facts into order, there seemed to be no easy explanation I could offer either my father or my younger self. There was no culprit to be caught, no handcuffs to be placed on the wrists of a single murderer or thief. The questions the story raised were like the heads of the hydra of Greek myth: cut off the head of one question, and several others grew in its place. How had JT Junior managed to remain in power for so long? How had so many clever, good people been led into such a cruel system? How had men like my father allowed themselves to become exactors and interrogators, bullying people into confessing to imaginary sins? And once they'd finally seen the system for what it was – the projection of an alcoholic's paranoia, delusion and hunger for power – what did they do about it?

# AFTERMATH

# I

In the hours after Aberdeen, the details of what had happened began to travel along telephone lines that branched throughout the world. James Gardiner telephoned my grandfather in Hove, one of many calls he made that night. He described the details of what had happened in the AiryLea bungalow, the showdown, the fact that the Aberdeen assembly had withdrawn from JT Junior, and that most other Scottish assemblies were expected to follow suit.

My grandfather, carrying the news like a grenade clutched to his heart, telephoned my father and summoned him. I imagine the two of them together in my grandfather's sitting room, under the framed text about Jehovah always watching you, my grandfather struggling to find the words for what Gardiner had told him. Though they would have been shocked and disgusted by what JT Junior had done, they would hardly have dared to think about the scale of the trouble that was about to begin.

My father and grandfather were by now high-ranking Brethren. My grandfather was a Stow Hill Depot trustee. My father had taken Meetings across Europe and North America. Whatever Stott father and son did now, whatever position they took, other Brethren – at least in the south of England – would follow. They prayed. They sought the Lord's will. And they decided that they would have to get the truth to as many Brethren across the world as they could, before any counter stories from New York set like concrete around them all, before the Hales supporters got hold of the Depot. The clock was ticking.

Two days later, on the afternoon of Tuesday, 28 July 1970, as hundreds of holidaymakers dozed in deckchairs on the Brighton seafront, 450 shocked Brethren brothers and sisters dressed in their best clothes, polished their shoes, put on their hats and headed for the Meeting Room on Vale Avenue, a large new purpose-built hall with high walls and two high, narrow slit windows on the northern edge of Brighton. There was only one item on the agenda for this particular Meeting: *Aberdeen*.

After all the phone calls and the secret meetings at our house or round the corner at my grandparents' house, after the praying, the late-night, lights-out conversations with their wives, this Care Meeting would determine how the Brighton assembly would act.

In our house, my mother must have put supper on the table as usual. She and I would have run the bath, spread out the towels on the radiators, heated the milk, sterilised the bottles, bathed and fed the babies, my brother bundled on my lap, my sister on my mother's, and tucked them into their cots as we always did. My brothers kicked their ball around in the garden in the twilight. Blackbirds sang in the lilac tree. It was just like any other night.

I asked my father, and later William, to describe the final Vale Avenue showdown. Forty-five years later, they still remembered every detail.

Brethren men filed into the lower front seats of the amphitheatre-shaped room. These front rows had been fitted with hand-held microphones every few feet. The women took up their positions in the upper, outer circles, where there were no microphones. William found a seat a few rows away from my father. His wife had stayed at home, too terrified to watch the inevitable confrontation.

When everyone had settled, John Railton, the self-appointed leader of the Brighton Brethren, and a JT Junior hardliner, reached for his microphone and stood to denounce the rumours from Scotland. It was a conspiracy, he declared. Satan was behind it. Stanley McCallum was behind it. How could anyone dare to say such things about the Man of God? It was an aberration.

William described how my father – still, I remember, only thirty-two years old – rose slowly to his feet. At six foot four, he towered above everyone else. Just as he'd agreed with my grandfather, he began to tell the Aberdeen story as he'd been told it, carefully, without drama, a simple relation of the facts.

John Railton shouted him down after he'd only spoken a few sentences. Declaring him 'not fit for the fellowship of God's son', he withdrew from him. When my father picked up his Bible, coat and hat and walked towards the door, no one followed.

'I drove home,' he told me, 'feeling as if I was going to be hit by a mighty bolt from the sky at any moment. It was a genuine physical dread.'

William was sure he was going to be sick. He was paralysed, glued to his chair, unable to stand. He watched as a man on the other side of the room stood to object to my father's expulsion. Railton withdrew from him too.

As William watched that man pick his way through the crowd towards the door, another man – my father's cousin-in-law this time – stood to protest, and was withdrawn from.

Now William found his feet, and gestured for the nearest microphone to be passed to him. He wanted, he said, to ask a simple question about the Man of God. He wanted some clarification.

'Can the Man of God,' he asked, 'do *anything*?'

Railton roared back: 'The Man of God is *pure*. The Man of God is pure.'

Now he declared William withdrawn from too.

William remembers a group of men sitting a few seats away, including two of his brothers-in-law, turning towards him. One of them said, 'Get out, you bastard,' and the chant spread slowly around the room. Soon everyone was chanting:

*Get – Out – You – Bastard. Get – Out – You – Bastard.*

William began the long walk to the door. He told me that he looked at the contorted faces of the chanting old men, one by one, as he passed them, reminding himself that the mortgage on his house belonged to one of them.

I remembered the story he had told me about how he asked his father where his uncle had disappeared to, and his father replying, 'Outside the door, son, there is only darkness.'

'I have grown afraid of the dark,' William had said.

Now here he was, all those years later, walking directly to the Vale Avenue Meeting Room door. There was no one outside among the parked cars waiting for him. My father and the others had gone, and no one had followed him out. He was entirely alone under that huge black sky. He told me he stood there, in the car park, for a long time.

He remembered, he said, every detail of the drive home through Brighton's streets that night. His head spun with panicked questions. Would he ever see his parents or siblings again? Where were he and his wife going to live when their Brethren mortgage had been withdrawn and they had to sell the house? Where would they go when his Brethren employers sacked him? What if his wife didn't want to come with him?

When he reached home, he told his wife he'd been withdrawn from. To his relief, she put her arms around him and said that if he had not walked out, she would have left him.

My grandfather, who was still in the Vale Avenue Meeting Room as the chants subsided, told my father the rest of the story.

John Railton, his blood high now that he'd expelled so many, now that he'd got the chanting started, took the microphone again. If Mr Taylor wanted to take *his* wife Eunice to bed, he said, he'd feel honoured.

He'd miscalculated. This was the straw that broke the assembly's back. My grandfather now rose to his feet. He could not, he said into his microphone, condone what had transpired in Aberdeen. If anyone in the room agreed with him, they should join him in walking out now. Half of the people in the Meeting Room stood up and headed for the door. Two hundred of them.

I wish I'd seen it.

# 2

My father parked his car on the drive, climbed the steps, opened the front door, and told my waiting mother that he'd been withdrawn from. She showed him the bags she'd packed, and told him, just as William's wife had done, that if he hadn't been withdrawn from she would have left on her own, and taken the children with her. My parents must have sat in the tidy sitting room together looking nervously at each other. Perhaps he poured himself a whisky. Perhaps they prayed.

Twenty minutes or so would have passed before they heard the sound of cars, voices coming up the front steps: my grandfather, my cousins, old people, young people in family groups or alone, William and his wife among them. I think of my mother opening the door, wondering where she'd find chairs for everyone, boiling the kettle, opening boxes of chocolate marshmallows, pouring tea, hoping the voices wouldn't wake the five children she'd spent so long trying to get to sleep. I sat at the top of the stairs out of sight, holding my stuffed rabbit, listening. My younger brother came to sit next to me, rubbing his eyes. Eventually we crept back to bed, falling asleep to the murmur of those voices downstairs.

They must have had to do headcounts. Who had walked out? Who was still in there? What were they going to do now? They'd have given thanks for their release; they'd have prayed for the Lord's guidance. They agreed that to start with they'd use the smallest Brethren Meeting Room at Edward Avenue, just a few streets away from our house. My grandfather still had the keys. The Lord would show them the way.

My father and my grandfather took the lead. The first thing they had to do, they said, was to get the truth about JT Junior out to as many people still 'inside' as they could reach. They'd use the printing presses at the Depot. Two of the four Depot trustees, it seemed, were now 'out', and my grandfather had the keys to the offices. Unless someone had already intercepted it, the audio recording of JT Junior's Aberdeen address would already be on its way to the Depot in the post. Someone needed to get there to pick it up. Once they had the tape, they'd transcribe it, gather all the witness statements, and print a pamphlet. They'd post it out to Brethren around the world, using the Depot's networks, before anyone in New York knew what was going on.

My father and grandfather couldn't have slept much over the next few weeks. Phone calls to and from Brethren around the world continued long into the night, every night. My father typed out the copies of the Aberdeen witness letters that James Gardiner sent from Scotland, and transcribed the bizarre, expletive-ridden and sexualised ramblings of JT Junior's Aberdeen address from the tape recording when it arrived at the Depot. That tape was important. JT Junior was claiming he had said nothing controversial in the Aberdeen address. The tape would be proof that he was lying.

No one at home was sleeping much either. My mother was feeding and minding, washing and dressing five young children, including three-month-old twins. She was keeping up appearances. Praying, cooking meals, sterilising bottles, and, when necessary, providing beds and food for the many sleep-deprived Brethren who came to our house to consult my father. She would have listened to him relaying the news as it unfolded, keeping a close eye on the way things were going. She'd been praying for years, she told me later, that we might all be released from a system that she knew was wicked. Now it had finally happened. The Lord had taken our family through the Brethren door and out into the world. My mother seemed different to me then, excited and bright-eyed. She didn't show her happiness and relief to visitors, but she couldn't hide it from me. I was always by her side, watching.

'For most of us,' my father wrote in the introduction to the pamphlet they'd decided to call *If We Walk in the Light*, 'it was like waking up from a prolonged bad dream. If we were honest we had to admit that, like Agur [*Proverbs* 30:2], we had been "more stupid than anyone".'

After Aberdeen, it was not disgust, or anger, or outrage that my father felt most acutely, but *stupidity*. But it's not my father and his wounded pride that haunts me. It's Elsie and Winnie Rhodes walking into that pond; fourteen-year-old Ruth pulling her father off her half-dead mother; it's Eva turning on the gas oven in the empty house, knowing she'd never see her sister again. How many decent people had been betrayed, tortured and tormented by this madman and his cronies, and this inhuman system they'd made?

The Exclusive Brethren had turned into a cult, and had played out their torments *in plain sight*, in the suburbs of provincial towns all around the world. How many non-Brethren teachers, doctors, coroners, psychiatrists, lawyers and judges must have seen glimpses of what was going on, and looked away for fear of causing offence? A doctor had once listened to me describe Satan as he appeared in my bedroom at night. Instead of asking me or my parents questions, he'd ordered a urine sample to be taken. A nurse at the hospital that cared for Rhina must surely have seen Eva's distress when she realised that the Brethren would not let her see her sister again. An administrator at the Egg Marketing Board had opened and read Elsie and Winnie Rhodes' letter in which the sisters had quoted the scriptures as explanation for cancelling their membership. He might have smiled at how batty religious people could be before he filed it away. Despite the strenuous efforts the modern Brethren make to seal off their people from any contact with the outside world, how many teachers, doctors, psychiatrists and judges are still turning a blind eye?

# 3

Eight thousand Exclusive Brethren members, including the two or three hundred defectors in Brighton, walked out of their suburban Meeting Rooms across the world – or were withdrawn from – in July 1970 or soon after. They formed a new schism, a group with no name. Later, people would call us the Non-Taylorite Exclusive Brethren. My parents and all the other adults must have been in a state of extreme shock. They would have felt lost, rudderless. They sought guidance from the Lord, as they'd always done. They'd been delivered from wrong-doing, but now they had to find their way back to the light and to the right road. After the agonies of the screw-turning years, all these families had to learn to live in a world they knew almost nothing about, and had been taught to fear. They would have to take stock, repent, pray, and start again. Within two years they'd split several more times.

Though my father was soon preaching regularly in Britain and Europe to small assemblies of Non-Taylorite Exclusive Brethren, he couldn't shake off that feeling of stupidity. It frustrated him that people weren't facing up to what had happened; a year after Aberdeen he gave an address about how some Brethren were already slipping back into the old ways, into the old sectarianism.

'What made us so weak and ignorant that we allowed these things to be imposed on us,' he wrote in a Brethren address published in late 1971, 'and then in many cases joined in the imposing ourselves? Even now, when our folly is manifest to all, we have still retained an unconscious tendency to condescend to other believers.'[1] He was still using the Brethren language; he was still preaching, but his certainties had begun to unravel.

In December 1971 he gave an address on Hayling Island, along the coast to the west of Brighton, near Portsmouth. After the preaching, William told me, he and my father drove back across the South Downs. A few miles from Brighton, my father took a detour and parked the car by the side of a road that looked out over the great gulf of Devil's Dyke, a dramatic notch in the Downs a few miles north of Brighton, said by local legend to have been carved by the Devil when he tried to let the sea in and flood the country. He had something he wanted to say, he told William. After he had switched off the headlights, and the darkness had closed around the car, he said, 'I don't think I believe anything to do with Christianity.'

When William described my father's strange confession, I felt once again as if I was looking through a keyhole, seeing something I wasn't supposed to see. What did those words *mean*? My father hadn't said, 'I don't believe in God'; he'd said he didn't believe 'anything to do with Christianity'. I wasn't sure what 'anything to do with Christianity' actually meant. Perhaps he didn't know either.

'He'd just been *preaching*,' William said, 'preaching to hundreds of Brethren at Hayling Island. He was good. People trusted him, looked to him to take a lead. But he hadn't believed a word of what he was saying.'

The fact that my father had preached without believing the words he spoke made William angry. Of course it did. Perhaps he was thinking that if my father had done this once, he might have done it several times. How hollow was he? I considered telling William that my father had not always meant the things he said, that he'd once given a preaching in which he'd broken an important promise he'd made to me, when he told people that I had asked if the Holy Spirit was the Lord Jesus's mother. But I didn't say anything. I wanted to defend my father. 'Sometimes it takes people a while to see things,' I said.

After all, hadn't this dreadful system forced so many Brethren to dissemble in order to survive? I wondered how many hundreds of Brethren children had feigned absolute belief in Brethren doctrine, rather than shame their parents. After a while it was impossible to tell what was authentic and what was performed, what you believed and what you merely said you believed. You began to wonder which parts of you were true any more.

I could picture those two still-young men, both afraid of the dark, looking out over the void, that violent slash in the landscape, trying to work out what to do and where to go, trying to be honest with each other. They must both have known what my father's words meant. They were, it seemed, going to have to go in different directions. My father's Christian beliefs – if they had ever been beliefs – were fracturing.

A few weeks later, in January 1972, William told me, he and my father both withdrew from the Edward Avenue assembly. They'd both lost their faith in the Brethren, but William was still a devout Christian, and my father wasn't. William and his wife had decided to join a new church. At that very last Meeting, the two men stood to read out the letters they'd written explaining their decisions.

I wish that my mother and William's wife had stood up to have their say too, for the very first and last time. I'd like to have heard that. But they'd spent their entire lives in a fellowship in which women never spoke, so by then it must have been psychologically impossible for them to speak in a Brethren Meeting. I like to think they had already cut their ties with the fellowship, that they were eager to go, but I imagine they were frightened. They did not know what the world was going to be like out there.

I didn't find my father's 'resignation' letter in any of the boxes. Perhaps he hadn't kept it. But, going by the preoccupations of the preachings he made around this time, it's likely that he talked about how Non-Taylorite Exclusive Brethren were gradually returning to their splitting and shunning ways, and how he didn't want to be part of that, because the Lord had shown him it was wrong. He would have known this was to be the last time he had the floor, so he would have taken his time over writing and delivering his last words. This was his Brethren swansong.

When he finished reading his letter, he would have walked out, taking my mother and all of us with him. I have no memory of the occasion, but I can still see the Meeting Room clearly in my mind's eye. We would have been sitting in the back row as usual, in our Lord's Day clothes, my mother at the end, next to the twins in their two pushchairs. When my father finished his speech, the Brethren probably launched uncomfortably into another tuneless hymn to cover the sound of our clatter and the bang of the door as we filed out after him with our hats, Bibles, coats and toys.

It couldn't have been easy for him. Non-Taylorite Exclusive Brethren were not as strict about separatism, so he knew we'd still be able to see all the family we were leaving behind – his parents, siblings, nieces and nephews – but we would not be Brethren any more. He knew the Brethren would say that he and my mother were turning their backs on the light, and consigning their children to the darkness. They would be praying for us all the time, for our return and our salvation.

William told me he saw my father on only four occasions after we left the Brethren. He and his wife met us in a park for tea in 1972, a few months after that last Meeting, and they came to see my father playing Richard the Lionheart in a production of *The Lion in Winter* a year after that. My father was very good, he told me. He had a strong stage presence. Seeing what a good actor he was, he added, had made him wonder whether he had been acting all through his Brethren life. I was thinking that too.

After that, he said, he and my father had lost contact for many years. He and his wife went to live in another country, and when they finally came back to England, William had tracked my father down to the Tunbridge Wells bedsit where he was living after he'd been sacked from the BBC. He'd been shocked by the state my father was in, how unkempt he was, but they'd talked for hours just the same, played classical CDs together, had lunch in the local theatre café. Then, decades later, he'd visited my father in the hospital in Bury St Edmunds six weeks before he died.

The remaining Non-Taylorite Brethren, including my aunt, my grandparents, and a few of my father's first cousins and their families, splintered into new groups as new leaders stressed slightly different ways of separating from the world. Each new faction came to be known by the name of its leader – the Rentons, the Frosts, the Walkers, the Strangs. They found new, ever-smaller Meeting Rooms, and broke bread together in their own particular ways. Each of them believed they'd found the right new path, and that they had returned to the light.

My grandfather, grandmother and uncle *went with* the Frosts. My aunt and her husband and small children *went with* the Rentons. For the rest of their lives they would disagree about doctrine and practice, and about the correct ways to 'withdraw from iniquity'. We still saw these aunts, uncles and cousins for dinners and occasional birthday parties, but it was often awkward. I always felt they were watching me, trying to judge how worldly I was becoming. I seemed to be always saying the wrong things, giving the wrong answers to their questions.

Eventually the Brethren Frosts subdivided yet again, into what they now refer to as 'Hard Frosts' and 'Soft Frosts'. They still shun each other. They are not allowed to attend each other's funerals or weddings. Sometimes I hear stories about trouble in the Renton ranks: a small group has risen up to defend someone who has been withdrawn from. Others take up the hardline separatist stance again. So they split. More people get withdrawn from. It's that shameful Red-Tiler and Blue-Tiler story all over again.

# 4

Perhaps in 1972 our parents thought we were too young to understand why we'd left. My brothers were eight and five; I was seven, the twins one. Perhaps they thought we hadn't been listening when they told us that televisions and radios were wicked; that Satan was in cinemas, newspapers, pop music, theatres; that the world outside our Meeting Room was evil to the core, and would corrupt us if we went anywhere near it. Perhaps they thought we'd be delighted when they installed a television set and a radio in our house, and took us to the cinema.

Perhaps they'd forgotten that they'd been telling us since we were born that the Rapture was about to come, and that if we had not given up our wills and desires and natural minds to the Lord, we'd be left behind when everyone we knew disappeared off the planet, and the bad people would be drowned, burned, buried alive.

But we children did not cast off our Brethren teachings so easily or quickly. I became, in this post-Aberdeen confusion, preoccupied with sin and salvation, particularly after my parents had left the Edward Avenue Meeting Room and began to take us to a succession of local churches.

In the spring of 1972, just months after we'd walked out of Edward Avenue for the last time, my parents started to take us to church services on Sundays. I was still expected to put on my Best Dress, but the neat pile of triangular headscarves that my mother had made for me, that I'd kept in my top drawer, disappeared altogether. We didn't have to get up in the dark any more. We were allowed to sleep until nine o'clock on the Lord's Day. We'd go to a new church for a few weeks, shake hands, smile, and then my parents would try another: the Baptists on Holland Road; the Methodists on Portland Road; even, eventually, the Anglicans on Nevill Avenue.

Once we were inside, we recited the Lord's Prayer alongside everyone else. The other people knew the words by heart, but we had to read them from the sheet we were given. We were supposed to memorise it, my mother said. My father didn't appear to like any of these new churches. He didn't seem to think the preachers were any good – I heard him complaining about the sermons to my mother. Within a few weeks he stopped going altogether, but my mother carried on taking us to the Anglican church on Nevill Avenue. My headscarves still hadn't turned up.

The way these other people worshipped bore no relation to the way we'd done things in the Brethren. But even if I'd felt able to ask questions, I wouldn't have known where to begin, and I was pretty certain my mother wouldn't have known the answers anyway. She looked just as bewildered as I was. These people were Christians, my mother said, just like us, but everything they did was different – the words they used for things, the places they put things, even the way they arranged their chairs. In this new world:

Churches had pulpits and altars.
The people were called congregations.
They sat in rows rather than in circles.
The women and children were allowed to sit with the men.
Some of the women wore trousers.
The men in the rows didn't preach.
Only the men in the pulpits preached, and they wore robes.
Only the very old women wore hats.
Someone invisible played organ music when we sang hymns.
People knelt to pray.
There were no headscarves.
There was a sheet of words we were supposed to follow.
Sometimes we were supposed to join in and say things all
    together.
They talked about 'Jesus', rather than 'The Lord Jesus'.
They read passages from the Bible that I didn't recognise.
They talked about 'Sunday', not 'The Lord's Day'.
They didn't talk about Satan, or the Rapture, or about Clean
    Houses.
No one was doing any 'withdrawing from iniquity'.

I was pretty sure they must have a completely different God up there. I couldn't see how *our* Lord would be happy to come in here, with all those pictures, crucifixes and statues.

At home, things were upside-down too. My father announced one Saturday afternoon, when my mother and I were polishing the brass, that he was taking my mother and us three older children to the cinema, to see *Gone with the Wind*. I glanced at my mother, alarmed, but she did not protest. It seems astonishing now, but I remember almost nothing of the film, apart from some shots of alarmed horses and the great fire that engulfed Tara, but I do remember reaching out for my mother's hand at the moment we stepped across the threshold into the richly coloured entrance hall; and later watching her face in profile, flickering in the light from the screen, rapt and terrified by turns, happier I think than I'd ever seen her.

It wasn't that I believed we were now Satan's people, or that we'd been plunged into some dark new world, or that the worldly people we were now allowed to talk to would trick and corrupt us – rather that someone had changed all the rules. It was like being lost in a town where all the signs had been changed into a language I didn't know. I remember sometimes reaching out to touch hard surfaces to see if I was awake.

There were other vertigo-inducing changes. Our meals and domestic routines and bedtimes had always been arranged around the times of the Meeting, especially on weekends. Without Meetings, our days were shaped differently. The twins were walking now, usually in different directions. My mother was grateful to have me mind them when she was busy. I'd carry them back into safe range when they strayed into the flowerbeds under the lilac tree, or would feed them when she'd carried their high chairs out into the garden. My two older brothers seemed delighted by all the new things they were allowed to do: the football stickers they collected and stuck into albums, the comics my father brought home for them, and the children's programmes on the television set. But they must also have been struggling to make sense of what was happening.

I found a picture of my brother and me in 1972. We are launching a hot-air balloon I'd made, with a basket fashioned from matchboxes. My Tribulation-survivalist fantasies had become more elaborate. Since I'd seen a full-size hot-air balloon drift across the sky above our house, I'd begun to wonder if I could engineer ways to escape flooding by using flight. When this balloon model got snagged on our television aerial I decided it was a sign of the Lord's disapproval of our new television set.

My father began to show a taste for art films. In September 1972, for my eighth birthday present, he brought home four reels of Zeffirelli's *Romeo and Juliet*. Swordfights, chickens, medieval Verona, velvet and satin costumes crackled and flickered through the projector and up onto the wall of our darkened sitting room. The words rose and fell, or fizzed like sparklers. But despite my father's careful explanation of the story – the star-crossed lovers and the feuding families – I couldn't follow what was happening. My brothers soon found excuses to leave the room. My mother left to put the twins to bed. Before I eventually fell asleep on the sofa, I watched my father's face caught in the light from the screen. He was transfixed, his eyes wide, just as my mother's had been in the cinema – but he was also mouthing the actors' lines to himself. Did he know the words to the whole play? *How* did he know them?

When I started a new middle school that year, I was allowed to attend school assembly for the first time. Assembly was worse than church. It wasn't that I disapproved, rather that I didn't understand the language of mild sentimental Anglicanism that my teachers used. There was a lot of talk about sharing, and loving your neighbour; we were expected to do a lot of clapping.

'I love God's tiny creatures,' we sang, 'That wander wild and free. The coral-coated ladybird, The velvet humming bee.' None of the Brethren hymns that I remembered had any animals or birds in them.

When I walked the school grounds – from the gym where we did PE, to the outdoor pool where we had swimming lessons, to the classroom where we practised Eleven-plus exam papers sitting at desks arranged in neat rows – I sometimes felt as if I was walking on the moon. I failed to find a way to explain to my teachers or the other children why I didn't know the rules of rounders or netball, or how to climb a rope. After years of being asked to leave the classroom for so many lessons, I still found myself waiting for a teacher to send me out. But now they didn't. Sometimes, when the classroom was very noisy, I wished they would. My teachers praised my abilities, particularly in reading and writing, in the school reports they wrote during these years, but they complained that I seemed to have a problem concentrating.

Many people assume that leaving a cult like the Brethren must be exhilarating. 'You had no TV or pop music or cinema,' they say, 'and then you did? It must have been amazing!'

But when you see interviews with people who have recently left cults, they describe feeling bewildered and frightened; their eyes dart around, searching for points of reference, metaphors that would get somewhere close to describing the feeling of being lost, not-at-home, without walls.

No one, of course, shrugs off years of indoctrination in one go. Many escapees went back to the Brethren after a few weeks, not only because they missed their families – which would be reason enough – or because they didn't have the skills to get work, but because the world frightened them. You can't just *refuse to believe* that the world belongs to Satan if you've heard it repeated over and over since you were born. It's under your skin. People also describe the difficulty of making choices – moral, financial, domestic, professional and emotional – because inside the Brethren there are virtually no choices *to* make.

The language that non-Brethren speak seems different, too. At eight years old, I did not know how to talk to the other children at school, or how to bridge the void between their world and mine. I was pretty certain the Rapture was still coming – after all, no one had told me otherwise – but I had no idea who'd be taken, now that my parents had started to watch television and films and go to other churches. I'd stand with my back to the wall in the playground watching the children skipping rope, singing their complicated rhymes, and I'd be conjuring Tribulation scenarios, imagining tidal waves sweeping across the tarmac, storms tearing down the playground walls and trees, the four horsemen galloping across rooftops, lights out and sea levels rising. *Icky Wicky Wai Cho, Chai Chickenora*, someone would be chanting; or a group of children would be creeping slowly across the playground, calling out, *What's the time, Mr Wolf?* They still didn't know what was coming. But nor did I any more.

I began to steal anxiously from the boxes my mother kept hidden in the house: packets of crisps, Kit Kats, marshmallows in shiny silver and red foil. Concerned about the weight I was gaining, my mother took me to buy tent-like crimplene clothes in bright yellows and pinks from a new shop in Brighton called C&A. My mother was still washing my hair in the bath. It had not yet been cut, and it hung down my back in two tight plaited ropes.

No one teased me much at school – they just avoided me. I was always the last to be chosen for teams, the first to stumble on the gym mat or to fall when we were supposed to leapfrog over the vaulting horse. My brothers didn't want me in their cricket matches. I was just a girl, and I didn't run very fast.

I read my way through the piles of library books I brought home from school and from the public library along the road: Russian, Cornish and Irish fairy tales, collections of short stories about Arthur and his knights. The girls fared far better in these stories than the girls in the Bible. Their fathers or brothers still exchanged them or married them off, or their stepmothers put them to work, but these girls often ran away, refused to do what they were told, stole keys, disguised them-selves, went where they weren't supposed to go – into the west wing of the castle, or down into the dungeons; they found out things they were not supposed to know. I began to write stories for my teacher about fairies, swords in stones, and snow girls.

I wasn't the only one flailing around with metaphysics and theology. My younger brother had become preoccupied with original sin. He and I would often wait for our mother to pick us up from school outside the Booth Museum of Natural History, a strange Victorian building a few hundred yards up from the school gates. Its steps were covered by a canopy, so we could take shelter there if it was raining. The road was on the edge of a park, and on the brow of one of the highest hills in Brighton, and from the steps we could look down over the whole of the town through the trees, and out to sea. I was sure I could make out the curve of the earth from up there, the water flecked with cargo ships and sailing boats.

One day I noticed that during the walk from school my little brother was flashing me dark looks. When we got to the steps of the museum and I asked him what was wrong, it all came out in a jumbled rage: 'It's all *your* fault. It's all *women*'s fault. If Eve hadn't made Adam eat the apple we'd all live *forever*.'

'He didn't *have* to take it,' I said. It was raining, my mother was late, and my shoes were wet. There wasn't much else to say. I was speechless with rage of my own. I couldn't counter the logic of the *Genesis* story. We'd been taught that every word of the Bible was absolutely true, that it was the *only* truth. He'd trumped me. The Bible had trumped me.

My brother and I didn't speak for days. I was furious about being blamed for stealing his immortality, and he was furious about having had his immortality stolen. There was no easy way to settle this dispute. We'd never discussed scriptures with our mother; that was our father's terrain. But he was hardly ever home now, and I wouldn't have asked him anyway – I'd resolved never to ask him about the scriptures again. I went back to my Brethren Bible to check the exact words in *Genesis*, but there were no exact words. That was always the trouble. It all depended on what you thought the words meant. Did the

Bible actually say that it was women's fault? Is that what the story of the forbidden fruit and the serpent meant? Was my brother right? Was it all my fault?

5

At home, my parents had started to dress differently. My mother had complied with the increasingly strict Brethren dress codes, wearing the compulsory headscarf or hat, and keeping her hemlines low and her necklines high. But she'd also dressed us and herself in the jewel colours that she loved, and that the older Brethren women disapproved of: reds and purples, cobalt blues, emerald greens and lemon yellows. She'd knitted me that red cardigan with shiny brass buttons.

Now she made herself new clothes in patterned silks and satins, with shorter skirts. She bought purple boots that laced up the front. My father bought her a white leather-and-fur coat. She wore her thick black hair just the same, piled on her head and pinned prettily into place, but she no longer covered it. I watched the way the sun lingered on its curls. She kept the Bible near her sewing pile, and still read it every day, quietly to herself. My father didn't.

He began to wear well-cut suits and slacks, occasionally a cravat. He grew a beard – Brethren men were not allowed facial hair – and shaped and groomed it. He wore a musky cologne.

He lost weight dramatically as I gained weight. He was handsome and dapper. He bought audiotapes of pop music, and played songs by the Seekers – 'The Carnival is Over', 'Morningtown Ride' – and Paul Simon – 'Kodachrome', 'Mother and Child Reunion' – in the car and in the house, very loudly.

Sometimes he'd play his favourite six or seven tracks over and over again. 'Listen,' he'd yell at us. 'Shut up for a minute and listen.' Sometimes he'd stop the car on the hard shoulder to make us listen. *And I dreamed I was dying*, sang Paul Simon, as the guitar moved to the crescendo, and my father turned the volume up as high as it would go, so the whole car shook, *And I dreamed that my soul rose un-ex-pect-ed-ly*. We'd sing too, as loud as we could, all together. Sometimes the lines and melodies seemed to have been set to repeat for days inside my head.

When my mother wasn't in the car, my father would let me climb onto the armrest between the two front seats and push my head and shoulders up through the sunroof while he drove. I'd fling my arms out wide like the wings of a bird, and he'd press his foot down on the accelerator and turn the volume up high. *And I dreamed I was flying*, I'd sing, *And I dreamed that my soul rose un-ex-pect-ed-ly* … the wind would take my breath away, and make my plaits fly out behind me.

Go faster, I'd shout, go *faster*.

In the summer of 1972 my father joined the Wick Theatre Company, an amateur group based in Southwick. Three actor siblings in their twenties, Vincent, Monica and Peter Joyce, gave him lists of music to listen to.

'He'd never heard the Beatles,' Monica told me on the phone from Corsica a few months ago. 'We couldn't believe it. He'd actually never heard the Beatles! That's how shut-off he'd been. How can anyone have lived through the sixties in Brighton and never heard the Beatles? I mean, he was like Rip van Winkle. He couldn't believe how beautiful everything was ... I made him tapes of all my favourite music, several every week.'

Wick players put on three plays a year in a barn that had been converted into a theatre in Southwick. Now my father would come home from the warehouse, eat the meal my mother had cooked for him alone in front of the television news, and disappear out again to a rehearsal. Sometimes he'd sweep into one of our bedrooms to play us a new song. Occasionally he'd weep in the half-darkness when he played 'Bridge Over Troubled Water', and that would make us cry too. The smell of his aftershave would linger in the air long after he was gone.

My mother was usually too busy to listen to music or watch television. If I came downstairs after bedtime for a glass of water, I'd often find her sitting over a pile of papers and accounts laid out on the kitchen table. She didn't complain, but she didn't want to be interrupted. She was doing the books, she said. That meant, I understood later, trying to work out where all the money was going.

When my father brought Vincent Joyce home to supper, I'd never seen my parents so animated. I'd never seen them laugh so much. My mother's eyes shone. Vincent was twenty-three, straight out of film school, charming, funny and handsome. He had a moustache. When he asked me questions about the books I was reading, I'd blush violently and drop my head, but he'd carry on talking to me just the same. I was nine years old. I couldn't stop looking at him. He agitated me. I was jealous when he talked to my brothers in the same way he talked to me. This made it all the more confusing when I spotted the crucifix he wore at his neck, which, I realised to my horror, almost certainly meant he was a Roman Catholic.

What was my father doing inviting papists into our house, and – worse still – eating with them? Had my mother seen the crucifix too?

In the Brethren we'd been told that all worldly people were dangerous, but some were worse than others. The Open Brethren, and the people who'd left the Exclusive Brethren, were the absolute worst, because they'd been shown the light but had turned their backs on it. Next came the Roman Catholics. They were idolators and fornicators, the people of whorish Babylon. They were spiritually corrupt and corrupting. I'd never seen a Roman Catholic up close before. That's why Vincent was so handsome and charming, I realised – Satan, they'd always told us, made very good traps. I determined to stop talking to him. Someone had to take a stand.

As my father became more hedonistic, I became more puritan. My mother had finally settled on the Anglican church on Blatchington Road, and she took us with her most weeks. In the Sunday school there was colouring to be done, and quizzes about Baby Jesus. I'd never heard the Lord Jesus called Baby Jesus before. Once I asked a few questions about Satan's dominion on the earth, and the kindly young teacher looked concerned and confused. I decided it was probably best not to ask questions here either.

Someone suggested that my mother move me to a new Sunday school, called The Crusaders. This was a much more serious puritan operation, much more in my line. Here we were crusaders, soldiers in some imaginary Holy Land. We wore shiny enamel badges in the shape of shields, with red crosses in the centre. There were oaths to be sworn, tests to pass, prizes to be won. I won a Bible in 1974, its thin pages interleaved with black-and-white photographs of the Holy Land.

I did not, however, take easily to the evangelising we were supposed to do in The Crusaders. Brethren had never been interested in recruiting heathens. When the old ladies who ran the Crusader classes told us we could only stop the Antichrist if we saved souls, I had to ask who the Antichrist was. I'd never heard Satan called that before. Ask me anything about the flight from Israel, or David and Goliath, and I could often quote chapter and verse. Ask me anything about Baby Jesus or the angel Gabriel or the Antichrist, and I'd be stumped.

I'd begun to have bad dreams. The voices I'd heard as a very small child had returned in different form. They'd turned into The Committee. The dreams were always the same: I'd be in a darkened room in some kind of semi-derelict warehouse, standing in front of a table behind which sat five men and one woman, in a sort of Last Judgement scenario. There was a heavy metal light on a stand behind them, like the ones I'd seen used in interrogations in films.

Why, one of them would ask me wearily, had I failed to achieve my mission *again*? Had I forgotten the reason I'd been sent to earth? Forgotten it *again*? Each time they asked, I'd tell them, 'Yes, I've forgotten.' I'd apologise. I'd stutter. I'd hang my head. They'd dismiss me, heads bent low, hands scratching out notes on forms. Then they would send me back to the waking world. This time, they'd say, *this time*, go and do what you're supposed to do. You're running out of time.

As I surfaced from those dreams, which looped like a song stuck on repeat in some forgotten anteroom of my brain, I'd resolve to remember – *this* time, *this* time, I would, I could, I will *remember* – but I'd wake, damp with sweat, to find that the crucial details of the mission had slipped through my fingers again, like sand.

# 6

Worldly families, I discovered, were different from ours. But the Marsdens were *very* different. I met Helen Marsden when I was nine. She sat next to me at school. She was shy like me, but she knew how things worked, so soon I was asking her to explain what certain things meant, and helping her with fractions and the endless practice tests we had to do for the Eleven-plus. She told the teacher when one of the boys who sat behind me kept putting the ends of my long plaits in his inkpot. She asked me to tea. My mother, no doubt both relieved and nervous, agreed.

It was the summer of 1973. As we approached the house, my mother and I were surprised by the high wooden gates, one of them leaning off its hinges, and the long, gravelled drive that wound steeply up from the road through a dense wood, beech and ash trees hanging low and dark. The vast Edwardian house appeared to be barely holding its own against the tangle of overgrown trees and shrubs. A rusty caravan sat in the trees opposite the front door, and we could see a bashed-up pale-blue Triumph car and bicycles in the open garage at the top of the drive.

As my mother and I stood at the top of the front steps, trying to work out if the elaborate bell-pull actually worked, a young boy called out from one of the gullies in the roof some-where high above us, warning us to get out of the way. Several tiny silk parachutes drifted slowly down past us onto the expanse of gravel and weeds, a kitten attached to each one. The kittens landed safely, unperturbed, as if they were used to it. Another child, in camouflage gear, his face blackened with mud or paint, appeared through the long undergrowth, saluted us, scooped up the mewling bundles, and disappeared back into the green.

Helen eventually poked her face through the dark crack of the door. Her mother, she said, was on the phone, otherwise she'd come and say hello. My mother excused herself, relieved not to have to talk or go in. She arranged to pick me up in two hours' time at the bottom of the drive. At the bottom of the drive at six o'clock, she repeated. She didn't want to have to risk being asked in. I understood that.

I stepped across the threshold into the unfamiliar faint smell of stale cigarette smoke and cats. Helen's great-grandfather had been a mayor, she explained, when she saw my astonishment at the size of her home. Her parents had inherited the seven-bedroom, three-bathroom Edwardian mansion in its huge grounds. It had been built for a large family, in the days when people had servants. It wasn't as tidy as it had once been, she added. Her parents were going to get some decorators in soon. I nodded. I'd already noticed the cracks in the ceiling, and the missing tiles in the hallway.

The vast Marsden house, with its east and west wings, butler's pantry and butler's lift, conservatory with broken stained-glass panels, rows of bell-pulls that no longer worked in every room, cellar, cobwebs and shadows, and wooded grounds with derelict summerhouses and swings, became my adopted home for almost two years. Though I loved my mother and father, I'd often pretend that Mr and Mrs Marsden were the real parents I'd once dreamed about. I fitted better there, I thought, than in my own home. I stayed more and more often, often for several days at a time.

My mother must have been glad to see my brothers and me making friends, but she was probably even more relieved to have us out from under her feet. She'd grown up in the country. Her houseproud mother had ushered all of her children out of their spick-and-span house whenever they were not needed to help turn the handle of the drying mangle or fold up the washing. When my mother wasn't in Meeting she roamed the country lanes, climbed trees and played alone in the woods.

Now that we were old enough to play unsupervised, my mother would see my brothers and me across the road to the park opposite when the weather was fine, passing us a picnic bag filled with crisps and bottles of orange squash and foil parcels of sandwiches. 'Off you go,' she'd say. 'I'll have your tea on the table for five o'clock.' Then she'd disappear back into the house with the twins.

My brothers would hammer their cricket stumps into the wide grassy spaces. Local boys we knew would drift over to take up their fielding positions. I'd take myself off into the hedges that ran along each side of the miniature railway line to look for birds' nests, or nestle into the roots of my favourite oak tree to read my books.

I preferred reading in the Marsden woods. The Marsden boys had built a rickety treehouse. To reach it you had to climb a rope ladder and then cross a rope bridge. With the sun filtering through the cracks in the side of the treehouse, and Helen reading her book a few feet from me, I'd be back in the hold of the ark again, just as I had been in the warehouse, listening out for the sound of gulls that meant we were approaching land.

The four Marsden children – the eldest sixteen, the youngest eight – ran as wild as the family cats. Nothing was watched here, nothing tended. Nature had been left to do its own thing. Helen's Irish mother smoked, gossiped, told stories about her life and about the elderly patients she tended in the old people's home she ran. She would tell us anything that amused or interested her. She swore sometimes. Helen's father, a solicitor, was quiet and shy. We didn't see much of him.

Towards the end of my first visit, I thought I saw Helen's mother cross herself. Then I began to notice the rosary beads and the statues of the Virgin Mary, the dusty paraphernalia of the Whore of Babylon on every mantelpiece. I tried not to look. I tried to turn my head away. The Marsdens, I realised, were Roman Catholics. Idolators, the Brethren would call them, Romanists. I'd already eaten with them. But how *could* they be Roman Catholics? They were so kind, and they didn't talk about the Pope. But then, that was what Catholics were supposed to do, wasn't it? They *lured* you into their traps slowly. They *seduced* you. Soon you'd be lost to the Lord. I determined to be vigilant. I would bring my Crusader badge and my Bible next time I came. But even though I knew they were Roman Catholic, when Helen asked if I'd come over again I said yes. One of the cats was due to have kittens any moment, she told me, and I wasn't going to miss that.

There were at least six adult cats in the house. All summer long the children – Helen and her two brothers and older sister – discovered new litters of kittens in cavities beneath broken floorboards, in cupboards, or in the cellar. The cats were half feral, and climbed in and out of grilles in cellar walls or through broken windows, carrying their newborn kittens in their mouths. If their nests were disturbed by Helen's little brother looking for recruits for his air assaults, the mother cats would find new hiding places for their kittens. Eventually Helen and

I would track them down. Then we'd work hard to keep Helen's brother from straying that way.

I slept in a spare bed in Helen's room, beneath posters of Donny Osmond and David Cassidy. Helen's mother referred to it as my bed. We played billiards with Helen's brothers in the billiard room. Her older sister had a boyfriend and was rarely at home, so Helen and I would steal into her room in the west wing and pull out any one of the several drawers that were full of lacy underwear, half-used make-up and hair rollers, which we'd borrow to curl our hair.

Sometimes when Helen's mother was reading a magazine in an armchair in the sitting room, scarcely visible, her hand would extend as I passed and she'd pull me onto her lap into a close and prolonged embrace. Helen would apologise, embarrassed. I didn't mind at all, I told her. Nobody did that in our house. But I didn't tell her that. Now that my father was often away at rehearsals, my mother was always busy running between cooking, shopping, sewing, cleaning, or doing paperwork. And we just weren't that kind of family. Everyone in our house was usually too busy or too cross about something.

If I was visiting the Marsdens over a whole weekend, I'd stay behind when the family went to church, and read my book. But one Sunday Helen asked if I'd like to come to Mass.

'You don't have to actually *take* the sacrament,' she said. I had absolutely no idea what she was talking about.

'Church,' Helen's mother said in her matter-of-fact voice. 'We can fit you in the car if you want to come.'

She said it quite casually, as if she were asking if I'd like to go bowling. She had no idea that to me being asked to go to a Catholic service was like being asked to step into a witch's oven.

'You can ring your mother to ask if you like,' she said, gesturing towards the phone.

'I'd like to come,' I said quickly, lowering my eyes, trying not to think of all those things the Lord had said to Satan when he'd tempted him in the wilderness. 'I'm sure my mother won't mind.'

After all, hadn't my father brought a Roman Catholic home to dinner? My mother *must* have known. So that meant Roman Catholics were all right now. And if they were all right, then going to their church must be all right too. If God didn't want me to go, he'd send me a sign before we got there, wouldn't he? As we drove to the church I looked about carefully, watching out for significant arrangements of letters in passing registration plates, or crows flying in groups of five, but I didn't notice anything.

The air in St Mary's church was thick with candle-smoke and incense, the light dim compared to the brightness of the Anglican church or the Meeting Room. There were crucifixes everywhere. Statues of Mary holding the baby Jesus, bleeding saints, clusters of candle flames. It was beautiful and hushed. I was just looking, I told myself. Just looking. But when the chants began, and everyone spoke the words together,

Lord have Mercy
Christ have Mercy
Lord have Mercy

I began to cry, overwhelmed by the music, the hymns, the chanting, the smell of the sweet smoky incense and the flickering of the candlelight. This was not a conversion comparable to the shuddering epiphany my father had experienced when he read that last page of *Mere Christianity*, but it was important. I'd never been moved in a church or a Meeting Room before. For a moment I had stopped striving to *understand*. I felt I'd crept into the presence of something beautiful, dark and strange, something I recognised but could not name. My sobs shuddered up through me like an earthquake. Helen's mother passed me a tissue and squeezed my hand. 'Bless you,' she said.

During the summer holidays, left to make up our own games, we played with a trunk full of Barbie and Ken dolls, all missing limbs and hair. We stole whiskey from the enormous drinks cabinet in the sitting room, decked ourselves up in chiffon from the dressing-up trunk, and danced on the lawn under the stars, or played hide-and-seek in the woods. Helen and I moved into the rusty caravan in the garden, making our own food, and when her brother came out to join us, we told ghost stories into the night. On Sundays, after church, the whole family ate together around the enormous dining-room table, scarred from the dripping plastic of a melting Action Man who had been set afire as he abseiled from one side of the room to the other.

We always Gave Thanks in our house, but the Marsdens didn't, so I was never sure when we were supposed to start eating. My father usually went on for a long time when he Gave Thanks; his voice would go up and down, and you could hear him trying to remember all the things we should be grateful for – that the Lord had shown us the way through something or other, that he had delivered someone or other from danger, that someone else had seen the error of their ways – and I'd be squinting through half-closed eyelids to check that my brothers hadn't been given bigger portions than me, or up at the painting of the milkmaid in her cobalt-blue apron to check that the milk was still pouring from her jug.

Now that my father hardly ever came home for dinner, my mother asked my brothers to Give Thanks. And because they didn't know what to say, they'd repeat something they learned at school which wasn't right at all – something like, 'For what we are about to receive may we be truly thankful.' I'd see my mother wince, but she didn't seem to know what to tell them to say instead. We were all embarrassed. I was glad that the Marsdens didn't Give Thanks at all.

# 7

My father and I were both 'adopted' by Catholic families after we left the Brethren. I was nine, my father was thirty-four. I found the Marsdens, and at the Wick Theatre Company my father found the Joyces.

'Your father came out of nowhere,' Vincent Joyce said when I tracked him down and went to see him at his home in Hove a few years ago. 'None of us had met anyone like him.'

I wanted to tell Vincent what he had meant to me, that he was one of the first grown-up worldly people I'd ever met, but I was afraid I wouldn't be able to explain why that was important, and how beautiful and dangerous he'd seemed to me back then. Instead I asked him what my father, who had only been out of the Brethren for a few months, had been like when they'd first met.

'He acted as though he didn't have much time left,' Vincent said. 'He wanted to stay up all night. He wanted everything *now*.'

I remembered the feeling I had when I entered the school library for the first time and reached for that copy of *The Secret Island*, certain I was going to be caught. I could hear the sound of the clock ticking, the minute hand juddering towards the number twelve, when the bell would ring and I'd have to put the book down and go to my next class. I understood why my father might have wanted to stay up all night with these new friends of his. Later, I'd wanted to stay up all night with mine.

'He was so tall,' Vincent said. 'He had a kind of spell. I mean, if you were at a party with him, you'd want to be in his part of the room.'

Vincent had known that my father had been in a religious group, had known he'd been a preacher, but they hadn't talked about that.

'Your father wanted to talk about films,' he said. 'Film-making, the theatre. He'd read more books and poetry than any of us. We talked a lot about poetry. Oh, and Bergman. Often until the early hours of the morning.'

I'd noticed the line of books about Ingmar Bergman on Vincent's bookshelf as soon as I walked into his sitting room. Vincent had been twenty-three years old when he met my father. He'd just left film school. If he had shown my father a Bergman film or two, they *would* have been up all night talking, because my father would have had so many questions.

Bergman knew about puritanism. His father had been a Lutheran preacher. All his life he'd been coming back to the metaphysical questions that had vexed him as a child. He'd made films about them. He wanted to know what it felt like for someone to lose their faith. What the silence was like that follows the disappearance of God. What it felt like if you kept on talking to God but he stopped answering.

My father must have been amazed to discover that this Swedish film director understood some of what he himself was experiencing. I wondered if he'd cried in front of Vincent when they watched Bergman films together, just as he'd always cry when he watched them with me ten years later.

As Vincent talked, my head flickered with Bergman stills: waves breaking against rocky outcrops, a tree bending in the wind, grey skies like gaping voids. Then I was back in a summer picnic that I'd forgotten. Vincent had been there, my mother and father and all of us children, others too. We were up on a hill above Devil's Dyke. I was lying in the sun on a picnic blanket, my head against my father's chest, listening to him practise his lines for *The Night of the Iguana*. Vincent was playing football with my brothers, my mother was in the distance with the twins. I could hear my father's heart beating in his chest, woven in with the muffled lines from the play, and behind that a kind of distant whooshing, like the waves breaking on a pebble beach inside him. I'd fallen asleep. When I opened my eyes, my father had gone. Dark clouds were passing across the sun. I cried out with a sudden sense of terror, as if I would fall and fall down the steep sides of the dyke and be swallowed up by the void of land beneath and sky above. Then I'd seen my father standing a few hundred yards away – alone – looking down there too. He had turned and smiled and waved, and the world had turned right-side up again.

My father auditioned for every play the Wick Theatre Company put on in the two years that he was a member, I reminded Vincent. And if he didn't get a part he'd sign up to do the sound effects, or help Vincent build the sets.

When I looked closely at the parts he played in those two years, it struck me that they reflected the different stages of my father's Brethren years. He'd been the Crusader prince in *The Lion in Winter* in 1972, the ex-priest in *The Night of the Iguana* in March 1973, and the duped Cassio in *Othello* in July 1973.

But as I listened to Vincent talk about the sets he'd built, and how they'd all dreaded the visits of the Fire and Safety Officer, and how good my father's sound effects were, I realised how absurd it was to think that the parts my father had been given

My father playing the ex-priest T. Lawrence Shannon in
Tennessee Williams' *The Night of the Iguana* in 1973

had somehow been chosen for him. If those plays had helped
my father to understand some things for the first time, he'd
been lucky. That was all it amounted to. It had been a fluke that
he'd washed up there, with the Joyces at the Wick Theatre
Company, just as it had been a fluke that Helen Marsden had
been told to take the desk next to mine. The fact that both
families had been Catholics was a coincidence too.

I still want to believe, however, that someone had designed
and built decompression chambers for my father and for me.
There are counsellors now who specialise in treating ex-cult
members after they've experienced long periods of mind
control. One of them told me it sometimes takes him years to
get his clients to return to normal levels of scepticism. He has

to keep on reminding them that there are many different ways of looking at things; he has to help them to think for themselves again. They used to call this process 'deprogramming'. But when I think of dancing under the stars with the Marsden children, and the music tapes the Joyce siblings made for my father, I wouldn't call it 'deprogramming', I'd call it 'decompression'. We'd been a very long way down to the bottom of some kind of sea. There was no easy way back up without getting the bends.

# 8

I may have resolved my problems with Catholics, but my growing body posed other kinds of metaphysical questions. It both fascinated and tormented me, as of course it does for many teenage girls. I'd put on weight. The body I'd always taken for granted as continuous with myself, that had once run, climbed and jumped, entirely unconscious of its movement through space, had turned into a body that bled, fell, stumbled, and burned with embarrassment. I was ten, and my periods had started. I was shy. When strangers or teachers spoke to me, I'd blush so that my face throbbed with heat, my skin stretched taut as if it – as if I – might split open.

But it was more complicated than that. In the Brethren we'd been told that flesh was blackened by sin, but also that flesh would be left behind, thrown off like an old coat, when the Rapture came. Brethren talked about sin all the time: how much we had, how much more the worldly people had, and how lucky we were that the Lord was going to take it all away. My periods, the blood and the abjection of those sanitary towels, only compounded my sense of my own sin. I wanted to throw my body off.

I once watched one of my father's beautiful Brethren cousins pass a strawberry from her mouth to that of her new husband as she sat at a table across from me at a family gathering. They thought no one had seen them. But I had. The passing of that strawberry between two mouths was one of the most shocking, daring and beautiful things I'd ever seen. That afternoon the cousin took me onto her knee and wrapped her warm arms about me, and told me there was no getting clean on this earth. My soul was black as black, and *always would be*. We had crucified the Lord, and only the Lord could undo that. I had to give myself up to him entirely if I wanted to be clean, if I wanted to be saved from all that sin. I had to welcome him into my heart.

Though I had never believed I'd be good enough to go up in the Rapture, I'd always taken it for granted that my 'me' was merely 'housed' in the body that looked back at me from the mirror. I did not call this inside 'me' a soul. Brethren never talked much about souls. But it had pre-existed my body, and it would outlive it. Now that we'd left the Brethren, it seemed my 'soul' would be stuck here forever in this ungainly body of mine.

Since leaving the Brethren, human bodies had come to seem especially strange to me. As I watched the twins sit and crawl, and then haul themselves up onto their legs and take their first steps, they often looked to me like monkeys. I started to notice eyebrows and nasal hair on grown-ups. My mother had one brown eye and one green one. Why would I never be able to grow a beard like my father? Why did humans have flat faces, and not pointy ones like dogs? Why did I have tiny hairs on the back of my middle finger and on my big toes?

I'd often heard Brethren preachers talk about an especially wicked man who'd gone around saying that humans had once been monkeys. Charles Darwin had been sent to earth by Satan, they said, to lead men away from God by putting evil ideas in their heads. It had always seemed a strange and beautiful idea to me, one I couldn't cast off. Though I'd been told it was heresy of the worst order, the idea that humans had once been monkeys seemed no stranger to me than some of the things that happened in the Bible: Lot's wife getting turned into a pillar of salt, Ezekiel making people out of dry bones, or God making Eve from one of Adam's ribs.

I must have been about six when I first looked up Darwin in the *Children's Encyclopaedia*. I wanted to know what the monkey man might actually have looked like. I didn't want to get caught, so I waited until my parents were busy with Brethren guests in the dining room before I slipped into the empty sitting room. I climbed on a chair, eased down the volume marked with 'D' onto the table, and spread out the closely-printed pages with my palms.

But there was no entry on Darwin in the D volume, just the sharp stubs of excised pages where it should have been. These were the volumes my father had described in his memoir, of course, which my grandfather had ordered and then censored with a razor blade.

Four years later, at the age of ten or eleven and no longer under Brethren rules or scrutiny, I went looking for Darwin again, this time in the school library's encyclopaedias. If this secret had been so carefully kept from me, I thought, it must be of unique importance. I was determined to find out for myself what this mouthpiece of Satan had really said. I found the entry and the photographs of the kindly-looking bearded man, who with all that eyebrow and beard hair looked more like a monkey than any man I'd ever seen. I read about natural selection, the survival of the fittest and evolution.

This was no flash of light on the road to Damascus, no conversion to some new kind of religion. There was so much I didn't fully understand. But strange images began to form in my daydreams. We'd been tiny water creatures once, Darwin had said, long before we were monkeys. We'd swum in a warm sea that had once covered the entire earth. Had we once been lizards and birds too?

The idea that we were all animals, moving and changing infinitely slowly through time into ever more fantastic forms, seemed both astonishing and beautiful to me, whether it was true or not. I began to think about the strange mirrorings and differences between the shape of my fingernails and those of my brothers, the curves of our noses, the tiny flaps of skin between my outstretched fingers, my ghostly similarity to my wilful great-grandmother. I imagined my body with fur or scales, my mouth tentacled like a coral, my arms as feathered wings.

Even if I didn't properly understand how natural selection worked, the world of flowing and endless forms that Darwin described made a dazzling counterpoint to the rule-bound, black-and-white, Manichean, sin-obsessed, flesh-loathing world of the Brethren. Darwin's version of a world in infinitely slow flux became a kind of poem that I'd keep coming back to for the next forty years. In this version of the world, nothing had purpose or design. Nothing drove or judged us. It was neither cruel nor kind, neither good nor bad. But it was a kind of miracle.

I'd sometimes stop at the Booth Museum of Natural History now on my way to the sports field on Tuesday afternoons. I'd climb the stairs where I'd once sheltered from the rain and go inside. The museum was usually empty. Glass-fronted display cases, banked five or six high, stretched all the way to the ceiling on every side. Bare floorboards made my footsteps echo.

Behind the glass, birds were pinioned amongst lifelike reconstructions of their natural habitats. Life looked both beautiful and bloody in those marshes, mountains and sand dunes: an eagle pulled out the innards of a lamb while the lamb's mother looked on; a vulture pecked out the eyes of a still-living rabbit. There were slaughtered animals everywhere, throats ripped out, eyes open, gazing up at pitiless painted skies. It turned my stomach, but I also found it shudderingly beautiful.

Notices around the museum walls explained that Edward Thomas Booth, a rich Victorian recluse, had set out to shoot, stuff and display a specimen of every bird in the British Isles. He died before he finished his project, but he'd still managed to collect hundreds of species. Once he realised he'd never be able to shoot one of every kind singlehanded, he recruited gamekeepers and game wardens all around the country to kill the birds he didn't have, and to mail him the dead specimens.

A sailor from the Newarp lightship in the North Sea had sent him wings taken from all the migrating birds that had collided with the light or got caught in the rigging. The list he sent Booth was a kind of poetry, I thought: Lark 520, Starling 348, Stormy Petrel 45, Brown Linnet 15, Greenfinch 21, Brambling 6, Fieldfare 2, Forktailed Petrel 1, Knot 2, Blackbird 20, Redwing 13, Chaffinch 15, Tree Sparrow 3, Rook 2, Snipe 1, Kittiwake 1. The parcel the postman delivered that day must have been enormous. I tried to imagine what 520 lark wings would have looked like: all those different shapes and colours and feather patterns, all those different birds.

The blood and guts and empty eye sockets of Booth's tableaux seemed to confirm something I already half-knew: that life was bloody, and that you had to watch your back or there'd be claws on you. But though Booth had tried to fix all those birds, lock them into his boxes, take them out of time, I now knew too, in a crude and stumbling kind of way, that everything was on the move, turning into something else, even if we couldn't actually see it with our human eyes. Even Edward Thomas Booth couldn't stop that.

# 9

Though we'd left the Brethren, my parents kept on hearing news about the bad things that were happening in 'the Jims', as they and my grandparents now called the Taylorite Brethren. The Taylor system hadn't stopped with JT Junior's death. Jim Symington, a pig farmer from North Dakota, had taken over as leader when JT Junior died. They called him 'the Elect Vessel' now, rather than the Man of God. Thousands of people were still in 'the Jims', including some of our aunts and uncles and cousins. From what I could tell, they were having unspeakable things done to them, and were doing unspeakable things to each other. People were still being forced to confess to terrible things; there'd been more suicides.

'He has a sister who's still in the Jims,' I'd hear people say to my grandparents, and they'd all look sad and cross. My mother's brother was still in the Jims, as was one of my father's favourite cousins. Those families had just disappeared from the landscape of our daily lives, as if they'd been rubbed out.

I was nine when I first heard my parents speak of the Andover Tragedy. We were in the car, coming back from somewhere. I'd been thinking about the clunky shoes my mother had just bought me for school. My father was driving erratically, talking fast to my mother with his voice raised and thumping the steering wheel from time to time. When I heard him talking about an axe, I leaned forward a little so I could hear better without drawing attention to myself. I'd read about axes in the fairy tales I'd borrowed from the school library. The woodcutter in 'Red Riding Hood' had an axe. He cut off the wolf's head with it.

People were dead, Brethren people. My parents knew them. But it was the axe I was interested in. And the feet. My father said the postman had seen Roger Panes's feet through the letter-box. Did that mean he was hanging from something, his feet swinging in mid-air in the hallway? I imagined those feet with socks; then with polished boots. For weeks afterwards I thought about those feet and the axe and the postman with his forehead pressed against the letterbox, looking in, but I was unable to put the pieces of the puzzle together. And they were always mixed up with those clunky school shoes I hated.

I found several newspaper clippings among my father's papers in his study a few months later. 'Father Ostracised by Sect Axed Family to Death', one headline read.[2] I slipped the clippings into my school bag. Once I was safely in my bedroom I closed the door and laid them out on the floor. I tried to figure the mystery out as if it had been one of the comprehension exercises they made us do at school.

The postman had not been a postman after all. He'd been a telephone operator. A relative had tried to ring the Panes's house several times but had failed to get through, so they had rung the telephone company to report a fault on the line. Someone had gone to the house, and when no one had answered, he'd knelt down, pushed the flap of the letterbox open, and seen those hanging feet. He'd called the police. The police had gone to the house and knocked the door down.

Det. Chief Insp. Stanley Atkinson and his officers found a man in blood-spattered pyjamas hanging from an electric cord attached to the banisters in the hall. They found Mrs Panes lying dead in a double bed in an upstairs bedroom. The newspaper said she had 'severe head injuries'. In my mind the Panes's house kept turning into one of the cottages in the woods in the fairy tales I was reading. I imagined bowls of hot porridge on the kitchen table; a cage with a child in it; a wolf dressed as an old woman. But this was a real town called Andover. It had policemen and telephone exchanges. It wasn't a fairy tale at all.

The policemen found three children with 'similar injuries' in other bedrooms, lying in bloodsoaked beds. In another bedroom they found a bloodstained axe with a seven-and-a-half-inch blade. I wondered why the reporter had measured the blade and written the measurements down like that. In that 'other bedroom', the paper said, there was a single bed that had been made up but not slept in. Was that important, that it hadn't been slept in? Was that supposed to mean something?

They found Bibles by the side of all the beds, and by the telephone in the hall. That didn't surprise me. This was a Brethren home. You'd always have Bibles by the bed and by the telephone in the hall. You'd have them in other places in the house too.

Blood on the walls, blood on the floor, blood on the hanging man's pyjamas and on his bare feet.

Roger Panes had left a note. He'd written:

There's never been such a wicked man. This house will have to be left empty or bulldozed. You go to the Brethren. I trust they will take you in. Cry to God for mercy for you all and the dear children. The Lord is coming very soon.

When he finished writing those words, he had folded up the piece of paper, put it in the pocket of his trousers, then folded the trousers and placed them on the chair by the bed that had not been slept in. Then he'd gone downstairs for the axe.

*You go to the Brethren*, he'd written. *I trust they will take you in.*

The police went to the local Brethren Meeting Room and found the name of a Mr Fennell, the Brethren leader in Andover, written on the board outside the door. They went to Mr Fennell's house to ask him some questions.

'Roger Panes,' Mr Fennell told them, 'was shut up during November 1973, because of the way he treated another member of the Brethren over a minor technical offence, and shut up that person wilfully.'

Roger Panes had been *shut up* because he'd *shut up* someone else. That made complete sense to me, but the journalists didn't seem to understand it. They tried to explain *shutting up* to their readers, but they didn't do a very good job. I would have done a better one, I thought. If someone didn't abide by Brethren rules, I would have told them, they were like lepers. The Bible laid out very clear rules about lepers. They had to stay in their homes, isolated, until one of the priests – like my father – decided they would no longer infect the rest of the assembly.

Sometimes it would take days, sometimes weeks, to get such a man clean again. Sometimes the shut-up person got sick.

'What was this minor technical offence that Panes had "committed" according to your statement?' the judge had asked Mr Fennell at the inquest.

'He shut up that person wrongly,' Fennell said. 'That was not right. It was contrary to the accepted code and violations of the Divine Principles involved in the Brethren.'

Back then – at the age of nine – the story had woven itself into my nightmares. But now, reading it again, I had different questions. Did the judge ask what had driven Panes to murder? Or did he decide it was best not to pry? Did he tell himself that he had a duty to respect religious practice – however extreme – in the name of the freedom of belief that had so long been enshrined in the British way?

The police, still searching for motives, interviewed the family doctor. Roger Panes had been ill for a while, the GP told them, checking his files. On 21 February 1974, eleven days before the murders, he'd taken an overdose and been rushed to hospital. When a busy doctor in A&E had spoken to Mrs Panes about her husband's mental health, she said that was 'between him and God'. Panes had been sent home.

No one, not the family doctor or the hospital staff, had thought to ask Roger Panes what had been going on. Roger Panes was religious. No one wanted to interfere. It must have been easier to look away.

Throughout that winter, the 'shut-up' Roger Panes would have sat on his bed listening to the sounds of his children playing on the other side of the unlocked door: Graham, seven; Angela, six; and four-year-old Adrian. He would have been able to tell the time by the coming and going of his wife's car as she took the children to Meeting or to school. He would have heard her telling them to hurry up, straighten their clothes, keep their voices down. He might have heard her crying. Daddy wasn't well, she might have said, as she placed his food on a tray outside his door yet again. Once a week or so he would have heard different cars on the gravel outside the house as a pair of ministering brothers arrived to interrogate him. Consigned to silence for so long, he must have been startled by the sound of his own voice.

'There's never been such a wicked man,' he wrote. They'd never get that house clean again. 'This house will have to be left empty or bulldozed.'

At the inquest, a hundred Brethren turned out to fill the gallery in their hats, headscarves and suits, carrying their Bibles. They'd been told to give a show of strength, a testimony of their faith. But someone must also have known that by occupying all those seats, they'd keep most of the journalists out.

When my father thumped his fist on the steering wheel that day, it was because the Roger Panes story had broken. After the Andover Tragedy we understood that there was no rescuing our family members and others who were still with the Jims. They might as well have been living on the other side of a great wall. They'd have to find their way out by themselves.

# 10

When I think of the life my father lived after Aberdeen, it reminds me of the whirlpool I used to watch in the plughole of the bath as a very small child, that spiralling tunnel I feared would suck me down with it into the darkness. My father had been running from it – whatever the 'it' was – all his life; now he was running like the frantic Tristram Shandy, leaping in and out of windows, stacking the chips, staying up all night: *faster, faster, before Death catches you.* When Death caught you – and he would – there'd be a reckoning. You'd be in trouble.

'If he'd let your mother keep control of the money after Aberdeen,' one of the cousins told me a year or so ago, 'things might have been different.'

Her husband corrected her: 'Your mother couldn't have stopped him. No one could have stopped him. After Aberdeen, your father was a different man.'

'He had a kind of excess about him,' Vincent Joyce said. While most people would come to Wick parties with a single bottle of wine, my father would bring a whole case. When Vincent told him about a new camera that had just come out, and that he knew he'd never be able to afford, my father went and bought it for him. If the whole cast went out for dinner after a performance, my father would foot the entire bill.

It must have been that hands-in-the-sweet-jar thing, I want to say. He must have felt that unless he could cram as many sweets as possible into his mouth all at once, someone was going to take the jar away from him. I knew what that felt like. I often felt the urge to grab everything, eat everything, read everything – *Quick now, be quick, they're coming* – before someone came and took the book or the sweets away, and then I'd be in trouble again.

My father was like that at home, too. Two years after we left the Brethren he decided it was time we moved to a much larger house. Although my mother agreed, she did not think we could afford to buy a house as big and showy as the one he settled on. But he bought it anyway. It had five bedrooms, an acre of land, a carved oak drinks bar as big as anything you might see in a small pub, a sweeping drive, and a double garage. That was important, because my father had started buying cars.

Vincent told me that the first time he visited us in our new house up on the hill there'd been two Jaguars parked on the front drive, next to the large emerald-green Ford Cortina estate my father had just bought my mother. My father told Vincent he couldn't decide which Jaguar model to buy, so he'd brought them both home to test-drive. He handed Vincent the keys and asked him to make the decision. One of the cars, Vincent remembered, had dual fuel tanks. He'd never seen a car with dual tanks before.

One of my father's cousins told me that my father had several accidents through the 1970s. He parked one of his cars on the drive outside our new house without properly engaging the handbrake, and it rolled down the slope and into a parked car on the road. Another time he drove into the back of a parked lorry as he was returning home from a rehearsal. He must have been drinking, I thought, remembering the empty bottles of Scotch I'd seen in the boot of the car.

My cousin had lowered her voice to a whisper: 'Sometimes I wondered if he'd been trying to … you know.'

She meant, I realised, *trying to kill himself*. It had never occurred to me before. He'd had so many accidents, so many near-misses; more than most people had in a lifetime.

He was also visiting another woman, and not telling my mother about it. I discovered this new secret of my father's by accident when I was eleven. When I wasn't needed at home, I'd taken to walking. It was an excuse to get out of the noisy new house full of quarrels and television, my mother's lists of chores, and my father's irritations. Even in this new world he'd found, he was still losing his temper at home. I would walk through the wood beyond the park, or along the muddy track that began at the end of the cul-de-sac that curled around the back of our house, and find a spot to sit and read.

The path followed a wooded ridge between suburban gardens and high fences. At one point a solid fence had been replaced with chicken wire, and from a bench near there I could look down onto several back gardens and across a pretty little estate – box-shaped new houses built around a green. I liked watching the people coming and going down there, neighbours talking over garden walls, children kicking balls around, women hanging out washing, men lighting barbecues as dusk fell. I liked knowing they couldn't see me. Sometimes I'd take my father's binoculars.

One Saturday afternoon, when my father was supposed to be away on a business trip and I'd slipped away to the bench on the high path, I looked up from my book to see my father's Jaguar drive into view and park among the cars around the green. I put my book away, leaned forward to see better through the gap in the fence, pressed the binoculars to my eyes, adjusted the focus. A smiling woman stepped out of the car with two children. My father climbed out of the other side with bags of shopping; neighbours looked up from their hedge-cutting or car-cleaning and waved. He called back, made a joke that I could not hear. They laughed.

What I had seen was interesting and strange, but it didn't occur to me to tell anyone, nor did I know how to interpret it. It was just another secret to be added to the others I had kept for my father. There was the radio I knew he kept hidden in the boot of the car in the days when radios were banned, the forbidden newspapers I saw him reading, the cinema tickets I found, the promise he broke. This new mystery wove through our new life in our new house like a red ribbon. I did not know what it meant, but I cherished it. It was my secret. I began to look for reasons to slip out again, to return to my watch post. I kept the binoculars by the back door next to my wellies.

Our big house, with its huge windows and garden, seemed to be waiting for something. At night, when I lay awake long after my brothers had fallen asleep, it sometimes felt to me as if the walls had become very thin, as if we might all blow away in the slightest wind.

# II

The tipping point of my parents' now-struggling marriage was not my mother's discovery of the woman I'd seen through the binoculars – my mother didn't know about her yet – or my father's disappearance into the world of theatre and art, or the vast sums of money he was spending. It was the trip we took across Europe in the summer of 1975.

It was the year Margaret Thatcher became leader of the opposition, the year the Yorkshire Ripper began his hammer attacks, the year the IRA bombed Green Park tube station. I was ten, nearly eleven, my older brother twelve, my younger brother nine, and the twins five. My father had rented a Dormobile, a shiny brand-new tank of a vehicle. He took us to see it in the showroom, demonstrating to my mother the seats that folded down to make beds, the tent that attached to the side, the roof that tipped up to make bunk beds in the roof, the stove and the fridge and all the clever storage spaces. It was, I thought, beautiful. It had everything. It was perfect.

It proved to be the chamber in which my parents played out the last scenes of their marriage, up front in the driving compartment, with us children crammed together with the luggage in the back. There were no grand outbursts, only the slow burn of anger: my father slamming doors, the electric crackle of sighs, dark looks, and sharp intakes of breath. We were on the road for three weeks – from Calais down through France and Switzerland to Italy, and back up.

The day we left, I pulled off a flake of nail that had come loose on my right big toe. By the time we reached Calais my toe had swelled and reddened. By Paris, it was oozing pus. My mother found the pink Germolene antiseptic cream in the first-aid kit she'd brought, but in the heat the cream just melted and ran off.

My father's obsession with covering distances in record times overwhelmed him again, just as it had overwhelmed Tristram Shandy. Every day after breakfast we five children took our seats in the back, crushed into the tiny foam sofas that became beds at night, two striped seats that faced each other. My father drove through most of the daylight hours without ever stopping for more than a toilet break.

In the absence of air conditioning, the temperature rose the further south we went. My bare thighs stuck to the seat; my toe throbbed and pulsed. The windows steamed up. We soon tired of playing I-Spy. My brothers settled into games of cards. We read books for as long as we could before the car sickness took over.

French fields slid by beyond the edge of the motorway, beyond the net curtains that were tied into bows. Then Italian fields, birds, steeples of churches built high on hills, vineyards. I was ill. My skin crawled and I had to pull a blanket around myself as the thermometer in the back of the Dormobile climbed higher. When we stopped, my mother prepared little bowls of warm water for me, with two capfuls of disinfectant, to soak my foot in.

I remember very little of the towns we visited – a flash of the twisting streets of Milan; a shop in a Swiss town that sold cuckoo clocks; the bronze horses in St Mark's Square in Venice, rearing black shapes against a deep-blue sky. My father kept a piece of paper on his sun visor on which he recorded daily tallies of the distances we'd covered and the times he'd clocked up. We covered 350 miles one day, five hundred miles another. We stayed in campsites on the edges of famous cities where we'd arrive just before nightfall. He would have driven for longer each day if he could, but he knew we had to pitch the tent before dark. My mother would cook up a meal from a packet and put us to bed.

Each day there were more campsites and more nightfalls and more records broken. My mother, dressed in pretty summer dresses she'd made for the trip, gripped the seat or the car door as we drove, her knuckles white, her face grey. Then I was sick, and the back of the car smelled of vomit and Dettol. My father tried to engage us with stories and history about the cities we drove through, and when he had to battle to make himself heard over the sound of our squabbling he'd yell and shout, and occasionally thump the steering wheel. Then he'd drive faster, and my mother would grip the handle of the door even tighter.

During the JT Junior years my mother had covered the seats of public toilets with carefully arranged layers of toilet paper before she'd let us use them. It was what her mother had taught her. Generally, it was better not to use them at all, she'd say, unless you were really desperate. In France the campsite toilets were often muddy holes in sheds. You were supposed to put your feet on each side of the hole and squat. She made us wash our hands again and again, but we still got 'runny tummy', as she called it, and then my father complained about having to stop all the time to find toilets.

The swelling in my toe had spread to my entire foot. By the time we reached the Alps I could not walk. On the San Bernardino Pass I put my swollen foot deep into the white compacted snow by the side of the road. I thought it might burn a hole through to the other side of the earth. I was seeing things now; the clouds made faces and animals above me. I stayed there, staring up at the peak of the mountain, my entire leg immersed deep in the snow for a long time, praying for something – and *to* something – I couldn't name.

My father was already drafting the letter he'd give to my mother a few weeks after we returned to England. Wouldn't they both be happier living apart? Hadn't the holiday proved that? After all that trouble they'd had in the Jims, he wrote, their marriage didn't stand much of a chance. He'd start looking for a flat as soon as he could.

# 12

Our mother sat us all down around the kitchen table before school and told us that our father wouldn't be living with us any more. He would live nearby, and he'd visit and take us out for the day. She was very matter-of-fact about it. Everything would go on much the same, she said, although we would probably have to move out of the big house into a smaller one sometime soon.

I would have liked to denounce my father, but I wouldn't have known where to start. He'd left my mother to manage everything; he'd gone to live somewhere else; he had another family no one knew about; there were all those broken promises, all those secrets and lies. Instead, I excommunicated him. I withdrew from him. I told my brothers to tell him, when he called to take us all out for the day over the coming weeks, that I was doing my homework. I disappeared to my room and closed the door, or I went to Helen's house and stayed as long as I could. It was more than a year before I spoke to him again.

By the time the estate agents came to put a For Sale sign outside the big house a few months later, my mother had found us a three-storey terraced house near the seafront in Hove, with five bedrooms, where she could take in language students as lodgers to help pay our school fees. We kids all shared two rooms up in the attic; my mother took the bedroom with the dangerous, about-to-crack-open ceiling on the middle floor. That left two respectable rooms for 'paying guests', as my mother called them. These guests began to arrive as soon as my mother was sure the paint on their bedroom walls was dry.

The floorboards were rickety, and my mother did not have enough money to buy new carpets or to pay a man to cut and lay the rolls of carpet she'd brought from the big house. She set up the sewing machine on the kitchen table at night to cut smaller curtains from the larger ones. A couple of our first guests, a middle-aged Swedish builder and his wife, alarmed by the forking ravines my mother had shown them in her bedroom ceiling, found a local plasterer to fix it.

The sea was so close we could hear the waves breaking on the shingle beach at night. Seagulls screeched like ghosts on the roof above our beds. On stormy nights the wind howled in the chimneys and rattled the windows.

When I wasn't needed at home, or staying at the Marsdens' house, I walked miles along the promenade, to the lagoon with the little boats, through the derelict buildings and rusting metal of the harbour at Shoreham, down across the mass of grey mudflats that the sea left behind when the tide was out. From deep under the mud, wormlike creatures had cast up sand coils, as if they'd sloughed off their skins. In the rock pools that the sea had gouged out around the edges of the concrete groynes there were crabs and tiny red sea anemones and seaweeds with beautiful names like bladderwrack and mermaid's purse. I brought home shiny streamers of it and hung them on the wall of our attic bedroom.

In 1976, the first year we lived in the new house, a heatwave turned everything to sweat and seemed to bring the hot sky down around us. Plagues of ladybirds covered the white hotel façades along the seafront. The buildings undulated and flickered with their moving bodies. They looked as if they were bleeding. When I walked across the garden to bring in the washing, ladybirds crunched under my heavy school shoes. They'd fly out of drawers, heavy, beautiful, lumbering things. I found them in my clothes and in my shoes. We had to keep the doors and windows shut to keep them out.

I read the Narnia books through that long summer holiday, and Laura Ingalls Wilder's *Little House on the Prairie* and *The Long Winter*. I wrote stories for the twins in which they built boats when floodwaters engulfed their town, or built log cabins to live out a long winter, or found ingenious ways of escaping monsters made of ice or seaweed. We watched episodes of *Robinson Crusoe* together on the television every morning. My fantasies of flight to a mysterious island opened up again. Now in my daydreams Jack and I would be weaving cabins and treehouses from young branches and twigs on a desert island. When Crusoe fixed his eyes on the horizon and blew into his conch shell in the hope that someone would reply, it was my mouth he blew through. I still imagined that a voice might reply from somewhere Out There.

That autumn, someone told my grandfather that my father had gone on holiday with 'another woman' only months after leaving my mother. My grandfather summoned my father and challenged him – 'What on *airth* were you thinking?'

Perhaps he expected my father to repent. Perhaps he even thought he could force his giant son to his knees and into prayer as he'd done years before; but my father didn't back down. Instead, now six foot four and twenty stone, educated and articulate, he shouted back, thumped his fists, raised his voice louder. He told my grandfather that he was going to live his life exactly as he chose, that my grandfather had no right, no *right*, to admonish him. He could go to hell.

Between them that day my father and grandfather whipped up a tempest that drove my grandmother running from the house. While my poor grandfather was in mid-invective, mid-sentence, mid-competition with his wayward son for the loudest, most outraged denunciation, he ruptured a plaque in his heart and fell to the ground clutching his chest. The paramedics who arrived half an hour later failed to revive him.

That was the autumn my father killed my grandfather.

That's not what anyone actually said, of course, but it's what my father believed, and what he thought other people were thinking. He'd never been able to forgive himself, he told me a few weeks before he died.

Kez had been right to get me to use the word 'Aftermath' for the third box file of my father's papers. These were violent aftershocks, earth shudders and rifts, occurring not along a natural geological faultline, but along a human-made one. I think of the paramedics trying to resuscitate my grandfather, my grandmother weeping and praying, my father looking on, ashen, the words he'd used to denounce his father circling round and round in his brain.

No one told us children until much later about the row that killed our grandfather. How could they? He had had a heart attack, they said. He'd gone to be with the Lord, our grandmother said. Coming so soon after my father's disappearance and in the muddied wake of Aberdeen, my grandfather's death left me winded and afraid. Where had he gone? Was he with the Lord Jesus? Why were they putting his body into the ground? What would happen to it when the Rapture came? Why was my father crying? I'd never seen him cry before. Brethren hadn't cried about death. It was supposed to be something to be glad about, because it meant the dead person was with the Lord.

At the Marsdens' dinner table in the weeks following my grandfather's death, something – a thought, an image, a question – would set me off into shuddering, gasping sobs, and I'd run for the refuge of the caravan. Eventually Helen's mother told me enough was enough. My grandfather had gone to a better place, she said. He was with Jesus. He was in heaven with the angels.

'But how do you *know*?' I wailed. Not knowing where my grandfather had gone tormented me. Was he really in heaven? He had believed in the Lord, I knew that, but he hadn't always been kind or good or right. Had he been good enough to get a place in heaven? Or was he in hell, being burned for ever and ever? If he was in heaven, would my grandmother be able to find him when she went up there in the Rapture? The mansion that the Lord Jesus had made had a thousand rooms. Where would she begin to look?

None of us knew for certain where my grandfather had gone, Mrs Marsden said firmly, and it wasn't for any of us *to* know. We'd find out in good time.

No one had ever talked like that in the Brethren. They'd have shot those panicked questions of mine down with the artillery fire of scriptural quotation. It was all right not to know, Mrs Marsden said. This was obvious to her, but it astonished me to hear it said in plain words like that. If it was true, it meant I didn't have to try to map the rooms in the heavenly mansion any more, or figure out who went where, or understand the degree of transparency of the Holy Ghost. There were things I would never figure out, Mrs Marsden said, no matter how hard I read my Bible. I was suddenly exhausted. I slept for twelve hours that night.

Would it have helped my father to confess to someone? Would it have eased his mind if he'd been shut up by Brethren priests until he'd come right with the Lord? Although his new acting friends would have told him his father's death was not his fault, he had to live with the guilt, muddle his way through it, or distract himself. He found consolation in the roulette table.

My brothers knew about the casino before I did, though they didn't know what it was, or what my father did there. After my grandfather's death, after I'd seen my father cry, I sometimes agreed to come out with him when he took my siblings out for the day, but my brothers were still seeing much more of him than I was. He'd bought season tickets for Brighton and Hove Albion, so on many Saturdays during the football season he'd pick them up and they'd be gone for a few hours.

Sometimes he'd take all five of us to a park or a carnival. Occasionally on the way back he'd park the car on a certain street, and leave us there for an hour or so while he went off to what he would call 'a business meeting'. My younger brother whispered that he was 'getting money' somewhere called 'Sergeant York's'. It was a secret, he said. He was going to get enough money to take us all to America. My father had new secrets, and I was curious. But the windows at Sergeant York's were too high to see anything through.

Years later, my younger brother told me that my father had promised him a day of treats for his twelfth birthday. This would have been March 1978. My brother had put on his favourite shirt and trousers, and washed and brushed his hair carefully. My father arrived two hours late. Once they were in the car he told my brother that first he had to make a trip to Sergeant York's, but as it was his birthday, he was going to give him all the money he won. They shook hands. He wouldn't be long, he said after he'd parked the car in the usual spot; just a few turns of the wheel, then they'd get going.

Two hours later he returned to the car, deflated and stony-faced.

'I guess it just isn't your lucky day, son,' he told my brother, slamming the door hard, and jamming the car into gear before taking him home.

'Poor fella,' my brother said when he told me this story years later. Of course he meant our father, not himself.

We continued to be baffled by our father's many derelictions right up till his End Days, but they fascinated us too. His behaviour was often so outrageous that we'd struggle to get people to believe us when we told them about it, or they'd look so shocked and upset that most of the time we just passed those stories between ourselves. Perhaps we thought that if we told them enough times, one of us might finally understand him.

# 13

I started at a new school just a few months after my grandfather died. I'd done well enough at the Eleven-plus to have won a full scholarship to a selective independent girls' school, housed in a grand building on a hill with a library on the very top floor that looked out over the sea. My school fees, uniform and books would all be paid for until I finished my A-Levels. My mother was both proud and relieved. My father had fallen behind with my brothers' school fees, so she'd had to take on more accountancy work and more language students as paying guests to try to keep up with the payments.

Helen telephoned to tell me she was going to the private Catholic girls' school over on the other side of Brighton. We'd be separated. At least she'd get to wear that lovely blue uniform, I told her, trying not to cry. My new uniform was a horrible bottle-green. We'd still see each other just as much, wouldn't we? I asked. And though she told me we'd be best friends forever, we both knew that those different-coloured uniforms would change everything. Brighton and Hove High School girls didn't mix with the girls from St Mary's. There wasn't any particular animosity between the schools, it was just that they were worlds apart.

My mother took me to have my hair cut for the first time the day we went to buy my new uniform. The hairdresser put me in the chair and cranked it up. She examined the two thick ropes of plaits I'd worn down my back since I was a very small child. Was I *sure*? I nodded. My mother nodded. The hairdresser still hung back.

'I can do it myself,' I said, as my mother flashed me a look that said, *Mind your manners*. I showed the hairdresser where I wanted the plaits cut, a few inches below my shoulders, but it was my mother she looked at when she made the first scissor-sawing assault on my hair. But the scissors wouldn't cut – the plait was too thick. That made my mother laugh, and then we were all laughing. The hairdresser went to fetch a bigger pair of scissors from the high shelf. And then it was done; the plaits unravelled, and my curls were trimmed into a shoulder-length bob. It looked good, I thought, and for weeks I was running my fingers through it, stealing glances in shop windows, wondering why I hadn't just done it myself years before.

I had grown tired of the foggy, upside-down, vertigo-ed dream world I'd lived in since Aberdeen. I'd begun to crave facts, certainties and meanings, walls that didn't crumble and give way when I pressed against them. Brighton and Hove High School for Girls was a gift for a child with a head full of difficult questions. It had been set up by two suffragist sisters in the latter part of the nineteenth century to teach girls the full range of academic subjects, including those – such as Greek and Latin and rhetoric – that had traditionally been taught only to boys. Most of my new teachers were sceptical of orthodoxies; many of them had travelled widely and read several languages; some of them were mavericks and misfits.

My history teacher, for instance, would write out difficult questions about the Corn Laws or the First Reform Bill on the blackboard and then answer them, sometimes giving the answers a right-wing spin, sometimes a left-wing spin. She'd take up a position, argue it, and then provoke us to disagree with her and put together an alternative case. I was a shy and awkward teenager, but in these classes, mesmerised, I'd forget myself, ignore the blood rising to my cheeks, and speak. Sometimes she praised me, no matter how much I blushed and stuttered out my answer.

'Put that in your essay,' she'd say. 'Then argue the opposite position. Make me think you believe both sides are true. Then show me why you think one side is more credible than the other.' Credible. Plausible. Non-orthodox. Empirical. The new words I was learning in these lessons brought my questions into sharper focus.

'Take nothing on trust,' she would tell the class. 'You have to make up your own minds as you go along, make them up as best you can. To do that you must be able to see several sides at once.'

'Questions,' she'd write out in looping letters on the black-board, 'are sometimes more important than answers.'

She didn't know I'd spent the first years of my life among fundamentalist Christians, of course. I was just one of the scores of young women she taught. We all had histories.

'The Bible is an old book written by human beings,' she said once, and I began to sweat, the heat rising up through my body to my face. 'It's been translated from one language to another to another. I'm not saying it isn't important, just that it was written in a particular time and place by particular people. Never trust anyone who tells you that they know exactly what it means.'

I remembered listening to my father talking about the *current* truth, the 'new light', the truth that was being unfolded to the Brethren alone by the Lord at that particular moment. If JT Junior told them that the Lord had sent him 'new light', they believed him. He had so much power. Someone like JT Junior could wipe out all previous truths with a 'new light' truth.

It wasn't just Mrs Marsden and my teachers who gave me answers – inadvertently perhaps – to some of the questions that vexed me. Over the next few years I gravitated towards a succession of outliers: musicians, poets, and people my mother would have called hippies. They didn't lecture me or tell me what I should be thinking. They asked me questions, exciting ones. They taught me to formulate more interesting questions than the theological ones that had always bothered me. They helped me find my way back to my beyond-the-pale father, and then

I began to ask him some of those questions too. They taught me how to argue back when I didn't agree with something.

When our Renton Brethren aunt and uncle invited me to spend a week of the summer holidays with my three girl cousins, one still very young and the other two close to my own age, I accepted. I was fourteen. I liked my cousins. The Rentons, I knew, were not like the Jims. My cousins had explained all that to me once, when I'd seen them at our grandparents'. They believed lots of the same things as the Jims, but they weren't so strict. They weren't supposed to eat at the same table with people outside their fellowship, I knew, but because I was family and not grown-up yet, they probably wouldn't worry about that. They were Christians, I told myself, trying to quell a sense of dread. They were good people, my blood; they couldn't do me any harm. My mother packed my Bible into my suitcase. When she dropped me off at the station, she told me that if my aunt and uncle asked me to go with them to the Meeting, I should probably go.

Life in the Rentons, it turned out, was much more permissive than in the Taylorite Exclusive Brethren, but it was still austere. My aunt and uncle and cousins attended Meeting several times a week; they had no radio, television or pop music; my uncle and aunt Gave Thanks just as we had done, and their talk always looped back, as I expected, to the Lord and the scriptures. When we were alone my two older cousins asked about the music I liked and the television programmes I watched and the boys I knew. I was, they told me, so very lucky not to be any kind of Brethren any more.

At every meal we ate together, my kindly aunt and uncle cross-questioned me about my belief and my knowledge of the Bible, as I knew they would. With my cousins listening nervously, my half-formed answers seemed shabby things. While I might have been able to defend a position about the impact of *laissez-faire* economics, or the degree to which the Great Depression contributed to the rise of fascism, my new rhetorical skills and facts counted for nothing here.

I wasn't at all sure what I *did* think about most of the things my aunt and uncle asked about. None of my school friends were interested in God or the Bible, or the nature of sin or grace or redemption, so while I often thought about those things, I hadn't talked to anyone else about them. I had wanted to, though. They still mattered to me. But now that I was actually being cross-questioned, I couldn't produce the certainties and opinions my aunt and uncle wanted from me. My head swam. I began to change the subject every time I saw it veer back towards the Lord and to me.

I managed only one small, rather inept, act of insurrection that week. When my uncle asked whether my science teachers had managed to persuade me that I'd once been a monkey, I told him I thought he was quite wrong about all of that, and that what Darwin thought was a lot more complicated. Of course my aunt and uncle had a set of polished counter-arguments about the age of the earth and the seven days of creation. I did not know enough to be able to refute them, but my history teacher, I told myself as I retreated from the table, would have called it *a good start*. Though I had better things to do with my time than defend Darwin's ideas against creationists, and though I had no intention of returning to the subject with my aunt and uncle, I knew I would have to read more books if I was going to understand how natural selection worked. I wasn't going to let myself flounder about like that again.

The elderly Renton Brethren assembly that my uncle and aunt's family attended in west London was very small. The men talked in just the same way I remembered, standing to speak in spasmodic flurries as the Spirit moved in and around the room and in and out of them, unfolding the nuances of the current truth. The women were still silent, sitting in rows at the back in their bows and hats, hands folded on their laps; the Spirit did not speak through Renton Brethren women either, and that still enraged me. The hymn-singing sounded the same. But I was no longer anxious to follow the angels-on-a-pinhead exegesis, and although I was struck by the fervour of their devotion, their absolutism and hard lines frightened me.

Something shifted inside my head in that west London Meeting Room. If the Apostle Paul thought that women should be completely subject to the rules of men, if he thought the Spirit was too good for them, then Paul was *wrong*. Hadn't he been just a man after all? A particular man in a particular place at a particular time? Hadn't he had flaws and prejudices, like all human beings?

What would I have been like, I wondered now, if my parents had joined the Renton Brethren? Or if they'd stayed in the

Jims? How would I have swallowed my rage and sense of injustice, avoided looking at all those contradictions? And what future would there have been for me as a Brethren woman? My two teenage cousins were not supposed to marry outside the Brethren. If they did, they'd drive a wedge between themselves and their parents. But, they told me, there were no boys in their Meeting young enough for either of them to marry. They were going to become old maids, they wailed, eyes wide. Did I know, they said again, how lucky I was?

# 14

I had a responsibility to do something with this freedom of mine, I told myself on my return home. I needed to do something reckless and brave. When my younger brother, then thirteen, told me he'd been inside the squatters' house on the other side of the road while I was away, and that there were drug dealers living there who had the most amazing record collection, I told him he *had* to take me there too.

Whenever we passed the squatters' house, my mother tutted at the unkempt garden, at the peeling paint and the tattered curtains hanging at the windows. I heard neighbours say it was a disgrace. The police should break in, they said, throw those dreadful people out and board the place up with those metal grilles they used. No one in the neighbouring Sackville

Gardens, they said, would stand for that sort of thing on their street.

So my brother and I hung about on the pavement outside trying to look inconspicuous for at least thirty minutes before we slipped down the side passage into the overgrown garden at the back of the squat. By the time we pushed through the long grass and shrubs to the door, we were covered in cuckoo spit, pollen and cobwebs. My brother knocked three times before a man in his mid-thirties with a moustache and shiny eyes appeared at a hatch in the boarded-up kitchen window. He looked like a picture of a leprechaun I'd seen once in a collection of Irish fairy tales.

'That's Chris,' my brother whispered. 'The other one's Alan.'

'Who've you brought with you today, little man?' Chris said as he shoved the door open with his shoulder. It was a joke, of course. My brother at the age of thirteen was six foot one. He was a handsome blond giant of a boy.

'This is my sister,' my brother said.

'Hello, sister,' said Chris. 'Do you have a name?'

There was something slow about the way Chris moved that made me think of the caterpillar on the toadstool from *Alice in Wonderland*. Alan, who we met later, was tall and mercurial. He had grown his straight hair long on one side to cover half of his face entirely. On the other side it was shaved. I'd seen the punks with their red, blue and green Mohican spikes all over Brighton. It was always hard not to stare at them. I tried not to stare at Alan.

My mother's house was pristine, threadbare and brightly coloured; theirs had broken sofas, marijuana plants and chess-boards. Books and records were scattered on the floor and piled high against the walls. Through cracks in doors I glimpsed mattresses pushed up into the corners of rooms, under more bookshelves and plants. Dust hung in the air where the sun slanted in. Soon my brother and I were visiting every few days, to return a book or pick up a new music tape they'd made for us. We'd slip down the side passage and into the garden, push through the overgrown shrubs and knock on the boarded-up back window.

Once we were inside, time moved differently. Chris and Alan's friends came and went to and from the house: artists, musicians and film-makers. They picked up work when they needed to, in a music shop or a bar or café for a few hours a week. My mother would have called them dropouts. The Brethren would have called them Satan's footsoldiers. They sold cannabis resin in small cellophane parcels – which meant, someone told me, they were definitely drug dealers. But they kept their promises. And they were kind.

I used the money I earned from my Saturday job at the newsagent's to buy charity-shop long silk floral dresses like those worn by the women I saw at the squat. I wore them with oversized sweaters and strings of beads. I lost weight. In the summer I wore Indian leather sandals, or sometimes went bare-foot. In the winter I wore Doc Martens boots. I bought joss sticks for my room.

At school I'd made friends with a beautiful Malaysian new girl. She noticed the henna I'd started using to colour my hair, and told me that in her country they made henna patterns on their hands. She was Hindu, and when I asked what that meant, she said no one had asked her that question since she'd come to Britain. She explained what her family practised and why, and told me why it was good to be a Hindu. She didn't know any Hindus in Britain. She and her brother and mother were living with their grandmother, who was Christian.

Why was she living with her grandmother? I asked. Her father had died, she said. Before they left Malaysia her little brother had lit the fire for the funeral pyre they burned him on. Why had it been her brother who had done that? I wanted to ask. Why hadn't they let her do it? Did Hindus consider her 'just a girl' too? But when she'd talked about the funeral pyre her eyes were full of tears, so I changed the subject.

In the last weeks of the summer of 1979, when I had just turned fifteen, when my mother was out at her new job working as an accountant in a neighbouring town, and the twins were busy or playing with friends, my brother and I would slip across to Chris and Alan's smoky living room. Over there in the half-light I didn't worry about blushing or stammering. No one noticed. We'd perch up against beanbags or cushions and play chess or backgammon, but mostly we were there, like everyone else, to listen to music. Alan played Kraftwerk and Roxy Music and Joy Division. Chris played Bowie, Lou Reed and Iggy Pop. I liked the music Chris played best. We drank tea, took occasional nervous drags from the joints people passed round, and listened to Chris and Alan argue about the new albums they brought home and played loud on their huge speakers.

'Did you feel anything *this* time?' my brother would ask as we crossed the road back to our house for dinner. And I'd shake my head. Neither of us dared inhale, so although I sometimes felt light-headed and heavy-limbed, I knew that, like him, I was never really stoned. It was LSD I wanted to take. I'd been asking Chris about the things he'd seen when he was tripping, but he said LSD wasn't good for people who had bad dreams. It was meditation I needed, he said, not acid. At fifteen, I was much too young to take LSD.

'When I'm sixteen then?' I asked. But he just laughed and shook his head.

He gave me a leaflet for a meditation course. I walked to the old Salvation Army Hall one Saturday afternoon after work, found the administrator for the adult education section, and signed up for twelve weeks of Sunday-afternoon classes, paying for them with my savings. When that course came to an end, I signed up for a communication class run by the same teachers. I sat cross-legged in a darkened room opposite my cross-legged partner while we repeated the phrase *All cows eat grass*. All language was inherently empty, the instructor explained, but we could learn to communicate deep and complex thoughts and feelings through apparently meaningless phrases.

For thirty minutes my partner would repeat the words *All cows eat grass* to me. Then for thirty minutes I'd say it to him. In between our weekly sessions we were supposed to practise this technique – locking eyes with strangers at bus stops, in queues and cafés – *It's cold today*, I'd say intensely. *Is the bus delayed?* What I was really saying in my mind was *Isn't life fasci-nating?* Or *I understand your pain.*

Now I practised making eye contact with every customer who bought sweets or a paper at the newsagent's I worked in on Saturdays, particularly the ones who were shy or in a rush. *That's twenty-seven pence change*, I'd say, smiling, projecting love, thinking of those cows eating grass. Every encounter, my meditation teachers reminded me, was sacred. Every man and woman on the other side of my counter had a deep secret place I was supposed to reach.

It was embarrassing at first, but I stopped blushing when I saw the powerful effects my newly fierce attention had on people. The most misanthropic customers found excuses to linger at the counter and talk. I began to extend the range of my questions. That shirt's a good colour on you – is blue your favourite colour? Why do you buy that particular newspaper rather than that one? Are you reading anything interesting? Have you ever memorised any poetry?

At the squat, Chris had begun to ask questions about my father.

'Why roulette?' he asked as he showed me how to roll the joint that everyone especially admired, the one that forked in the middle and was made of six long Rizla papers. 'I mean, is there something about a roulette wheel that's different from slot machines?'

I'd been so spellbound by the question that I missed seeing the way he made the fork in the middle of the joint.

'Was there a connection,' he asked, 'between your father losing his belief in God and starting to gamble?'

'I don't know,' I said, thinking about the tallies of black and red numbers I'd seen scattered on scraps of paper around the car. How could anyone know?

'He has a number system,' I said, crumbling the resin down the middle of the long trough of tobacco cradled in Chris's hand.

'If he really thinks he can predict what number is going to come up next,' Chris said, 'that's *amazing*. I mean, if he does – and your father is smart, right? – then he believes humans can predict the future. Does he think he still has a hotline to God?'

'I don't know what he thinks,' I said. 'I haven't asked him about that.' I hadn't really asked him about anything.

'Would he *mind* you asking?' Chris said, as he showed me how to make the little twist of paper at the end to keep the tobacco and the weed in. 'I mean, could you ask him questions like that?'

# 15

They'd put *Macbeth* onto the O-Level syllabus, I told my father on the phone the next time he called. Could he take me to see a performance? The teachers had said we were supposed to see at least one production if we could.

He'd seen Anthony Hopkins play Macbeth in 1972, and Helen Mirren play Lady Macbeth in 1975, but the very best performance of the play *ever staged*, he said, with his usual maddening hyperbole, was the Ian McKellen–Judi Dench RSC production, which he'd now seen four times. It was on again at the Young Vic. Good thing I'd mentioned it. He'd get us tickets.

I'd once dreamed of railing at my father for his broken promises, for the fact that he'd made life so hard for my mother, but now I wanted more than anything to know if he thought the future was knowable. As soon as I got into the car he put on a tape of the Hollies' 'The Air That I Breathe', and I had to bite my lip so that I wouldn't cry. Chris and Alan would have said that the Hollies were trite, but I didn't care. I was sure he'd put on that song just for me.

In my mind I was up on the armrest again, my body through the sunroof, my arms outstretched like a bird, the wind whipping my plaits against my face.

Before, I'd always been in the back seat with the twins. Now I had the front passenger seat all to myself, and had the run of the glove compartment where my father kept his precious tapes. 'Have you still got "Kodachrome"?' I asked coolly as I rummaged through it. '"Mother and Child Reunion"?'

We'd set off late, so soon he was driving at ninety miles an hour up a crowded A23 towards London. Even as the rain began, he was overtaking all the other cars, his foot pressed down hard on the accelerator.

For the first twenty minutes or so I put on all the old songs my father had played repeatedly in the upside-down days after we left the Brethren: 'Bridge Over Troubled Water', 'Morningtown Ride', 'Sinner Man': *Sinner Man, where you gonna run to?* I told myself he must be remembering all the same things I did from those days, but Chris's voice was in my head: *None of us really know what's going on inside other people, right?* Perhaps Chris was right. We were all dreamers; life was a dream.

I was relieved when, somewhere north of Crawley, my father slowed down a little and began to lecture me about the play. How much did I know about *Macbeth*? he began, but he wasn't really interested in my answer. He wanted to tell me about everything he had in the *Macbeth* drawer in the filing cabinet in his brain: every interpretation Wilson Knight had ever made of the play, the connection to the Scottish witchcraft trials, what hubris meant, what the tragic flaw meant in relation to the play, Shakespeare's obsession with sin and blood and stains, and the relationship between the stains and puritanism.

'If Macbeth had refused the call of the witches,' I asked him, desperate to stop the flood of his talk, 'if he'd *not* actually killed Duncan, would Birnam Wood still have come to Dunsinane?'

My father stopped talking. He smiled.

'Interesting question,' he said. He was thinking.

Then he turned the music down and began to recite Yeats's 'Leda and the Swan' slowly, assuming I was keeping up, getting his inference, understanding how the complex poem answered the question I'd asked.

As he reached *A shudder in the loins engenders there*, his voice began to break. The rain was now hammering the windscreen in great lashing strokes. *The broken wall, the burning roof and tower* …

The wipers screeched across the glass, because the rubber had perished and he hadn't bothered to replace it. We were swerving towards the side of the road, and he was still beating out the rhythm on the steering wheel …

*And-Ag-a-mem-non-dead.*

Suddenly we were in a ditch, white fog lights and red hazard lights refracting and splitting through the rainwater, the long rising and falling of truck horns as they swerved around us.

While we sat waiting for the towtruck, the rain running like a dark river over the car, he'd started up a monologue about Yeats's gyres, by way of explaining how the poem answered my question. His words spiralled out and spiralled back, just as his preaching once had. You just had to keep up, concentrate.

I might have been furious with him for nearly getting us killed, for making us miss the play, for lecturing me, but I wasn't. I had my father to myself, and I wanted to understand about the gyres, and the patterns the rain made on the windows in the dark were so beautiful.

'Yeats believed,' he said, 'that time was like a necklace of intersecting spirals.'

He tried to draw the shape in the air with his huge hands, but he couldn't make it work, so he reached into the inside pocket of his jacket and sketched the pattern on the back of a betting slip:

'The spirals of the new gyre start to spool outwards here,' he said, adding arrows to his diagram, circling the axis points with his red pen, 'just as the last gyre is coming down into its end. See? Each new gyre of history starts with a kind of violent annunciation at an axis point: Zeus turned into a swan; he seduced Leda. That's there at the axis, here. And then the gyres open out: Leda gave birth to Helen; then Helen's beauty brought the Trojan wars into being. It spirals out and out – see? – until everyone's caught up in it. Then a new axis point opens inside the gyre here – see? The angel Gabriel visited Mary. That's another collision between man and god, of course. Mary gave birth to Jesus, and Jesus ended up crucified, and before you know it, two millennia of Christianity have come into being. It spins out and out, and this time the burning walls are monasteries and abbeys and country churches …'

I'm thinking of the wings beating above the two staggering girls, Mary and Leda, already pregnant, already incubating, feathers everywhere.

'History spirals out from moments of violence like that,' my father continued.

'It was rape,' I said. 'Not seduction.'

'What?'

'You said Zeus seduced Leda. He didn't – he raped her.'

'History isn't *kind*,' he said, as though I was being sentimental. 'It's violent and unstoppable; it builds to bloody crescendos.' He was beating out the rhythm on the steering wheel again:

*And-Ag-a-mem-non-dead.*

We're all caught up in history, I thought, like the girl on the swan god's nape.

After the towtruck finally arrived and pulled us out of the ditch, and we got going again, and when my father had parked and managed to persuade the ushers to let us creep into the back of the theatre, we caught McKellen doing his 'Tomorrow, and tomorrow, and tomorrow' speech. I began to see it all more clearly: the gyres and the witches and the whole relentless unravelling. Macbeth knew exactly what he was doing. Even if he suspected there'd be a price to pay for his apparent invincibility, for seeing out his course, he just *didn't know how to stop.* He turned himself into his own private gyre. My father was doing that too. He didn't know how to stop either.

'I am in blood Stepped in so far,' Macbeth mutters to himself, 'that, should I wade no more, Returning were as tedious as go o'er.'

He imagined himself wading through a river of blood. He was up to his thighs in it. But it was too far to go back, so he told himself he might as well just keep going, let the gyre run its course, because he couldn't stop it.

My father must have felt that way too, I thought, when he looked at the final demands that piled up unopened on his desk, when he looked at the pattern of numbers he believed he'd discovered. Neither he nor Macbeth knew what lay ahead, but they had to run their course.

Did my father think the future was knowable? I still didn't know, but I could understand why he might have wanted to believe that it was. It was all going to come right, he thought: with that One Big Win at roulette he'd be redeemed, lifted off the earth as it crashed and burned into the thunder and lightning, earthquakes and plague of the Tribulation.

# 16

Through the winter of 1980 my father drove me to see plays in London, in Bristol, and in small theatres along the south coast. We talked about music, morality, Bergman and Shakespeare, his gambling system, his new diet, about the books I was reading. But I still couldn't find a way of putting into words the questions about God and free will that I wanted to ask. He brought me books to read each week, ragged copies from his own growing collection and new ones he'd buy from local bookshops, including those he kept returning to: novels by E.M. Forster and Saul Bellow, Joyce's 'The Dead' and Sterne's *Tristram Shandy*.

Our conversations were not always easy. Those early years of locked doors, banned books and secrets had made me curious in a starved, urgent kind of way, convinced that the now-open door would swing shut at any moment, that the grown-ups would suddenly repent of their looseness or indiscretion, or that the page I was reading would be torn out before my eyes. And though I wanted to know what he thought, I hated being lectured at. I'd spent too much time not being allowed to ask questions or interrupt. He'd spent too much time expecting not to be interrupted, particularly by women.

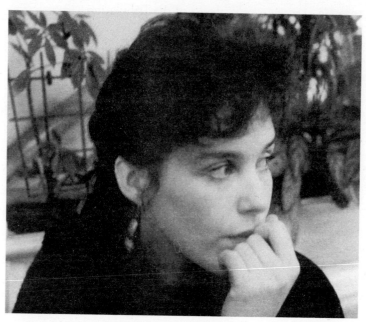

A photograph of me taken by my father in a
theatre foyer in 1980

We disagreed; sometimes one of us would shout 'Nonsense!' or 'Don't be absurd!' or even 'Bollocks!' I got better at challenging him. He got better at appearing to listen while still maintaining his position. And running through everything was always a shared feeling of urgency, a sense that time was running out.

At home, my mother and I did not speak of the defection that had broken our close domestic alliance. I was often away from home now, not just with my father but with friends, drifting around the vintage clothes shops of Brighton, reading in a park, working at the newsagent's, or listening to music in Chris and Alan's squat. I no longer helped out much around the house.

My mother made me a bedroom in what had been the pantry so that I could study for my exams away from my siblings. It was a surprise. She'd squeezed a single bed and a chest of drawers in there, made a desk from an old sewing-machine-table base to which she had attached a long slab of wood she'd found in a skip and varnished to a high shine. Behind the bed she hung a curtain to hide the pantry shelves. She made it out of the blue-and-green-striped fabric she'd salvaged from the old bedspread on her and my father's bed. She'd cleared a space for my school books on the shelves between the plastic boxes of oats and the rice and the boxes of Smash powdered potato. I was delighted. We were both embarrassed when I hugged her. The boiler hummed on and off through the night, but I no longer had to put the light out before I wanted to.

I did not tell my mother about my father's notebooks, and the columns of red and black numbers he was showing me. His system was almost perfect, he said. He was working on the last details. He was winning. He'd point out the repeating patterns he saw in the columns of numbers, circling the ones that came up at regular intervals. I could not see the patterns he described, nor did I think that numbers acted in such predictable ways – but there was no telling him that.

*Did* he think the universe was ordered, and that he had found a way of reading it? When he described his intricate system, he behaved as if he was sharing a great confidence, an alchemical formula, the secret of the philosopher's stone. If he could predict numbers, I wanted to ask him, then why couldn't he predict other things?

I found another column of numbers in the back of his notebook. It was a list of his winnings and losings. I ran my fingers down those columns. He was, of course, losing much more than he was winning. So the system wasn't working after all. How, I longed to ask him, could he know one thing – that he was losing vast amounts of money – and still believe another – that his system was infallible?

I had to come to the casino with him, he told me. He had to *show* me how the system worked; then I'd see for myself. He picked me up from school one afternoon when I knew I wouldn't be missed. I had brought a change of clothes in my sports bag, as we'd agreed, clothes that would make me look older than my fifteen years. 'None of that hippy stuff,' my father had said. 'Something smart.'

The doorman called him by his first name, shook his hand, refused the £10 'tip' my father offered him, a bribe that, I guessed, was supposed to make him overlook the fact that I was underage. The red-velvet-upholstered alcoves, mirrors, and dim light inside made the interior seem a place of perpetual midnight. A group of men in expensive suits sat at the bar with cocktails. Four or five older men were playing roulette, shadowed by glamorous, much younger women with loud laughs who didn't play. A croupier saluted my father ostentatiously. He fetched a high stool for me and placed it in the corner of the room so I could use the high shelf there to keep a list of the winning numbers. He took out a roll of £50 notes from his inside pocket.

The way my father moved around the roulette table, sliding coloured chips from the pile in front of him to the numbered squares, slipping backwards and forwards from his chips to the wheel, was different from the way the other players moved. He looked as if he could make these moves in his sleep. The others cheered when they won. He was silent, rapt, his eyes shining.

The numbers were stacking up in the patterns again, he told me, glancing at the list I was keeping. Could I see? There was the red seven, a black thirteen, two red nineteens. Opposite me, in the half-light, an old woman in a white fur coat pushed £50 notes down a hole in the roulette table with one hand, very slowly, passing her chips from square to square with the other hand, as if she was moving underwater.

When my father won, he collected his winnings from a hatch at the back of the room in rolls of notes held together with red elastic bands, but instead of leaving, he started feeding the notes straight down the hole again, buying more chips. It would take me fifty hours to earn a single one of those notes at the newsagent's shop, I whispered as he leaned over me to check the list of numbers again, but he was already back to the roulette table dance. Soon he seemed to have forgotten I was there at all.

I began to visit him after school in the new smaller flat he'd taken near the Stott and Sons warehouse. I could walk there on my way home. It smelled of cigarette smoke, old newspapers, off milk, socks and kitchen rubbish. I washed up. I cleaned. I made a pile of his dirty clothes and left notes telling him to take them to the launderette, with diagrams about how to get there and information about how much change he'd need to take with him. I threw the mountains of newspapers in the bin, making sure to cut out the crosswords first. He liked doing crosswords when he couldn't sleep.

He took me to see a performance of Ibsen's *The Wild Duck* at the National Theatre in London. I was sixteen. In the car, he explained Ibsen's idea of the Life Lie with great care and attention. Life lies, he said, were the lies people told themselves to make life bearable.

The Ekdal family in *The Wild Duck*, he explained – father, mother, teenage daughter, grandfather – were poor but happy. They keep going, he said, because they have delusions. The grandfather thinks he's a great hunter. The father is convinced he's on the verge of creating an invention that will make him famous and pay off all the family debts. The daughter thinks her father is a great man. These were their Life Lies.

'So Ibsen,' said my father, 'sends in a visitor, Gregers, an old friend of the father's. Gregers exposes all their Life Lies, and tells them a few more things they would rather not have known. Then Ibsen makes us watch what happens next. It's not good, of course. But that's the point: Ibsen isn't sure we should make people see how deluded they are.'

How could my father see intricately complex patterns in the black and red numbers of his columns, but not have seen his own Life Lie reflected back in Ibsen's mirror that evening?

'I just need one big win,' he told me again as we drove back through the night. He'd begun to rant about how the new partners at Stott and Sons were fleecing the business. 'Just one big win will make everything come right.'


# 17


My mother noticed the whited-out entries on the cheque stubs, and the ragged holes in the income and outgoings ledgers. Though my parents had separated, she was still working in the Stott and Sons office down at the warehouse. She must have guessed that the stubs had something to do with my father's afternoon disappearances, but she could not have known the scale of what would unravel when the partners decided to bring in specialist accountants to take a closer look at the books.

It took the partners, the accountants and the police several weeks to gather the evidence needed for my father to be charged. He'd been embezzling money for years, fiddling the books to pay for his gambling. For some reason he'd stopped trying to cover his tracks in the last months of 1980. Did he want to be caught? Did he want someone to make it all stop?

The police investigation was secret, but my father must have sensed the walls closing in. He hadn't been sleeping for some time; he complained of stomach pains; empty bottles of whisky rolled around in the boot of the car and under the passenger seat; he kept boxes of antacid tablets in the glove compartment, and took seven or eight at a time; his skin looked grey.

There'd been another suicide. Anna Napthine, a young Brethren wife and mother, had hanged herself in London. My father collected the newspaper reports and added them to his file.

'They've learned *nothing* since the Andover Tragedy,' he said, passing me the clippings. 'The journalists don't get it, of course. They never do.'

He'd had to ask around about Anna Napthine, he told me. He'd phoned some ex-Brethren to find out what happened.

Jim Symington, the Elect Vessel, had decided that there was a backlog of sins that now had to be 'cleared' if the Brethren were going to get clean enough for the Lord. He'd gone over old tapes of Meetings to identify people who'd been trouble-makers, or who'd asked difficult questions back in the sixties

and seventies. Hundreds of sinners had not been properly disci-
plined the first time round, he'd told the Brethren, so priests
must root out these people in their local Meetings and put
them under seven days of 'assembly discipline' to get them
properly *clean.*

London Brethren, my father said, had put Anna Napthine
on their list. Years before, she'd 'confessed' to adultery but had
not been 'shut up' at the time, so now they told her it was time
for her to get properly right with the Lord. They'd shut her up
for much longer than the now-statutory seven days, although
no one knew why.

In her bedroom, isolated from her family for weeks,
tormented by her own thoughts and the visits of the priests,
Anna Napthine got sick. Her husband took their two young
children to the local park one afternoon, and when they came
back to the house they found Anna's body hanging from a ceiling joist.

'They're completely *unshameable,*' my father said.

Symington, my father told me, had preached about the
suicide in a ministry Meeting in Australia the following day. He
told the Brethren that Satan had used Anna Napthine as a
weapon to stop them from doing the Lord's work: 'The devil
urged her to do that to counter the Lord's demand for a review
and an adjustment of defective assembly administration.'[3]

My father looked stricken and depleted.

'How many more?' he asked.

That winter of 1981, after he'd been arrested, charged with
embezzlement and fraud, and released on bail pending trial, my

father played me the Bergman 'Faith' trilogy: *Through a Glass Darkly*, *Winter Light* and *The Silence*. He sat on the floor of his flat, among the discarded newspapers, drinking his way through another bottle of whisky, pausing and replaying scenes to puzzle out their meanings to me, and to himself. I was sixteen.

In *Winter Light*, a priest who has lost his faith gives communion to the last two or three remaining members of the congregation of his remote Lutheran church in midwinter. Although he goes through all the rituals and preparations, he's tormented by God's silence, God's failure to say something back.

We watched the light move around the empty church up on the screen, slanting in through windows, lighting the priest's tormented face as he gave his sermon or collapsed in exhaustion in the vestry. We watched him berate and entreat God, perhaps trying to provoke him into sending some kind of sign. In one shot, the priest stands looking out at the snow falling across the fields, his face lit up. This is all there is, Bergman seemed to be saying, just the light on the snow. But look how beautiful it is. We are too busy fretting about the next world to see this one in all its strange beauty.

When a tortured young man, the father of a young family, comes to talk to him, the priest stops just short of telling him that there is no God. The young man disappears into the snow, and is later found hanged. The priest, racked with guilt, takes communion just the same.

We watched *The Silence* the same afternoon. It was even more haunting and incomprehensible, scored by the sound of clock hands ticking and fans whirring. Two sisters and a ten-year-old boy, travelling across Europe on the brink of war, wall up in a two-room apartment in a semi-derelict central European hotel. The elder woman is dying, self-medicating with vodka and cigarettes, and trying to finish a manuscript. The child, whose mother is the younger sister, goes wandering in the corridors of the hotel. He meets a troupe of Spanish dwarves, and stares out the window as a lone tank rolls down the road at night.

'No one *says* anything,' my father said. 'That's the thing. Everyone's locked into the silence. Everyone's trapped. They're all talking into a void.'

Especially the boy wandering the corridors, I thought. Especially him.

That boy reminded me of the boy my father had once been, the boy who had collapsed on the steps of his house when he thought his mother and sister had been taken in the Rapture and he'd been left behind, the boy counting up the Bible letters in the Meeting, longing for time to himself, hectored by the father voices he heard in his head and beguiled by the mother voices. But when the silence finally came for that child, it had engulfed him.

'I've met a boy,' I told my father, just weeks before his court case. We were sitting in his flat. I could still smell the smoke from the previous night's bonfire in my hair. I had twenty minutes to get back to school for my afternoon history class, and because my father was in a hurry to show me *Through a Glass Darkly* he didn't ask me any questions about the boy. We watched the film, and I missed my history class.

I'd met the boy at a bonfire party a couple of weeks before. In the summers, my friends and I roamed the seafront promenade like flocks of birds gathering on wires. Emma lived in the next street, and her parents took in language students too, but they were much younger and wilder than the ones who boarded with us. They invited us to parties on the beach, where they gathered in large numbers around a bonfire after dark. We'd bring our friends. That night we were sitting on old blankets thrown over the pebbles, drinking cheap white wine, smoking weed, talking about university applications. I'd missed too much school, I told them. My teachers must have predicted very low grades for me. I'd had four rejections out of my five applications. Someone was telling me I should think about signing up for a kibbutz instead.

I'd been watching the boy over on the other side of the flames playing his guitar, his enormous brown leather jacket pulled around his hunched body, his long fingers picking out chords. He wrote his own songs and music, I heard someone say; he was in a band. His name was Tom.

A week later, Tom had walked me home from another bonfire party. We sat on a bench looking out over the ocean, the full moon making a road across the water to us. Seagulls drifted overhead like ghosts. We stayed there talking until a line of pink gradually widened along the horizon and the sea slowly disgorged the great fireball of the sun. He told me he was leaving home. His parents didn't understand him. They were philistines, he said, and I asked him if he knew who the Philistines were. When he said he didn't, I explained, and then he kissed me. My father was about to go to prison, I said, watching his dark eyes open wide. When I crept back into the house after dawn, I was relieved to find I'd not been missed.

# 18

I was afraid of what my father might do in the days leading up to the court case, I told Tom. Especially with Marsha and her children away on summer holiday, and him staying in their house all by himself. Marsha had been my father's girlfriend once. Now she was just his friend. My father was not well. He'd asked me to stay with him there, to keep him company, now that my exams were finished. My mother didn't think it was a good idea, but who else was going to do it?

I packed a bag. My mother drove me to the edge of that leafy estate where my father's one-time girlfriend still lived with her teenage children. She made me promise to call her if I needed her.

'Just keep it ordinary,' Tom said. 'Just use your instinct. Watch films. Keep him talking. Call me.'

There were books he wanted to talk to my father about, he said. He'd come over. I told him it was probably better if he didn't.

This was the house I'd watched from my seat up on the hill. I'd never been inside. My father had often invited me to meet

Marsha. I'd like her, he said. She was smart, and she knew all sorts of things about books and music and films. But I'd refused. I didn't want to meet the family I'd seen through my binoculars. I didn't want those neighbours to see me getting out of my father's car, walking along the path that he'd walked with them. I didn't want to put myself into that world.

But now I was inside. There were pictures of Marsha with her ex-husband and children. There were pictures on every wall: babies, portraits, holidays. There were photos of my father with her, and with her children and their friends. Those were her books on the shelves, that was her music collection next to the record player.

That week my father drank from the moment he woke until the moment he fell asleep on the sofa twelve hours later. He'd bought a case of whisky. He woke in the night and paced the house, clutching one of his battery-operated radios. When he started talking about killing himself – how he was fit for nothing, how he was so ashamed, how he'd never forgiven himself for killing his father, for leaving my mother – I made more tea, gave him films to watch, or talked about anything and everything that came into my head.

Tom tapped on the window one night, and I invited him in. He and I sat at the top of the stairs, my father asleep downstairs on the sofa under the rug I'd pulled over him. When Tom saw the checklist I'd made of things to hide from my father – the knives in the kitchen, the painkillers in the medicine cabinet, the keys to the car – he told me I was being way too over-dramatic. I think you mean *melodramatic*, I said.

A week later, my father was given a twelve-month prison sentence that would, my mother told us, probably be reduced to three months. There'd be no more running for him now, I told Tom. He was safe. He had a new iron room, I said, and then had to explain what an iron room was. Tom asked why anyone would want to build a church from corrugated iron. I told him it was complicated, and that one day I'd explain. My father would be fine, I repeated. He'd have books and pens and paper. He could finish that play he'd started writing.

Why would they call a prison 'Wormwood Scrubs'? I asked Tom, but he wasn't much interested in what I knew about the Bible, so I didn't tell him that Wormwood was the name of the star in the Book of Revelation that blazed like a torch, fell from the sky, and poisoned all the rivers and springs. The waters turned bitter, and many people died. Falling stars, comets and poisoned waters were all signs that the End Times were coming.

It was July. School had finished. I was in love. My father was in prison and he was safe. And York University had offered me a place to study English literature.

The largest bundle of the letters Kez found in the envelope my father had labelled 'Prison Letters' were from Tom. During my father's time in prison, Tom and I were walking the streets of Brighton at night, sneaking into the back of gigs so we didn't have to pay, lying under the stars on the beach in the early hours of the morning talking about books, God, music, swimming at midnight, waiting for our A-Level results. Through all of that, Tom, who'd met my father only once before the court case, had written to him every day he was in prison. And my father had written back. That surprised me. They'd written to each other about T.S. Eliot, about Camus and Sartre, about transcendentalism. Tom told my father not to worry about my silence – that though I wasn't writing to him, I was thinking of him. I was busy, he wrote, with all the various part-time jobs I had: 'two pubs and a shop … She often talks of you.'

I *was* busy. But the real reason I didn't write to my father in prison was that I'd had enough, and I was furious with him. Not because he'd shamed the family – that hardly seemed important – but because it seemed to me that he'd played straight into the Brethren's hands. I knew that the news of his prison sentence would be travelling down Brethren networks. The Jims would be using him to tell the same old story: look what happens when you leave. Look what happens when Satan gets hold of you. They'd be using my father's story to frighten more teenagers into compliance. Look what happened to Roger Stott. *Outside the door, son, there is only darkness.* My father had written the Brethren the perfect morality – or immorality – tale, and there was no undoing it.

I needed new air. In August, Tom wrote to my father to tell him that my A-Level results had been unexpectedly good. York had confirmed my place. Classes started in the middle of September, just two weeks after my father's release date. I had, he wrote, already started packing.

# 19

When people asked me about what happened to my father after prison, I'd tell them he'd landed himself a job at the BBC. For ten years he worked as a researcher for religious programmes, and then he was promoted and made three brilliant films. He interviewed George Steiner and various eminent bishops for his first film, *A Brief History of Hell*, I'd tell them proudly. He'd even met the Pope. He'd worked with Susan Sontag on his second film, *Just an Illness*, which was about illness and ideas of divine punishment. In his last film, *The Isle is Full of Noises*, he used poems by Yeats and Heaney and Hughes to show how ancient spirits and gods haunt our landscapes.

And I'd be thinking to myself: he never let up, did he? He'd spent all his post-Brethren years trying to figure out what had happened to him – in his memoir, his plays, his poetry, the books he read, and then in his BBC films. When I listened to myself describing my father's post-prison years like that, it sounded like a redemption song: the lost man who gets back on his feet and makes something of himself.

But his life was more complicated than that. There were other sides to it; there always are. I'd try to avoid telling people about how he'd continued to steal or borrow from my brothers and me and from his friends so he could keep returning to the roulette wheel, that he'd been sacked from the BBC for financial irregularities, that he was still gambling online on his deathbed.

We all knew how that particular part of his life story was going to play out. So I wouldn't tell people that he and I had been estranged on and off over the years, that I'd stopped talking to him when he came out of prison and I went off to university, and again when he conned money out of family members and lied to cover his tracks. But, I remembered now, the silences between us had never lasted for long.

He'd say the gyres were still opening up, and that we were all caught up in them, especially him, and that he couldn't help himself – but I don't see it that way. To me the world is made up of delicate branching webs and connections. That way of seeing comes, I think, from reading Darwin and George Eliot in my second year of university; and, when I fell prgnant, thinking of the child growing inside my womb and that miraculous network of neural pathways forming in both his new brain and my older one. We *were* all 'netted together', just as Darwin had said. Everything we did had an effect on the people around us.

I thought of those networks again when, decades later, I found my sixteen-year-old daughter Hannah crying outside a temple in Jaipur. She'd seen me praying at the Hindu shrine, she said, and because I'd brought them all up in a secular way, my prayers had felt to her like a kind of betrayal.

'Does that mean you believe in God?' she asked, her eyes swollen and dark. I cursed myself. I should have talked with them more about God and religion and souls, I thought. We'd talked about other difficult subjects like love and sex easily enough. I'd told myself it was best to leave them to puzzle out their own beliefs about God, not for me to tell them what I thought; but the truth is I probably wouldn't have known what to say.

A woman had said to me once, I told Hannah on the bus to Pushkar, that there were some mysteries we'd never figure out. I saw mysteries everywhere now that I was older. Not just about God, but in the science I read about – in pure maths, in animal behaviour, in studies of consciousness and the mind and memory. The more we find out, the more mysteries we seem to discover, I said. I was thinking of my mother greeting the moon. 'Hello moon,' she'll say as she closes the curtains on the night, 'there you are again.'

When I lost myself praying in the temple in Jaipur, I told Hannah, it was because in India I felt that mystery of who we are and where we've come from and where we are going like a fire in my blood.

'I look at you,' I said, 'and I think about all the voices and questions in your head, and your brother's head, and your sister's head, and the thousands of miles of neural pathways you have between you – and that's a miracle too. There are things we'll never know.'

'You taught us that,' she said, and we were both crying now. 'You taught us that it was OK not to know.'

When our Muslim guide asked if we wanted to join the Hindu ceremony on the banks of the holy lake at Pushkar to mark New Year's Eve, it was Hannah who volunteered first. She wanted to sit and watch the sun set on the last day over the holy

lake with all those other people, she said. And when the setting
sun made a burnished road across the lake and the lake birds
rose all together as the temple bells began to ring out, and the
drumming began, I told her it had reminded me of the night
of my first kiss. She laughed. It had made her think, she said,
of how little we are.

When I think of my father now, I often think of two jars. The
first is made of transparent plastic. It sat on a shelf in my son's
attic room at Christmas twenty years ago, a treasured, closely-
guarded jar, half full of brightly-coloured cellophane-wrapped
sweets. Jacob had vacated his bedroom, begrudgingly, for his
grandfather's visit. Though he liked Dodge, as we all called him
by then, and thought of him as a bit of a legendary scoundrel,
he didn't much want to give up his room, especially at
Christmas.

In the days leading up to Christmas, my father quickly filled
my son's room with the detritus that he always scattered around
himself: newspapers, empty wine bottles, notebooks full of
columns of numbers. I dared not look. I knew how this would
end up. My son would be outraged, despite the fact that at the
age of twelve he was, like his grandfather, a detritus-scattering
boy, his room on a normal day full of abandoned clothes and
the tangled wires of computer equipment. So I steeled myself
when he came to find me in the kitchen on Christmas morning, beckoned me to follow him upstairs to his room, and
gestured through the half-open door with an expression of both
horror and intense admiration.

There, among the old newspapers and discarded clothes, amid a scattering of sweets and empty wrappers, was the sweet jar, now filled with bright-yellow liquid.

'Someone's been sleeping in my bed,' Jacob said, reciting the words from 'Goldilocks and the Three Bears', his eyes shining. 'Someone's been peeing in my sweet jar, and they've filled it right up.'

We closed the door quietly and took ourselves back downstairs to the kitchen, where my father was holding forth about Yeats or Dylan Thomas again. My then-husband glanced up from basting the turkey with a look of exasperation.

Through the eating of the turkey, and the paper hats, and the toasts, and the exchanging of gifts, Jacob returned again and again to the sweet jar. He came to tell me it was *still there*. The next day, after we'd driven my father to the station and said our goodbyes, and he'd told Jacob that he'd send him Seamus Heaney's new collection, my son and I went back up the stairs to the attic bedroom together. The jar was on its original shelf, the sweets back inside. We stood there, he and I, staring at the jar that was now misting up with condensation.

'Good old Dodge,' Jacob said. 'Sound. Nice work.'

And of course I wanted to say something about how a man might steal, embezzle and betray, and you'd still want to be in his part of the room. That a man might be both *sublime* and *abject*; and I thought, if Jacob asked me what that meant, I'd say that my father could be downstairs talking about Yeats or free will, and upstairs peeing in his grandson's sweet jar. But I knew there was no way I could explain that yet. Jacob would have to figure some of those things out for himself. We high-fived instead.

The second jar was the same shape and size as Jacob's sweet jar, but made of opaque red plastic. The woman at reception at Cambridge Crematorium asked me to sign for it as she passed it across the desk. It had my father's name on it, and the date of his cremation. The red of the plastic was dark: somewhere between blood and wine, the texture slightly mottled.

'That's him?' I said. 'That's all of him?'

Had they really managed to get all of him in there? His bones, sinews, bile, arms, legs, and that scar that ran from his ear to his Adam's apple?

'They removed your father's pacemaker first, of course,' the receptionist said, checking her files, as if she thought I was complaining of being short-changed. Did I want to take that away with me too?

No, that's not it, I wanted to say. It's just that he was so *big*. He'd stand in my kitchen reciting poetry or explaining why Poliakoff was the second-greatest playwright currently writing for British television, or describing the pattern he'd seen grow-ing in the columns of numbers he'd made, and it would be so hard to get around him, he took up so much space. I'd ask him to sit on a chair so I could cook or get to a baby, and he *would* sit, but then he'd spring back up again to reoccupy the middle of the room.

Instead, I signed the form she gave me to say I'd taken the ashes but not the pacemaker.

It was raining. I put the red jar on the passenger seat of my car, and turned the ignition so that the wipers cleared the wind-screen. We sat there together, he and I, in the cemetery car park, while I waited for the rain – and my own sobs – to subside. Now there was only the red jar with the lid screwed tight.

'Say something back,' I said. 'Just say *something.*'

There was only the sound of the rain on the roof, the wind-screen wipers screeching against the glass, and the caw of a crow from a nearby tree.

But I hadn't tuned in. I wasn't listening.

'Yeats, you see,' my father was saying, 'believed that time was a necklace of interlinked spirals.' And he's drawing the gyres on his betting slip, circling the axis points with his red pen, 'See?' And he's slipping seamlessly from Leda and the swan to the angel appearing to Mary, and on to the crucifixion.

'Sooner or later,' he's saying, 'the burning walls of Troy become the burning walls of our monasteries and abbeys and country churches …'

And I'm saying: 'Does that mean you still believe in God?'

# 20

I haven't seen a Brethren family for several years now. There are 45,000 Brethren around the world, but they keep to themselves; they blend in. So I was surprised when Kez found an assembly last summer in rural Norfolk, just a few miles from the house I'd rented in Norwich.

I'd read Mark Cocker's *Crow Country* and bought myself a pair of binoculars so I could go off on weekends to the marshes and broads. Sometimes Kez would come with me. It was summer, the wrong time of year for the great rook displays, the Strumpshaw Fen birdwatchers told me, but if I was patient I'd see bitterns, marsh harriers and kingfishers instead.

I spent several Sundays listening out for the mating boom of the bittern on the marshes, but failed to hear it, so I decided to go further north, out of the Yare Valley and up onto the broads. Kez said she'd join me.

A few days later she rang to say that if we left really early on Sunday morning we could park outside the Brethren Meeting Room at Salhouse and watch them all go in to break bread before we went off to find the bitterns. She'd found the Norfolk Brethren Meeting Rooms on Google Maps a few weeks before. There were only two: a small one in Salhouse, and a huge one in Rackheath.

'It's perfectly legal,' she said, when I protested. 'The Meeting

Room is right next to the station car park. We could watch from there. We wouldn't be trespassing.'

'But we'd never see over the wall,' I said.

'This one seems to be made of some kind of metal with gaps,' she said, 'with shrubs along the inside. You can see through in places. I've checked on Google Street View.'

We drove through the streets of an eerily empty Norwich at 5 a.m., heading north. A thick blanket of fog hung across the fields, pooling in pockets in the lower ground. When a young fox crossed the road in front of us, the fog curled around him like currents in a river.

As we approached Salhouse down a farm track called Muck Lane, floodlights on the horizon lit up the morning sky. That was the car park of the Meeting Room, I told Kez. I remembered the lights at Vale Avenue in the early morning. They'd hurt my eyes when my father lifted me out of the car half-asleep.

The Meeting Room was a dark wooden building with blacked-out windows. It stood in a sea of tarmac built on fenced-off land adjacent to the railway station car park. Once we'd parked, we peered through the chain-link fence between our car park and theirs. Their car park was full. We were too late. The Salhouse Brethren were already breaking bread. They must have started at 5.30, I told Kez, half an hour earlier than the time we broke bread when I was growing up.

While we waited for them to come out, Kez pulled up the previous evening's episode of *The Archers* on her phone and played it through the car speakers. Helen Archer was in prison, awaiting trial for having stabbed her abusive husband. She'd just had her baby. We both wanted to know if she was all right. Kez passed me the binoculars.

Eventually the Meeting Room doors swung open. Twenty or thirty men and boys came out first, each of them dressed in a dazzlingly white shirt and black trousers. The effect of all those white shirts against the dark building was startling, like the foam on the top of a wave that was moving in our direction. Behind them, women with brightly coloured headscarves tied at the backs of their necks ushered small children towards cars. One of the women, spotting our car, walked straight towards us and peered through the metal fence.

I gasped, and reached for the button to lock the doors. Kez laughed.

'She can't see us through the glass, remember,' she said. 'It's tinted.'

The woman glared at our darkened windows. We looked at her. After a few seconds she turned and climbed into her car. Kez grabbed my hand. 'I won't let them get you,' she said. We both laughed.

We waited for the last of the cars to leave, and then drove slowly through the village in the fog. Clusters of Brethren men and boys carrying Bibles came into view and then were gone. Soon the big cars and the men in white shirts had disappeared completely. We were alone in the dawn on the outskirts of Salhouse.

'Now it's time for the bitterns,' Kez said, pouring coffee from a flask and unwrapping the sandwiches we were supposed to save till lunch.

As we walked the path around Salhouse Broad, passing the binoculars between us, scanning the reeds for reed buntings and listening out for the elusive bitterns, the little girl in the red cardigan kept appearing in my mind's eye. I wondered if there were girls like her in the Meeting Rooms now, sitting in the back row among the women, trying to work out how transparent the Spirit was; and if those girls sometimes wondered, as I had done, why the women didn't just stand up and stamp their feet and shout.

The morning sun felt warm on my skin. Birdwatchers and walkers were gathering. All around us giant oaks and elms puffed up their colossal greens into blue sky. Cuckoos called from distant fields. We saw a kingfisher flash past and a pair of herons take to the air together, but still we didn't hear the bitterns.

My children have grown up very differently from me. My son Jacob, born during my second year at university, was raised in a commune of intellectuals and writers; my daughters Hannah and Kez are not afraid to ask questions, or speak up, or take to the streets together to demonstrate about the refugee crisis. The gyre is not inexorable. They've been raised to love this world of ours. They do not believe in absolute Good or absolute Evil. They'll fight to protect this fleeting life and each other, and to make the world more just and kind.

My aftermath has been slow, which is why, I think, I have spent so much time reading in libraries and talking about literature in university seminar rooms, writing books about

Charles Darwin and teaching classes on feminism. The iron room of my father's world swung open to the skies when, at the age of ten, he was allowed to keep Arthur Mee's *Book of Everlasting Things*. Since that first burst of joy and terror I felt when I reached for the turquoise spine of the school library copy of *The Secret Island*, or tracked down Darwin in the school encyclopaedia, I have spent much of my life in libraries: Cambridge University Library, the English Faculty Library, Cambridge Zoology Library, and now the British Library. I read erratically sometimes, veering from poetry to science to history to fiction until I find myself caught up in something. It might be seventeenth-century glassmaking, or Darwin's barnacles, or what happened to Londinium after the Romans left it derelict, or the hunting patterns of peregrines.

I haven't had that dream about The Committee for a while, but I'm certain they'll be back. Next time I'll have a few things to say. For fifty years they've summoned me back to their iron room to hector me with questions about why I've failed to do what I was sent here to do ... Have I forgotten *again*?

Next time, I'll take a few paces across the room and grasp the iron handles of that heavy interrogating light of theirs with both hands. The beam will sweep across the room, shadows contracting and stretching until I have them all pinioned in its glare.

'I don't have to remember what I was sent here to do,' I'll say, 'because I wasn't sent here *to do anything*.'

I'll borrow some phrases from V.S. Ramachandran's book on consciousness.

'My brain is made up of atoms forged billions of years ago in the heart of countless far-flung stars,' I'll say. 'Those particles drifted for eons and light years out there in the universe, until gravity and change brought them together in my skull to form the tangle of atoms that make up my brain. Now I can wonder about the gods, or life after death, or consciousness and where we've all come from and where we might be going to, and I can sit outside under the stars talking with my children and their friends and wonder about my ability to wonder. You'll never build an iron room strong enough or big enough or dark enough to stop that. There'll always be a crack where the light gets in.'

I had gone to fetch my children – Kezia who was then twelve, Hannah fourteen, and Jacob twenty-three – so they could say their goodbyes to their grandfather. He hadn't spoken for days, I told them. He hadn't opened his eyes or moved. Even when I'd read him the whole of *Four Quartets*, his favourite poem, his face had not flickered. His breathing was shallow. 'He's our tribal leader,' Jacob said. 'I can't imagine him not being there.'

Up on the fens, the snow was falling again; the setting sun had cast a red glow across the white fields. We drove slowly up the lane, following the line of the river until the pink tower of the Mill came into view over the brow of an incline. My brother and stepmother were cooking dinner in honour of our visit, an elaborate cassoulet from one of my father's recipes. The sitting room in the Mill tower where my father lay was warm and fragrant, the table laid out with candles and open bottles of wine.

But when the children took their positions around the chair, and Jacob called his name – 'Dodge,' he said, softly – his voice cracking with tears, my father's eyes opened. I took Kez's hand.

'I'm sorry I can't talk now,' he whispered, struggling to catch his breath, 'but in a little while I'll unfurl my wings and then fly a little, you'll see.' Then he disappeared back under the morphine.

It was the last thing he said.

Four days later the owl began its slow, ghostly flight down the riverbank towards him.

# ACKNOWLEDGEMENTS

Many people have helped me to write this book. Ex-Brethren have checked facts, tracked down source material, provided photographs, notes and diaries, explained obscure Brethren doctrine or told me their family stories. Most of these people, several of whom appear with substitute names in the book, have chosen to stay anonymous. For many of my informants remembering was difficult. Their determination to answer my questions despite that difficulty kept me going when the task of finishing this book occasionally seemed impossible. I particularly thank 'Frank', 'Ruth' and 'William'. They became a chorus in my head as I wrote, just as they had been for my father.

I am grateful to Ian McKay for his friendship, encouragement, patience and the speed with which he checked my account against his records, archives and his books of ministry during the two years of the book's evolution. Thank you also to Graham Johnson of the Christian Brethren collection at Manchester University Library who provided archive material.

The trustees of Hawthornden Castle International Writers Retreat gave me a month-long fellowship to finish the book and turned a blind eye to my occasional excursions to remote graveyards and fishing villages. Thank you to Hamish Robinson for an early-morning drive to the local GP's surgery after the wasps attacked.

Thank you to my friends Tiffany Atkinson and Petra Rau, who were also my readers and who, like so many of my colleagues at UEA, take risks with form and breach disciplinary boundaries in endlessly inventive ways. Tiffany helped me to understand embarrassment and even, occasionally, to find pleasure in it.

I thank Alex Stein for her twelve-week course on the Social Psychology of Cults and Totalitarianism, taught at the Mary Ward Centre in London, and to the group of people in the class that summer. Most had children in cults or had lived in cult communities. I am grateful for their stories and for the reading Alex gave us – books and essays from Hannah Arendt to Peter Lipton and extracts from Alex's own work on brainwashing all helped me to understand the Brethren as a cult and to see how cults work.

Don Paterson convinced me it was time to begin, showed me both how to start and, after a duration, how to end.

I thank Rebecca Carter, my agent at Janklow & Nesbit, for seeing what I couldn't yet see and for her unique insights and instincts along the way. I am grateful to my very brilliant editors – Helen Garnons-Williams of Fourth Estate and Cindy Spiegel of Spiegel & Grau – for understanding what the book might be, and for challenging me through every draft to go further and to find answers to questions I did not yet know how to formulate. Thank you too to Robert Lacey of Fourth Estate and Kelly Chian of Spiegel & Grau for putting the book through such scrupulous and eagle-eyed copyediting and into production.

My thanks finally go to my grown-up children Hannah, Kezia and Jacob for reminding me why this book mattered. Kezia chivvied and challenged as I wrote and was often ahead of me with the torch finding the way. Jacob and Hannah read and improved drafts. I could not have written this memoir without my brother Benjamin, who is one of the kindest and wisest men I've ever known. And finally my thanks go to my father for leaving me such a complex and rich inheritance, and to my mother for keeping the family ship afloat in the often mighty turbulence he left in his wake.

*Rebecca Stott*
*March 2017*

# NOTES

**Reckoning**

1. See Michael Bachelard, *Behind the Exclusive Brethren* (Scribe, 2009).
2. Philip Cooney, 'Brethren Still a Cult in Rudd's Book', *Sydney Morning Herald*, 23 August 2007.
3. Bachelard, *Behind the Exclusive Brethren*, p.3.
4. Billy Kember and Alexi Mostrous, 'Extreme Sect Secures Tax Breaks', *The Times*, 17 March 2015.

**Before**

1. Carl E. Olson, 'Five Myths About the Rapture', *Crisis* (Morley Publishing Group, 2003), pp.28–33. Although it is understood that about 50 per cent of contemporary Americans believe in the idea of the Rapture, there was no common notion of a pre-Tribulation Rapture before the eighteenth century. Olson writes: 'Vague notions had been considered by the Puritan preachers Increase (1639–1723) and Cotton Mather (1663–1728), and the late-eighteenth-century Baptist minister Morgan Edwards, but it was John Nelson Darby who solidified the belief in

the 1830s and placed it into a larger theological framework.'

2. Cited in Norman Adams, *Goodbye, Beloved Brethren* (Aberdeen, 1972), pp.31–2.

3. James Grant, 'The Religious Tendencies of the Times', *Sword and Trowel*, June 1869.

4. See Ian Smith, *Tin Tabernacles: Corrugated Iron Mission Halls, Churches and Chapels of Britain* (Salisbury: Camrose Organisation, 2004), and Alasdair Ogilvie, *Tin Tabernacles and Others* (PhotoStroud, 2009).

5. John Nelson Darby, *Collected Writings*, Vol. 41; cited in Bachelard, *Behind the Exclusive Brethren*, p.21.

6. See Brian P. Levack, *Witch-Hunting in Scotland: Law, Politics and Religion* (Routledge, 2007); for all my information on Eyemouth I have relied on Peter Aitchison and John Hume Robertson, *Children of the Sea: The Story of the Eyemouth Disaster* (East Lothian: Tuckwell Press, 2001).

7. 'Scotch Bankrupts', *Herald* (Glasgow), 26 August 1885.

8. See T.M. Devine, *The Scottish Nation 1700 to 2007* (Penguin, revised edition 2012), and Peter Aitchison and Andrew Cassell, *The Lowland Clearances: Scotland's Silent Revolution 1760–1830* (Birlinn Ltd, 2016).

9. Callum Brown, 'Protest in the Pews: Interpreting Presbyterianism and Society in Fracture During the Scottish Economic Revolution', in T.M. Devine (ed.), *Conflict and Stability in Scottish Society, 1700–1850* (Edinburgh, 1990).

10. For Brethren accounts of the Glanton division see two pamphlets in particular: D.L. Higgins, *The Glanton Crisis Explained* (London: G. Morrish, c.1915), sets out the London position; W.T.P. Wolston, *'Hear the Right': Plain Facts Regarding Alnwick and Glanton, Edinburgh and London* (privately printed, 1908), sets out a defence of the Alnwick Brethren. Both can be found on the website of archive materials, brethrenarchive.org.

11. Napoleon Noel, *The History of the Brethren* (W.F. Knapp, 1936), pp.40ff.

12. See Peter Bladin, *A Century of Prejudice and Progress: A Paradigm of Epilepsy in a Developing Society – Medical and Social Aspects, Victoria, Australia, 1835–1950* (Epilepsy Australia, 2001), and M.J. Eadie and Peter Bladin, *A Disease Once Sacred: A History of the Medical Understanding of Epilepsy* (Eastleigh: John Libbey, 2001).

13. Kathleen Taylor, *Brainwashing: The Science of Thought Control* (OUP, 2004), p.126.

## During

1. See Bachelard, *Behind the Exclusive Brethren*, pp.272–85.

2. 'Doctrine that Divides', *Anno Domini*, BBC Everyman, dir. Peter France, 1976.

3. J. Taylor Junior, *Letters*, Vol. 2, p.324.

4. Roger Shuff, *Searching for the True Church: Brethren and Evangelicals in Mid-Twentieth-Century England* (Milton Keynes: Paternoster, 2005).

5. Quoted from a letter in the author's possession.

6. Stephen Bates, 'Secretive Sect Softens Ban on Outside Contact', *Guardian*, 15 March 2003.

7. J. Taylor Junior, *Readings at Nostrand Avenue and Other Ministry*, Vol. 1 (1970), p.2.

8. Email in the author's possession.

9. Email in the author's possession.

10. Gerard Kemp, 'Brethren Drove Them to Suicide', *Daily Mail*, 24 July 1962.

11. Stanley Milgram, 'Behavioural Study of Obedience', *Journal of Abnormal and Social Psychology*, Vol. 67, No. 4 (1963), pp.371–8.

12. Robert Stott (ed.), *The Way Everlasting* (Kingston: Stow Hill Bible and Tract Depot, 1958).

13. 'Notes of a Meeting in Connection with Stow Hill Depot, 1962, held at Alexandra Palace, London, 12th July, 1962'. A copy can be found at www.brethrenarchive.org.archive/ later-exclusivism/raven-section/taylorite/ notes-of-a-meeting-in-connection-with-stow-hill-depot.

14. Manuscript in the author's possession.

15. J. Taylor Junior, 'The Service of Song and Other Ministry: Notes from Meetings at Haywards Heath and Croydon, 1963', in *The Ministry of J. Taylor Junior*, Vol. 25, p.91.

16. Unpublished manuscript of 'Notes Taken from Meetings 1957–1970'. Document in the author's possession.

17. Alan Clarke, 'The Compliance Officer' (unpublished manuscript in the author's possession), p.138.

18. Ibid.

19. See Michael Bachelard, 'Schooling', in *Behind the Exclusive Brethren*, pp.215–45.

20. http://www.discourses.org.uk/History/TheAberdeenIncident.pdf.

21. The account that follows is assembled from two documents: witness statements assembled in Robert Stott, *If We Walk in the Light* (Stow Hill, 1970); letter from Ted Steedman, http://wikipeebia.com/wp-content/uploads/2013/02/Steedman_letter.pdf.

22. Letter from Ted Steedman, http://wikipeebia.com/wp-content/uploads/2013/02/Steedman_letter.pdf, p.2.

23. Ibid., p.3.

24. Ibid.

25. Ibid.

26. Robert Stott, *If We Walk in the Light*, p.3.

27. Ibid. Nicodemus was a Pharisee who helped prepare Jesus's body for burial. I have no idea why JT Junior is invoking him here, or why he refers to 'Eric' as Nicodemus.

28. In 1987 the Brethren brought a lawsuit against the author and publishers of a book published in The Hague in which the Kers testified to the good character of JT Junior. Their testimony is online at wikipeebia.com/wp-content/uploads/2013/02/Kertestimony.pdf.

## Aftermath

1. Roger Stott, ministry in possession of the author.
2. See Martin McGregor, *The Town that God Forgot* (lulu.com, 2011); 'Father Ostracised by Sect Axed Family to Death', *Daily Telegraph*, 21 March 1974.
3. *Ministry of J.H. Symington*, Vol. 95 (Minneapolis, 26 August 1981), pp.134–5.

# SELECT BIBLIOGRAPHY

**Archives of Brethren Materials**

Christian Brethren Archive, John Rylands University Library of Manchester University

www.mybrethren.org

Archive of materials on the Plymouth Brethren: http://www. brethrenarchive.org/archive/

**Books About the Brethren**

Adams, Norman, *Goodbye, Beloved Brethren*. Aberdeen: Impulse Publications Ltd (1972)

Bachelard, Michael, *Behind the Exclusive Brethren*. Carlton North, Victoria: Scribe Publications (2008)

Bailey, Michael and Redden, Guy (eds), *Mediating Faiths: Religion and Socio-Cultural Change in the Twenty-First Century*. Farnham: Ashgate (2011)

Baylis, Robert H., *My People: The History of Those Christians Sometimes Called Plymouth Brethren*. Wheaton, Ill.: H. Shaw (1997)

*The Brethren Movement Worldwide: Key Information 2011.*
Lockerbie: OPAL Trust for International Brethren
Conference on Mission (2011)

Cutler, Margaret Grace, 'Diary Account of JT Junior Edicts,
1959–70'. Unpublished record, from Papers of Margaret
Grace Cutler, Box 141, Christian Brethren Archive, John
Rylands University Library of Manchester University

Dickson, Neil T.R., *Brethren in Scotland 1838–2000.* Milton
Keynes (2002)

[Dronsfield, W.R.], 'The Brethren After 1870'. Christian
Brethren Archive, John Rylands University Library of
Manchester University, Neil Dickson Collection, Box 115,
2/16/9

Goodall, Felicity, *A Question of Conscience: Conscientious
Objection During the Two World Wars.* Sutton (1997)

Ironside, H.A., *A Historical Sketch of the Brethren Movement.*
Neptune, NJ: Loizeaux Bros (1985)

Neatby, William Blair, *A History of the Plymouth Brethren.*
London: Hodder & Stoughton (second edition, 1902)

Noel, Napoleon, *The History of the Brethren.* Denver, CO:
W.F. Knapp (two vols, 1936)

Pickering, Henry, *Chief Men Among the Brethren.* Neptune,
NJ: Loizeaux Bros (1996)

Rowdon, Harold H., *Who Are the Brethren and Does it
Matter?* Exeter: Paternoster (1986)

Scotland, N., 'Encountering the Exclusive Brethren: A Late-
Twentieth-Century Cult'. *European Journal of Theology*,
Vol. 6, No. 2 (1997), pp.157–67

Scuff, Roger N., *Searching for the True Church: Brethren and Evangelicals in Mid-Twentieth-Century England*. Milton Keynes: Paternoster (2005)

Tonts, M., 'The Exclusive Brethren and an Australian Rural Community'. *Journal of Rural Studies*, Vol. 17, No. 3 (2001), pp.309–22

Wilson, B.R., 'The Exclusive Brethren: A Case Study in the Evolution of a Sectarian Ideology', in Wilson, B.R., *Patterns of Sectarianism: Organisation and Ideology in Social and Religious Movements*. London (1967), pp.287–342

Wilson, Elisabeth, '"The Eyes of the Authorities Are Upon Us": The Brethren and World War I', BAHNR, Vol. 3, No. 1 (2004), pp.2–17

## Memoirs

Arnott, Anne, *The Brethren: An Autobiography of a Plymouth Brethren Childhood*. London: Hodder & Stoughton (1970)

Field, Marion, *Don't Call Me Sister!* Woking: Petra (1993)

Field, Marion, *Shut up Sarah*. Godalming: Highland (1996)

Gosse, Edmund, *Father and Son: A Story of Two Temperaments*. Ed. Michael Newton. Oxford: Oxford University Press (2004; originally published 1907)

Thomas, Ngaire, *Behind Closed Doors: A Startling Story of Exclusive Brethren Life*. Auckland: Random House (2005)

Virtue, Noel, *Once a Brethren Boy*. Auckland: Vintage (1995)

Wood, Christine, *Exclusive By-Path: The Autobiography of a Pilgrim*. Evesham: James (1976)

# PICTURE PERMISSIONS

p.8 Still from Ingmar Bergman's *Det sjunde inseglet/The Seventh Seal* © 1957 AB Svensk Filmindustri. Still photographer: Louis Huch

p.40 'Grandpa Mallalieu', portrait in Stott family possession

p.44 John Nelson Darby, from print in author's possession

p.49 'The Iron Room' in Kenilworth, courtesy of J. Heatley and the Kenilworth History and Archaeology Society

p.56 Fish-gutters at Eyemouth, courtesy of Kevin O'Brien

p.66 Eyemouth Harbour, courtesy of Kevin O'Brien

p.83 David Fairbairn Stott and family in 1925, courtesy of Ruth Pallister

p.102 Ada-Louise in her twenties, from photograph in author's possession

p.114 Methodist Central Hall, Westminster, from photograph in author's possession

p.119 Ada-Louise and Hugh Wasson in the 1950s, from photograph in author's possession

p.125 Roger as a child, from photograph in author's possession

p.131 Roger as a teenager, from photograph in author's possession